# THE TURKISH COOKBOOK

Ghillie Başan

# THE TURKISH COOKBOOK

Exploring the food
of a timeless cuisine

LORENZ BOOKS

# Contents

Introduction 6

An abundance of ingredients 36

Meze and salads 94

Soups and hot snacks 138

Vegetable dishes 176

Beans, peas, lentils and pilaffs 212

Fish and shellfish 252

Meat and poultry 294

Sweet snacks and jams 336

Nutritional notes 376

Index 380

Acknowledgements 384

# Introduction

Turkey is a country of extraordinarily beautiful landscapes and bountiful seas through which its fascinating history and culinary culture are vividly weaved. There are few places in the world where the cuisine is so rich and diverse, where the traditional merges so effortlessly with the modern, where the people are so friendly and proud of their heritage, and where the hospitality shines like a bright beacon.

Above **Surrounded by sea on three sides, with the narrow Bosphorus as a link, Turkey acts as a geographical and cultural bridge between Europe and Asia.**

Opposite top **A timeless tradition: a cup of coffee with a piece of Turkish delight.**

Opposite bottom **Colourful dips and salads are often enjoyed with *rakı*, the national aniseed-flavoured spirit.**

# Greet a Turk and you will eat

The Turks are passionate about their cuisine. If you ask them about their favourite dishes, they will chat animatedly for hours describing the fresh, crunchy salads, scented with herbs; glorious, garlicky dips made with yogurt; succulent vegetables stuffed with aromatic minced lamb and pine nuts; meat balls and kebabs; breads and savoury pastries; and the sumptuous and divine milk puddings and syrupy pastries packed with nuts and bathed in syrup. They are so proud of their diverse culinary culture that it gives them pleasure to share it with you and it is their generous hospitality that draws me to the country again and again.

When I first went to Turkey in 1984, I was struck by the luring aromas of cooking in the streets and the bustle of the spice bazaars but the most striking thing of all was that everywhere I went I was offered a glass of tea, a nugget of soft, scented Turkish Delight and if there was a pudding or pastry shop nearby, someone would fetch a piece of melt-in-the-mouth pistachio *baklava* – simple gestures of hospitality at the bus station, in a bank or shop, in the street or at the market. There is a lot of truth in the saying: 'Greet a Turk and you will eat'.

And wherever you go in Turkey there truly is something delicious to eat. Whether you are in the busy streets of Istanbul, in a small village in Anatolia, on the slopes above Bursa, or in a tourist resort in the Mediterranean, the enticing aroma of grilling, baking, and spices fills the air – warm bread rings covered in sesame seeds; deep-fried mussels with a garlicky sauce; roasted chestnuts, almonds and pistachio nuts; savoury pastries filled with melting cheese; lamb roasting on a spit; aubergines smoking over charcoal; and the scent of fresh peaches. You can try the famous Ottoman puddings in Istanbul; juicy apricots stuffed with rice in Cappadocia; anchovy pilaff along the Black Sea coast; fiery kebabs served on a sword in Adana; and the hallucinogenic honey of Kars in eastern Anatolia.

Every town and city has a market, where you will find a wealth of fresh, seasonal produce, such as plump olives and crunchy pickles, juicy figs, ruby-red pomegranates, ripe melons, strings of dried red chillies, and leafy herbs, which are sold like bunches of flowers. The beauty of Turkish food is that it is seasonal and abundant. Traditional recipes have been handed down from generation to generation and modern chefs add their own twists. There is something for everyone in this never-ending moveable feast.

Turkey, itself, is as thrilling as its food. With one foot planted in Europe and the other immersed in Asia, the country acts as a geographical and cultural bridge between the two continents, a fact that is vividly represented in the diversity of the cuisine.

Turkey is a land of contrasts. It has the fortune to be surrounded by seas on three sides and is home to numerous lakes and rivers and vast irrigated, fertile plains with rich grazing pastures for cattle and sheep, so agriculture and fishing are key contributors to the country's economy and food bowl. There are high mountain peaks to climb, glorious blue sea to swim and sail in, fast-flowing rivers meandering through the land, tea and cotton plantations, bountiful orchards and endless fields of roses, sunflowers and wheat. The diverse landscape is dotted with impressive mosques, ancient Roman and Greek ruins, troglodyte cave dwellings, remote hilltop settlements and rustic villages where donkeys are still laden with firewood, oxen still till the soil, and the children are often the most cheerful souls you will ever meet. Climatic variations in the region are striking too – long, cold winters grip the east and hot summers scorch the south – conditions that play their part in determining the type of food that can be successfully grown in each area.

To get a taste of Turkey, Istanbul is the place to be. It is where Europe and Asia meet. Divided by the Bosphorus, the busy waterway that flows from the Black Sea through the middle of Istanbul to the Sea of Marmara and out into the Aegean, you can have a cup of coffee in Europe in the morning and hop on a boat to have dinner in Asia. All roads, by land and sea, lead to this majestic city. Once the seat of the vast Ottoman Empire, Istanbul has become a vast melting pot of different cultures. As it is the centre of commerce and trade in Turkey, many people have migrated here from the far-flung corners of Anatolia (the Asian part of Turkey), Europe, the Middle East and the Black Sea countries, bringing with them their own culinary traditions and local flavours. In one spot you can experience the history and the journey of the food – the famous spice bazaar is called Egyptian; the ubiquitous red chillies are often linked to Aleppo; there are Jewish *köfte*, Arab kebabs and Lebanese *kibbeh*, Circassian chicken and Russian salad, sautéed liver from Albania, and spicy dumplings from Mongolia. This unique city never fails to surprise and tantalise the taste buds, nor the adventurous spirit. Day and night, it is intoxicatingly alive with the endless street and water traffic, the honking of horns, the resonant call to prayer, busy restaurants and bars with live music, indoor and outdoor markets, vibrant student life, football matches and festivals, and, of course, the alluring smell of food cooking in every street. Istanbul is a city that never sleeps.

Founded on both its ancient Anatolian traditions and its sophisticated Ottoman heritage, the influences drawn from its history are very apparent in the vibrant contemporary cuisine of modern Turkey. There are those who do not sway from the traditional recipes and methods while there are others who, bursting with creative flair, have a desire to come up with something new. In essence, that is what Turkish cuisine is all about: constantly developing, but also never forgetting where it comes from.

Top **Passengers can enjoy splendid views of Istanbul from the Bosphorus and the Golden Horn as the ferries cross from Europe to Asia.**

Bottom **Mediterranean bliss in a quiet cove near Antalya.**

# Culinary history

While the food of Turkey is inevitably linked to its diverse geography and climate, it could be said that the country's turbulent history has also played a key role in shaping the cuisine. Constantly in flux, the culinary traditions combine the ancient with the contemporary and the religious with the mystical, embodying the many cultures that have had an impact on the region over the centuries. These include the ancient Persian and Arab Empires, the influences of Islam and the Ottoman Empire; and today, the growth of urbanisation and tourism.

## Ancestral roots

The early ancestors of modern-day Turks originated in the Altay mountains in Central Asia, from where they drifted towards Anatolia, encountering and adopting different culinary traditions along the way. Some of these were based on the use of animal products, such as the milk and meat from horses as well as the many different wild animals that were hunted. In common with other nomadic tribes of the period, the early Turks would also have made unleavened bread from wheat flour and would have drunk *ayran*, a yogurt drink, and *kımız*, fermented liquor made from the milk of their mares.

When these nomads arrived in Anatolia around the 10th century, the region already had its own rich culinary heritage, influenced by the Hittites, the Romans, the Byzantines, the Arabs, the Mongols and the Crusaders who had passed through the region. The legacy of these influences was a cuisine that made use of the ready availability of beans, wheat and lentils, which were cooked with oil extracted from plants.

The early Turks adopted and further developed this cuisine, melding their own characteristics and culinary techniques with those already present in the region. Evidence of this early Turkish cuisine can still be found today among the Kazan and Tartar communities in central Anatolia. Here, many early dishes have survived, including *mantı*, a noodle dough, *yufka*, the thin sheets of flat bread, and *tarhana*, fermented dried curds that are used for making a traditional soup.

## The impact of Islam

Following the death of the Prophet Muhammad in 632CE, a new Arab empire rose in the Middle East. As the Golden Age of Islam flourished between the 8th and 12th centuries, the Arabs invaded and conquered

Top **The nomadic herders of central and eastern Anatolia take their sheep to the high pastures to graze in the Kesis Mountains.**

Bottom **A farmer with oxen ploughing his field in the age-old way.**

vast territories in Central Asia, imposing religious restrictions on all aspects of the cultures they encountered, including those of Turkey.

During this era there was a cultural awakening throughout the Middle East, as the seafaring Arabs brought back silk and porcelain from China, ivory and gold from East Africa, and spices from the East Indies. With the arrival of spices came a great deal of culinary creativity and the advent of instructive literature on recipes, etiquette and the health properties of certain foods, all of which had an impact on the cuisine of Turkey. Around the same time, Mahmud al-Kashgari wrote the first important literary document, a Turkish-Arabic dictionary, which detailed and recorded aspects of the cuisine, such as the early nomadic Turks' love of yogurt, and their cooking methods for recipes such as *yufka* and *mantı*.

Top **The minaret of the tomb of the Rumi at the Mevlana Museum in Konya, Anatolia.**

Bottom **Holding on to an important cultural tradition, the dervishes who whirl out of religious conviction only perform at *semas* (ceremonies) in Konya and Istanbul.**

## The Seljuk period

By the 11th century, the nomadic Turks had formed a warrior aristocracy, which resulted in the establishment of the Seljuk (Selçuk) Empire in Konya from where they ruled Greater Syria for most of the 12th century. The culinary culture at this time was influenced by the sophisticated cuisine of Persia. Many important aspects of this food culture were recorded by the poet and mystic, Mevlana Celaleddin Rumi. Among the recipes listed in his works are dishes consisting of meat cooked with a variety of vegetables, such as leeks, spinach and turnip; *helva* made with grape molasses, *pekmez helvası*; the jelly-like, saffron dessert, *zerde*; and a number of pilaff and kebab dishes, all of which are cooked to this day.

Rumi's writings also reveal the abundance of produce that was available then, such as marrows (large zucchini), celeriac, onions, garlic, chickpeas, lentils, apples, quince, melons and watermelons, dates, walnuts, almonds, yogurt and cheese. Wheat flour was used to make *tutmaç*, traditional noodles that are cooked with yogurt or meat; *yufka*, the thin sheets of flat bread; *börek*, the savoury pastries and pies that the Ottoman Palace chefs later developed into wondrous creations; and *çörek*, small ring-shaped buns. It was around this time that the Turks began to understand and record the importance of eating healthily, devising a system of balancing the warming and cooling properties of certain foods, based on the ancient Chinese principles of yin and yang.

**The Mevlevi Order** | Following the death of Mevlana in 1273, the Mevlevi Order (of whirling dervish fame) was founded. They established strict rules of kitchen conduct and table manners, most of which are still adhered to in modern Turkish society. In their teachings, the kitchen was regarded as a sacred hearth and it was there that new apprentices matured and learned under the Guardian Master Cook, the Sheikh Cook, and the Sheikh Stoker.

In order to join the Order, the apprentices had to be prepared to shed their social upbringing and pride, and spend long hours in the kitchen, which was regarded as a temple in which every individual had a clearly defined role, such as sherbet-making, pickle-making, bread-making, even dish-washing.

Mevlana's personal cook, Ateş Baz-ı Veli (the original Guardian Master Cook), was considered so important that he was buried in an impressive mausoleum, a privilege usually reserved for royalty. Now a shrine for gastronomic pilgrims, it is said that if you remove a pinch of the salt from around the mausoleum, your cooking will be blessed.

Top **The Nilüfer Hatun Imareti, Iznik, was built as a soup kitchen in the 14th century.**

Bottom **A traditional table and seating, with low table and cushions, in Istanbul.**

## The Ottoman period

The most significant change in Turkish cuisine came about during the Ottoman (Osmanlı) Empire. Lasting for 650 years, the Empire was first established in Bursa in the 14th century by a Turk called Osman, the son of a pagan chief. It later spread and at the height of its power, it controlled huge swathes of south-eastern Europe, the Middle East and north Africa.

Once Constantinople (now Istanbul) was conquered by Mehmet II in 1453, the Topkapı Palace became the centre of the Empire and all culinary activity. By this time, the Turks had developed a sophisticated cuisine, which merged traditional nomadic traditions with new techniques and ingredients from Persia.

Mehmet II was a gourmet of the highest order with a penchant for indulging in lavish feasts, prepared in the Palace kitchens by carefully selected chefs from Bolu. These kitchens were divided into four main areas. The most important of these was the Kuşhane – the birdcage kitchen – named after the small cooking pots in which food for the Sultan was prepared in small quantities. The second most important kitchen was the Has Mutfak, where food was prepared for the Sultan's mother, the princes, and privileged members of the harem. The remaining two kitchens produced the food for the lesser members of the harem, the chief eunuch, and the other members of the Palace household. The head butler of the Palace was responsible for the kitchens and each one had its own head chef.

During the reign of Mehmet II, the Palace kitchens boasted a huge staff of specialist chefs, such as the *börekçı*, the maker of savoury pastries; the *baklavacı*, the maker of sweet pastries; the pickle-maker, the *helva*-maker, the meatball-maker, the pudding-maker, the yogurt-maker, the bread-bakers, and so the list goes on.

The tradition of specialisation in the kitchen that was launched by the Mevlevi Order in Konya reached its height during this period, as each chef strove to produce the most exquisite and tasty dish imaginable,

resulting in a plethora of sophisticated and creative dishes that became known as the Palace (Saray) cuisine.

As the Ottoman Empire expanded its territories during its six-century rule, it also increased its culinary repertoire by flamboyantly adopting and adapting the recipes it encountered in the Balkans, the Mediterranean region, North Africa and much of the Arab world. During the reign of Süleyman the Magnificent, creations from the Palace kitchens reached such heights of indulgence that various dishes with sensuous names emerged – such as 'young girls' breasts' (*kız memesi kadayıf*), 'ladies' navels' (*kadın göbeği*) and 'ladies' thighs' (*kadınbudu köfte*) – dishes that are still part of Istanbul's cuisine.

While the culinary creativity of the Palace was at its peak, a similar level of industrious ingenuity was taking place in every Ottoman *yalı*, the grand houses inhabited by the distinguished members of Ottoman society, and in every wealthy household that could afford a chef. There was even an element of competition in the streets, as the *kelle-paçacı*, the maker of sheep's head soup, and the *gözlemecı*, the pancake-maker, vied for trade and praise among all the other makers of sweet buns, rice dishes, meatballs and Turkish Delight. This was a time when cooking was regarded as an art form and eating was a pleasure, a legacy that is at the root of Turkish cooking today.

In the 16th and 17th centuries, the Ottomans persuaded the Spaniards, the other key players on the world stage at that time, to return from the New World via the North African coast, so that newly discovered ingredients, such as chilli peppers, tomatoes and maize, could be brought into Constantinople. These new ingredients were quickly absorbed into the sophisticated Palace cooking, from where they filtered throughout the Empire, shaping a large proportion of the Mediterranean cuisine.

While the Ottomans ruled, the very best ingredients were brought to Istanbul, ensuring high standards of food at every level. When the Ottoman Empire collapsed after its defeat in World War I, its culinary influence remained evident to the west of Constantinople but, as the Empire had never really penetrated eastwards into the heart of Anatolia, the local dishes managed to survive there unaffected by the Ottoman influence.

**Past meets present** | To put Turkish food into perspective it is instructive to go back to the origins of the nation, and its subsequent history, but there has always been room for creativity and the generation of new culinary ideas and techniques – the Ottomans were fine examples of that – and the moveable feast of Turkey continues to evolve and reinvent itself. With such a rich and diverse culinary culture, shaped by the movement of peoples and empires, exploring the cuisine of modern Turkey is a journey in itself. Every time I visit the country I come across something new.

Top **The marble upper terrace at the Topkapı Palace with the ornate Baghdad Kiosk and the gilded Itfar Pavilion where the Sultan was reputed to break the fast (itfar) after sunset during the month of Ramazan (Ramadan).**

Bottom **Some of the splendid Ottoman houses, each one a distinct *yalı*, on the Bosphorus.**

# Food traditions

The Turks are masters at combining several of the most important things in life: food, family and friends. Everywhere you go – a quiet village on a mountaintop, a leafy neighbourhood of a city, or a busy marina in a coastal resort – there will be a family or a group of friends seated in a courtyard, a doorway, a balcony, by the beach or beside the road, anywhere they can set up a table to balance a few dishes upon. One of life's little pleasures is to sit by the Bosphorus in Istanbul, listening to the calls to prayer resounding across the water, as you tuck into a spread of delicious meze dishes with a beer or a bottle of a wine and the company of good friends. As the Russian cargo tankers slip silently by and the old ferries transport people from Europe to Asia, you can get a sense of what it must have been like to rule the seas as an Ottoman Sultan but also feel part of modern day life as it unfolds around you while you eat.

The concept of sharing, visiting, hosting and eating has long been part of the social culture. Medieval documents vividly record feasts that would last for as long as forty days and forty nights. In addition to the traditional wedding and circumcision feasts, there were many others hosted by statesmen, noblemen, and the rulers of the Ottoman Empire. These elaborate meals would generally take place at long or u-shaped tables laid with silver and gold candlesticks, urns and pitchers, some of which were decorated with jewels, and large bowls of fresh grapes, plump figs and pomegranates. There were specific table seating arrangements and a regular flow of dishes, such as a sour soup, roasted legs of lamb with peas and plain pilaff, stuffed savoury pastries, sweet pastries, clotted cream and sweetmeats.

Feasts were not entirely exclusive to the wealthy though, as the very same hosts would also provide food for ordinary folk, presenting them with a wide selection of dishes, and there was an important Ottoman tradition of feeding the poor. This took place at imarets, which were places of charity often attached to mosques, where students, travellers and poor people would come in their hundreds and thousands to eat. Simple foods, such as loaves of bread, plain pilaff, soups, *aşure* (a pulse and grain pudding), and *zerde* (a jellied saffron and rice pudding), were served daily at these imarets, which housed a kitchen and dining hall. Next door there was often a *tabhane* (an alms house), which provided accommodation for the elderly and weak, as well as for travellers or migrants seeking work. That idea of providing food for others continues to this day in the same manner, at some mosques but also in the home with the custom of setting an extra place at the table just in case an unexpected visitor, possibly a stranger, comes to the door – no one should leave hungry.

Top **An overhead view of the Golden Horn. Istanbul fuses the modern and traditional, East and West.**

Bottom **Preparing flat breads and accompaniments for a family meal in a village home.**

Top **Traditional sweets on display in an Istanbul pastry shop.**

Bottom **Tulip-shaped glasses of black, sweet tea.**

## Giving sweet gifts

In addition to the hosting and sharing, there is also a tradition of giving from the guests. It is polite to arrive with a gift of something sweet – often *helva* or *baklava* – beautifully packaged and ideally from the best pastry or pudding shop in the town. By bringing a sweet gift the guest bestows good fortune and prosperity on the host.

During the Ottoman period, guests would bring a gift of *keten helvası*, which was similar to candy floss, and to contrast the sweetness, pickles would often be served with it. *Helva*, in fact, played an important role in the feasts and social gatherings of the time. There were specific *helva* parties dedicated to its consumption. Particularly popular during the winter months, these parties were a form of entertainment for family, friends and neighbours, who would congregate in each other's houses to eat a variety of foods, such as stuffed chicken, savoury pastries, pancakes, and poached apricots filled with cream. The end of an evening always culminated in a bowl of *helva*, usually made with flour or semolina, and then coffee would be served. A great deal of merriment was had by all at the parties, as games were played, songs were sung, stories and proverbs were recited, and the adults conversed late into the night – this was termed 'helva conversation', *helva sohbeti*, which was also the name given to the parties. During the reign of Ahmed III (the Tulip period) the *helva sohbeti* were so popular that the wealthy households transformed them into large-scale entertainment with professional musicians and comedians.

## Mealtimes and etiquette

When it comes to the mealtime, there are some rules of etiquette that are still adhered to. This varies from village to city and from family to family but there are hints of tradition wherever you go.

The early Turks of Central Asia ate on a leather sheet, a *kenduruk*, which was spread out on the floor, or on the ground if eating outside. In the 11th century this evolved into a large tray, *tergi* (*tepsi* in modern Turkish), made out of wood, copper or silver, which was raised on a stone or a wooden trestle to make a low, round table. All meals were eaten at this table and the family would gather to sit around it on cushions.

Before eating, a large jug of water and a hand-washing bowl would be placed by the low table to ensure everyone washed their hands. The mother of the household would then place the food on the table in bowls and copper dishes. In a wealthy home, a servant would bring in the food and the family meal would usually begin with a soup, followed by a savoury pastry or pilaff, and a vegetable dish. In a poorer household, there might have been only one dish. At the end of the meal, the water jug and hand-washing bowl would appear once again, and the men would then be left to enjoy tobacco and coffee or tea. In rural Anatolia, families still eat in this manner.

During the Ottoman period, communal meals were traditionally the domain of men who ate in institutions such as the military, dervish lodges, or rest houses. A bowl of soup with some bread or boiled rice would be placed in the middle of the low table and each diner would use a spoon to dip in. Since the soup was the main dish, it had to be wholesome and nourishing enough to sustain everybody for the day. The meal would end with a prayer and a pinch of salt on the tongue to thank God for the food.

In a traditional Turkish household, some of these rules of etiquette are still followed, such as the washing of hands before and after the meal, respecting the prayer that will be recited before and after eating, and popping a pinch of salt on the tongue before and after as well. In addition, strict etiquette can extend to the use of two hands to break bread and only three fingers to pass the food to the mouth.

Knives are rarely present at tables – most dishes have been prepared in a manner that avoids the necessary use of one – and an individual never passes a knife to another without spitting on it first, otherwise it is believed a fight will ensue. Any coughing, sneezing, or picking of teeth with a toothpick must be done with the head turned away from the table and a hand covering the mouth.

It is also polite to compliment the hostess or host on their food after you have finished eating, by saying "elinize sağlık" ("health to your hands"); the idea being to acknowledge that gifted hands have produced a stunning spread, and long may that last.

Top **It is considered polite to use three fingers to raise food to the mouth.**

Bottom **There are many varieties of olive, prepared in countless ways and enjoyed at breakfast, as part of meze, and with a drink as a snack.**

# Meze

The tradition of meze dates back to the ancient Greeks, Romans and Persians, as well as the medieval Arabs and Ottomans. Until relatively recently, it was a custom enjoyed by men alone – traders, travellers, noblemen, kings and Sultans. Traditionally, a table of meze would have been laid out to accompany spirits with the aim of achieving a 'pleasant head', not to fill one's belly but to delight one's palate, as the word meze is thought to have originated from the Persian word maza, which means relish or taste (beyond Turkey the word is spelled mezze). Often loosely translated as hors d'oeuvre, appetisers or snacks, the versatility of meze enables it to be all of these things and more, enjoyed at any time of day. With this in mind, many Turks tend to have meze in the evening when time is not pressing and a glass of cloudy *rakı* can be sipped at leisure. Whether your meze consists of one simple dish or an impressive spread (read more overleaf), it is about the pleasure of sharing.

# The pleasure of meze

Sharing a selection of meze dishes with friends is my favourite way to eat. The sight of so many delicious-looking, freshly-prepared dips, salads and stuffed vegetables never fail to make me feel hungry: heavenly, garlic-flavoured, smoked aubergine purée; springy cracked wheat salad with tomato, mint and flat leaf parsley; crushed green olives with coriander seeds; small green bell peppers stuffed with aromatic rice, pine nuts and currants; spicy walnut purée with pomegranate syrup; artichokes and broad (fava) beans in olive oil; a sweet, tangy *tahin* and lemon purée; light, crisp, cigar-shaped pastries filled with white cheese, mint and dill; plump mussels coated in a beer batter and deep-fried; tiny, tasty fish *köfte* flavoured with cinnamon and dill; thin strips of warm, grilled aubergine and courgette served with a cooling, garlic yogurt; and whole juicy mushrooms cooked with pine nuts, spices and fresh herbs. Each and every plate of temptation is classed as meze.

The most primitive form of meze is a small plate of *çerez*, which usually consists of a dainty serving of dried fruit, such as white mulberries, or plump olives with a squeeze of lemon juice, or even just a selection of nuts, roasted pumpkin seeds, salted sunflower seeds, or roasted chickpeas (*leblebi*). Full of protein and minerals, and delicious when freshly roasted, nuts have long been eaten as appetisers because they are reputed to increase one's toleration of alcohol. Other simple but popular meze dishes include sweet, juicy melon cut into golden chunks and served with cubes of white cheese, and *ezme* dishes, which consist of ingredients that are beaten, crushed, mashed, pounded, puréed, or pressed into a paste, perfect for scooping up with bread. Not all dishes that are pounded or puréed are called *ezme* – some have their own names like *humus*, made with chickpeas; *tarama*, made with fish roe; and *fava*, a dish of puréed broad beans. When it comes to fruit and vegetables each season offers its own special gems, such as fine slices of fresh quince with a squeeze of lemon; the unripe, firm, tart-tasting green plums (*erik*) that are dipped in salt; the sweet ruby pomegranates dripping in juice; watermelon, figs and cherries; as well as fresh salads prepared with sun-ripened plump tomatoes, purple carrots, turnips and radishes, broad beans and artichokes. Meze and salads go hand in hand, as many salads are served as meze, and some pulped and puréed dishes are called 'salad', even if they do not resemble one.

The wonderful thing about meze is that there really are no rules. The pleasure of meze is not regulated by timing or order of dishes, just the understanding that the food should be served in small quantities to be savoured and shared at a leisurely pace, and that one should rise feeling contented and comfortable, not stuffed.

Opposite **Meze dishes and backgammon in a café.**

# Religious days and festivals

At the root of the modern culinary culture, there is the role of Islam. Although not every Turk is a follower of Islam, some culinary habits, hours of prayer, days of fasting and religious holidays and events are based on Muslim practices so they can have an impact on people's lives whatever their beliefs. These Muslim practices include fasting during Ramazan, only eating halal meat, refraining from eating pork and drinking alcohol, and the consumption of traditional foods to celebrate religious days and rites of passage. The principal religious events in Turkey are Ramazan, the month of fasting; Ramazan Bayramı (Şeker Bayramı), a three-day festival at the end of the month-long fast; Kurban Bayramı, a festival to mark the near-sacrifice of Isaac; and Muharrem, the first month of the Muslim calendar. The other social events and ritual ceremonies involving food and feasting include circumcisions, weddings, childbirth, funerals, and various local gatherings, such as the celebration of the spring harvest. The customs and rituals associated with the faith gather families together to cook and celebrate, lending certain foods a sacred significance.

Perhaps enforced by the Koranic verse "To enjoy sweets is a sign of faith", there seems no limit to the capacity and creativity of pudding- and pastry-making in the name of religious or social duty. *Helva* is prepared for commemorative occasions, such as births and deaths, as well as moving house, graduating from school, the commencement of military service, and many harvests and festivals. *Zerde*, a jelly-like, saffron-scented rice pudding, *helva* and *baklava* are all traditionally prepared for weddings and circumcision feasts in the belief that by eating something sweet, a sweet life will be ensured. The Sweet Festival, Şeker Bayramı, that marks the end of the month of fasting, is testament to the importance of sweet things.

## Islamic rules

In the holy book of Islam, the Koran, there are four categories of food that are strictly forbidden: any animal that died in a manner other than by having its throat cut (non-halal meat); the blood from an animal's body; all forms of pork; and the meat of an animal that is sacrificed in the name of any other god. The consumption of other creatures, such as reptiles and beasts of prey, are not restricted in the text but Islamic scholars consider them harmful so they are not on the culinary menu. Although it is considered lawful to "fish in the sea and consume the catch", only a small proportion of Turks tuck into shellfish.

Opposite **The Blue Mosque in Istanbul is a triumph of architectural harmony and elegance laid out in a classical Ottoman design, and is one of only two mosques in Turkey to feature six minarets. Illuminated in the evening light, it looks magnificent. Officially called the Sultan Ahmed Mosque, it has acquired the 'blue' in its name from the stunning design of Iznik tiles and stained glass windows in different shades of blue that line the interior walls and domes.**

The Koran also forbids any form of alcoholic drink, although the text refers to "wine", providing the opportunity for argument among those who wish to consume *rakı*, or other local spirits. The words of the Prophet Muhammad are: "That which causes any form of inebriation is wine and any kind of wine is forbidden." The restrictions imposed by the Koran are waived on the rare occasion of severe hunger or thirst, or an illness that occurs in a situation where it is impossible to stick to the strict Islamic rules.

**Ramazan** | The ninth month of the Muslim calendar, which follows the lunar year, is called Ramazan (Ramadan) in Turkey. This is the month of fasting that is observed by all Muslims. Fasting during Ramazan is regarded as an act of piety – this means that no food or drink may pass the lips during the period between the early morning meal, Sahur, eaten an hour before the morning prayer, and the call to the evening prayer, when the Itfar meal can be enjoyed.

In some neighbourhoods and villages, there is a festive atmosphere during Ramazan as friends and relatives visit each other and share in the ritual meals. However, modern life requires that business carries on as usual, so tempers can run wild during the daytime, especially if Ramazan falls during the hot season. The only exceptions to the rule of fasting are infants considered too young to undergo the rigours of fasting, pregnant women, the sick and elderly, and travellers.

Traditionally, the meals taken during Ramazan are Sahur, a little breakfast taken pre-dawn, and Itfar, to break the fast at the end of the day. The breakfast normally consists of special breads, such as Ramazan *pide* or *simit* (the round bread rings), accompanied by various jams, cheese and olives, as well as cups of blessed water.

The meals of Ramazan generally include light soups, seasonal vegetables cooked in olive oil, stuffed vine leaves and peppers, meat stews, *baklava*, and flat breads such as *pide* and *güllaç*, the paper-thin sheets soaked in milky rose-flavoured syrup. The Sahur meal is lighter on the stomach and always ends with fresh fruit or fruit compôte, *hoşaf*, to leave the mouth refreshed rather than thirsty for the long day of fasting ahead.

**Ramazan Bayramı** | When the month of fasting draws to a close, it is time to celebrate with another festival, Ramazan Bayramı, also known as Şeker Bayramı, the Festival of Sweets – basically a three-day sweet fest. Again families and friends visit each other, but the streets are festive, too, with an abundance of street sellers, merriment and fireworks. In addition to the savoury dishes, this festival is celebrated with a myriad of sweet dishes, such as *baklava* and *kadayıf*, as well as *helva* and *lokum* (Turkish Delight) and other forms of confectionery, including sugared almonds and boiled sweets or candies. Children are given sweets

Top **Spongy flat breads like this are often served at Ramazan.**

Bottom **Light soups and stuffed vegetables are typical dishes served at the Iftar meal to break the fast.**

wherever they go, and boxes of *lokum* are presented to guests, hosts and friends when people visit one another. For such events some people will drive to the other side of a city to get the freshest *baklava* from a famous *baklavacı* that uses ghee or a high-quality butter in the pastry, or they will fetch the creamiest milk dessert from the most reputed milk-pudding shop, *muhallebici*, and they search for the most moist *helva* from the *helvaci*.

**Kurban Bayramı** | The holy festival of Kurban Bayramı is another important event in the Muslim calendar across the Islamic world, as it marks the near-sacrifice of Isaac.

At Kurban Bayramı sheep are herded through streets, villages and markets, where families gather to buy one to take home and sacrifice it ritually. The family will then choose cuts of meat and offal (innards) to make special dishes to mark the event and give the rest to the poor in the neighbourhood.

The prepared dishes will include *işkembe çorbası*, the traditional tripe soup that is served with a splash of vinegar or pickles; *kavurma*, which involves frying the meat in its own fat; a pilaff made with the sheep's liver; *köfte* and kebabs; *kıkırdak poğaçası*, a delicacy made by boiling the fat tail; and *bumbar dolması*, a dish of grilled intestines stuffed with liver, onions, spices and currants, which is similar to the street speciality, *kokoreç*.

**Muharrem** | On the tenth day of Muharrem, which is the first month of the Islamic calendar, the martyrdom of Hüseyin, the Prophet's grandson, is commemorated with prayers in the mosques and the sharing by families and friends of *aşure*, a magnificent fruit and grain dessert that is also associated with the legend of Noah's Ark. It is believed to have evolved when provisions ran low on the Ark and Noah suggested that all the remaining dried fruit, nuts and grains should be boiled together. Following tradition, it is made in vast quantities so that it can be shared with everyone. The preparation and sharing of *aşure* can take place at any time from the tenth day onwards and each household uses nuts, grains and dried fruits of their choice then shares it with friends and neighbours. Sometimes particular members of the family are appointed to make this dessert every year, as their version is considered to be unbeatable.

**Kandil** | There are five religious feast nights called Kandil nights, when the minarets of the mosques are illuminated. The dates and months of these nights are determined by the Arabic calendar, which follows the lunar year.

On the twelfth night of the third month, Rebiülevvel, it is the Prophet Muhammad's birthday; the first Friday of the seventh month, Receb,

Top **A skilled maker of *kadayıf* swirls fine shreds of the pastry dough on a revolving stovetop.**

Bottom ***Aşure*, the fruit and grain pudding which is associated with Noah's Ark and served at Muharrem, varies according to personal preference or availability of ingredients – some like it plain, others decorate it elaborately.**

marks the Prophet's conception and is particularly significant as it is the night that people believe their prayers will be answered; the twenty-seventh night of the seventh month marks the Prophet's ascension to heaven; the fifteenth night of the eighth month, Şaban, is the Night of Privilege, when the angels note and consider the future actions of individuals for the ensuing year; and the twenty-seventh night of the ninth month, Ramazan, is the night of Power, when the Koran was revealed to the world. This last night, known as Kandil Gecesi, is the most celebrated and joyous of all the Kandil nights, as people gather in the streets to enjoy fireworks and festive foods. Perhaps because it occurs towards the end of the month of fasting, devout Muslims are usually in the mood to feast extensively and have fun. Kandil foods include *lokma*, pastries soaked in syrup, *baklava* and *helva*.

Top **Semolina *helva* with pine nuts is prepared for special occasions.**

Bottom **There are many types of Turkish Delight, some made with roasted pistachios, hazelnuts or walnuts, others delicately flavoured with scented oil and water such as lemon and rose.**

**Hidrellez** The spring festival, Hıdrellez, takes place in some rural regions of Turkey. Generally, it is an occasion for families to gather in the countryside and celebrate together with typical picnic food, such as stuffed vine leaves, *kuru köfte*, and pilaff dishes containing chunks of meat. A great deal of merriment is had by all, as the women prepare the picnic, the men cook the meat on the *mangal*, the children run about and play in the woods and fields, and the whole family dance and sing together after eating.

**Circumcisions** In modern Turkish society, circumcision remains an important event. It usually takes place when a boy is between the ages of five and eight years old.

Proud parents dress their boys in a white jacket, trousers and a cape and often a group of boys will face the circumcision together. Before the event, the boys are sometimes marched through the streets to the beat of a drum and, after their ordeal, which is carried out by a religious person or a doctor, they lie on a bed in the middle of a room, often in some degree of discomfort, while the family and friends gather to feast and dance. All the guests bear gifts of sweetmeats, money, and good-luck talismans for the boys. Plenty of sweet dishes are served at these feasts, as well as stuffed vine leaves, meatballs, pilaff, and *keşkek*, a porridge-like mixture of bulgur wheat and meat.

During the Ottoman period, the circumcision feasts of princes lasted for days, even weeks and, on occasion, these celebrations would be combined with the marriage festivities of the princesses. Guests would arrive from faraway corners of the Empire to be met by high standards of hospitality. When Mehmed IV had his sons Mustafa (Mustafa II) and Ahmed (Ahmed III) circumcised, he also arranged the marriage of his sister, Hatice Sultana, who was only seven years old at the time. The celebrations for this occasion lasted for almost one month and involved thousands of dishes, including 50,000 chickens.

**Weddings** | In both urban and rural Turkey, no wedding would be complete without a great deal of feasting and dancing. Depending on the region, the bride may be transported to her wedding on the back of a donkey, in a horse-drawn cart, or in the family car, and she is almost invariably dressed in white.

Many of the wedding dishes are associated with other social events, such as births and religious festivals, but among the wealth of meatballs, stuffed vine leaves, savoury pastries and myriad vegetables on offer, there will always be rice in the form of a pilaff, sometimes served in a ceremonious mound or encased in pastry, *perdeli pilav*, and in the traditional pudding, *zerde*.

Some of the dishes are prepared to welcome the bride into the groom's household or, as in the case of *içli köfte* (mother-in-law meatballs), to ensure the bride's lips are sealed with discretion. Others, such as the rice grains in pilaff and the seeds of pomegranate, symbolise fertility and the birth of many children. Trays of confectionery, such as sugared almonds and Turkish Delight, as well as *helva* and *baklava*, will be offered by hosts and brought by guests to ensure a sweet life for all.

Before and after an Ottoman wedding, confectionery was served to women in the harem and to men in the selamlık (the female and male areas of a palace or house). At the end of the ceremony, the guests would be splashed with rose water and served a fruit or almond sherbet in silver goblets. The ensuing banquet would be lavish, with every type and shape of bread, rice piled in a dome dripping with butter, and whole roasted lamb, or leg of lamb with almonds. The day after the feast, the women would gather for *paça günü* ('sheep's hooves day'), at which they would eat sheep's hooves in a soup or stew sent to them by the groom. The bride would wear a special dress for the occasion, at which musicians and dancers performed.

Top **A special red drink, *lohusa şerbeti*, is offered to guests celebrating the arrival of a new baby.**

Bottom **Beautifully fragrant rose water is used to sprinkle over guests at traditional weddings.**

**Births** | On the second or third day after the birth of a child, a sweet red drink, *lohusa şerbeti*, is prepared to mark the joyous occasion. Flavoured with cloves and coloured with cochineal, this drink is served to visitors who come to congratulate the mother and bring gifts for the baby. In some traditional households, a *kına gecesi*, a henna night, is still held on the seventh night after the child is born. Traditionally, this was when neighbours and friends were invited to dine, play music and sing.

**Funerals** | When someone dies, neighbours prepare simple food, such as savoury pastries, pilaffs, and meat stews, for the family of the deceased during their period of mourning. On the day of the funeral, however, the grieving family prepares a helva made with semolina and pine nuts, *irmik helvası*, to offer to visitors who have come to pay their respects. In some Anatolian households, the family may also prepare *helva* or *lokma*, fried pastries soaked in syrup, to offer to the spirit of the deceased.

# The Turkish kitchen

Turkish cuisine is often cited as one of the best in the world and it is easy to see why. A land of rich produce combined with Anatolian and Ottoman traditions, Turkish life revolves around food, almost to the point of obsession, as the people are united in pride for their culinary heritage. You can actually feel that passion as you travel around the country and become immersed in the seasonal cooking of each region.

**The centre of the home** | The traditional kitchen was split into two sections: the pantry and the cooking area. The pantry was usually dark and ventilated, so that the goods remained fresh for days or even months. Jars of jam, honey, *pekmez*, pickles and cooking oils were placed on a stone step along the base of one of the walls, and the *pastırma*, *sucuk*, onions and garlic hung from hooks along the wall. Fresh fruits were also hung in muslin or cheesecloth bags for storing and preserving. The dry goods, such as flour, sugar and bulgur wheat, were stored in sealed copper and earthenware pots to keep the ants and weevils at bay. As these foods were used daily, they would be placed somewhere accessible, near the doorway connecting the pantry to the cooking area.

Inside the cooking area you would normally find a basin and a fountain for washing, shelves for the storage pots, pans and crockery, and a wire-mesh meat safe, used for keeping flies off the cooked dishes.

Located in the same part of the kitchen, near the kitchen hearth or stove, you would find a wide, round wooden board or low table. Surrounded by cushions and sited in the optimum spot for the swift transfer of pastries to and from the oven, this table would be required for rolling out huge wheels of *yufka*. This difficult art is still practised today, but can really only be successfully achieved by using an *oklava*, a long, thin rolling pin designed for the purpose. Nearby, stacks of round, shallow baking tins or pans, *tepsi*, would be at hand, ready to be lined with the sheets of *yufka* to make the pastries so enjoyed by Turks.

**Stoves and ovens** | A *mangal* (a charcoal stove) would be used for cooking a wide range of dishes in a traditional kitchen, while a coke-fed stove (*maltız*), or a hearth, was used for dishes that required an intense heat. As the *mangal* was portable, it could be used in the open doorway, or outside in the courtyard, which is where you often see them today – in people's yards, on their balconies and taken on picnics in the countryside. Any bread-baking or roasting would take place in the family *tandır*, a pit dug in the earth, or in the village *fırın*, a large communal oven. For some festive occasions, a whole sheep or goat would be cooked on a spit over the family *tandır*, to be shared among friends.

Top **Preparing traditional pastry dough – *yufka* – using a long, thin rolling pin called an *oklava*, in the hearth area of a rural kitchen.**

Bottom **Popular street and village food cooked over a hot domed griddle, *gözleme* are traditional flat breads that can be enjoyed sweet, sprinkled with sugar or drizzled in honey, or savoury with fillings of spinach and cheese or minced meat.**

Top **The *mangal* is in constant use for grilling and barbecueing, and many are small enough to be portable on picnics.**

Bottom **A traditional oven-baked savoury pastry, *saç boreği*, prepared with layers of the paper-thin sheets of *yufka*.**

**Kitchens today** | When you step into the village kitchens of central and eastern Anatolia very little has changed since ancient times. Only basic tools are used, such as wooden spoons, deep ladles, heavy enamel pans or tin-lined, copper pots. Earthenware casserole dishes (*güveç*), or concave roof tiles (*kiremit*), are used for roasting and baking cuts of meat and fish in the communal oven.

A copper yogurt urn lined with tin is still used to make yogurt whenever it is required. As Turks consume a lot of yogurt, this can be on a daily basis. Depending on the region, these yogurt urns can be very attractive, like the elegant tulip-shaped ones from Trabzon, or plain like the stout, bucket-shaped urns used in Van.

A sturdy mortar and pestle, usually made out of stone, brass, or iron, is used for crushing spices and lighter, wooden ones, often with a convenient handle, are used for crushing garlic with salt to create a creamy mixture that is beaten into yogurt and other dishes.

Brass coffee grinders and the long-handled *cezve* are the necessary equipment for making Turkish coffee, while the double-tiered tea-pot system and dainty tea glasses, which are often shaped like tulips, are the required utensils for making tea. The teapot system is a crude form of Russian samovar, enabling tea to be made all day long by continually filling the top pot with boiling water from the bottom one.

Long metal, copper, or aluminium skewers for grilling meat can be plain or elaborate, depending on the location and the wealth of the family. Some are decorated with the Turkish symbol – the star and sickle moon motif – while others display designs of tulips, or a pomegranate with seeds to symbolise prosperity and fertility.

Long, thick kebab swords are also a feature of kitchens in the southern region of Turkey, where fiery mince kebabs are cooked around them as the sheath to the sword.

**Rural and urban kitchens** | Cooking practices differ slightly in towns. Many urban dwellers have fairly simple kitchens at the back of the house in which the family meals will be cooked, but little baking is done, as urban dwellers rely on the neighbourhood specialist bakers for their selection of breads and pastries. In the city, urban Turks also enjoy going out to the pudding shops and pastry houses for their sweet snacks. With such a vibrant restaurant scene in the cities, dining out is commonplace.

In rural parts of Anatolia, recipes are still handed from mother to daughter and many of chefs in restaurants are men, but this is no longer as black and white as it used to be. In places like Istanbul, Izmir, Ankara and the tourist centres in the south, there are a growing number of female and foreign chefs, an influx of cookery books, TV cookery programmes, and cookery schools. Some chefs specialise in Ottoman or Palace cuisine; others keep regional cooking alive by holding on to their traditional roots and techniques.

# An abundance of ingredients

The Turkish kitchen is a unique tapestry of exciting tastes. Life revolves around food, and with daily markets bursting with vegetables and fruit, bunches of herbs and baskets of pungent spices, crates of gleaming, fresh fish, and cheeses stacked into towers next to buckets of yogurt, it is easy to see how food has become an obsession. Cooking in Turkey is a passion, and most of the dishes are wonderfully versatile, and simple.

# Vegetables

To my mind, the vegetable produce in Turkey and the dishes prepared with them are some of the best in the Mediterranean. The variety is simply astounding, and I always feel I am eating healthily as the Turks are fascinated with the health properties of the food they eat and vegetables play an extremely important role in this. For example, aubergines are believed to be beneficial for fighting infections of the ovaries, courgettes for combating intestinal parasites, onions for ulcers, cabbage for stomach pains, and garlic for blood circulation and overall good health. It is not unusual to find baskets of dried medicinal herbs and vegetables, their seeds and roots, beside piles of fresh vegetables. Throughout the Seljuk and Ottoman periods, many recipes were based on the ancient Chinese yin and yang theory that some vegetables 'warm' the blood whereas others 'cool' it. As a result, Turkish cooking possesses more healthy vegetable dishes than most other cuisines.

Visiting the market is very much part of the day's activities in most households. Choosing the vegetables for lunch or supper can be quite time-consuming and a lot of fun, while the cooks pick over the vegetables on display and haggle with the sellers. Often the vegetables available will dictate the meals of the day, as there might be an unexpected selection of fresh beans bursting from their pods, or the regal-looking, young globe artichokes artfully prepared for cooking. Cucumbers are peeled at the markets and sold as a refreshing snack, and giant cos lettuces are taken home to be placed in a jug of water on the table, so that everyone can help themselves to a long crunchy leaf and sprinkle it with a little salt – a delightful way to enjoy lettuce, particularly on a hot day.

**Artichokes (enginar)** | In botanical terms, the globe artichoke is really just a rather splendid-looking thistle that happens to be edible. The tall plants are cultivated throughout the Middle East and Turkey, where the regal-looking globe is regarded as a delicacy. Turks rarely eat the scales; instead, the globes are trimmed down to their hearts, or bottoms. In the markets, the fresh artichokes are sold on their stems so that they can be stood in a bucket of water, like a bunch of flowers, until ready to use.

When preparing the globes, they need to be rubbed with lemon juice and plunged into cold water to prevent them from discolouring. The most traditional method of cooking artichokes is to poach them in olive oil, either on their own with dill, or with broad (fava) beans, almonds and tomatoes, both of which are called *zeytinyağlı enginar*. Another version involves stuffing the artichokes with aromatic rice and wrapping them in vine leaves before poaching in olive oil.

Top **Carefully selecting vegetables from a stall at a rural market.**

Bottom **Classic summer vegetables destined for the traditional *zeytinyağlı*, olive oil, dishes.**

Top **Plump, fleshy aubergines ideal for smoking.**

Bottom **Place the aubergine directly on to the gas flame to char the skin and smoke the flesh.**

Aubergines/eggplants (patlıcan) | Sometimes referred to as 'poor man's meat', aubergines are cooked in numerous ways in Turkey. During the Ottoman period, the Palace chefs were known to have prepared aubergines in at least 40 different recipes, and some Turks claim there are at least 200 aubergine dishes in the country.

Generally, the aubergines of the region are purple, or almost black, in colour and range from the large, bulbous ones that are shaped like boxing gloves, and the long, slender variety that are ideal for *dolma*, to the small teardrop-shaped ones, which taste lovely smoked. Smoking aubergines is common practice in Turkey, where the distinctive-tasting flesh is bound with olive oil and plenty of freshly squeezed lemon juice and made into a variety of delicious meze dishes, such as *patlıcan ezmesi* and *patlıcan salatası*, or it is beaten into a cheese sauce to make the unique dish, *beğendi*.

Every part of an aubergine is used in Turkey, including the skins, which are hung up to dry in the sun and then threaded on to strings and sold in the markets. Reconstituted in water, the skins are stuffed in the winter with an aromatic pilaff or spicy bulgur wheat mixture, or poached in a little olive oil and lemon juice to make a dish that is a speciality of the *güney* cuisine from Gaziantep and Antakya. Another speciality from that region is jars of pickled aubergines stuffed with hot peppers, and if you travel westwards along the coast to Adana, you will come across a most unusual jam made with baby aubergines.

**Frying aubergines** Prior to frying, whole aubergines are generally partially peeled in stripes, a little bit like the markings of a zebra, and then submerged in a bowl of salted water for 30 minutes. Similarly, aubergine slices or cubes are soaked in salted water first and then drained. The idea here is to draw out any indigestible juices that may be present and to soften the flesh slightly. Both the whole aubergines and the slices must be thoroughly drained and, in some cases, squeezed of any excess water before they are dropped into the hot oil.

**Smoking aubergines** To smoke aubergines easily and effectively, you need to have a gas cooker or a barbecue or charcoal grill. First, place the whole aubergine directly over the gas flame, or over the hot charcoal. Leave to soften, turning from time to time. Over a gas flame the skin will become charred and flaky, whereas the heat from the barbecue or charcoal grill toughens the skin like leather. When the aubergine is soft (that is, so that you can press it down easily with your finger), place it in a plastic bag to sweat for a few minutes. To extract the smoked flesh, you can slit the aubergine open lengthways and scoop it out, or you can hold the aubergine by its stalk under running cold water and peel off the skin using your fingers – if you do the latter, make sure you squeeze out the excess water at the end.

**Beans (taze fasulye)** | Runner beans, string beans and green (French) beans all come under the banner 'fresh beans' (*taze fasulye*). Only fresh borlotti (*barbunya*) and broad (*fava*) beans have their own names – this may be because they are used in their dried form too. All the fresh green beans are cooked in the same way, the principal and most delicious method being to cook them in olive oil with a little tomato and dill, *zeytinyağlı taze fasulye*.

**Beetroot/beet (pancar)** | The most popular way to enjoy beetroot in Turkey is to pickle it in a mixture of vinegar, garlic and salt. Baby beetroot are pickled whole and the large ones are sliced. Slices of beetroot are added to jars of pickled turnip to colour it a pretty shade of pink. Beetroot is also often enjoyed as a meze dish mixed with yogurt.

**Carrots (havuç)** | The south of Turkey is one of the few regions where you can still find red- and purple-skinned carrots, which have a slightly peppery taste, more akin to a radish than a regular orange carrot. These special carrots are best appreciated as a grated salad, dressed in a little lemon juice.

The orange colour of most carrots is due to the high content of betacarotene and these carrots also contain a fair amount of natural sugar, making them both pretty to look at and sweet to taste. A popular vegetable in the Turkish kitchen, the long, tasty carrots add a splash of bright colour to many dishes. They are grated or chopped and combined with yogurt; tossed in salads and pilaffs, such as *kaşgar pilav*; cooked with lentils, beans, or other vegetables in stews; sliced and pickled, steamed and puréed to make *ezme* or *köfte*; and poached with sugar to make a sticky *helva* or a delectable jam.

**Celery (kereviz)** | Celery stalks are mainly braised with meat, or they are grated and combined with coconut in the refreshing southern salad, *kereviz salatası*. The celery root, on the other hand, is employed in a number of meat and fish dishes. Generally it is diced and cooked with potatoes and carrots, to which it adds its own distinctive flavour.

**Courgettes/zucchini (kabak)** | The courgette is an immature marrow (large zucchini), which is believed in Turkey to be cooling to the blood and, therefore, requires balancing with warm herbs, such as dill and mint. The young, fresh, bright-green courgettes are crisp and slightly perfumed, and are best tossed raw in salads or cooked very lightly. At the beginning of the season, young courgettes are often sold with their papery, yellowy-orange flowers attached, and these can be stuffed with aromatic rice or bulgur wheat. The courgettes in the Turkish markets are always green or creamy-coloured with a marbled effect. They are rarely much longer than 18cm (7in), as they should be firm and tender, not

Top **Beetroot is particularly used in meze dishes and for pickling.**

Bottom **Courgettes are often stuffed with rice or minced meat.**

large and spongy, or watery. They are often cooked with tomatoes in stews or egg dishes, alternatively they can be deep-fried and served with a nut sauce, *tarator*, or garlic-flavoured yogurt; stuffed with aromatic rice in a similar manner to aubergines; or combined with white cheese in the mint- and dill-flavoured patties, *kabak mücver*. The larger marrows, on the other hand, tend to be more watery and are stuffed with minced meat, or cooked in stews. The seeds of the marrow are roasted and eaten like pumpkin seeds or nuts.

**Cucumbers (salatalik)** | Generally, the cucumbers of Turkey are much the same size as courgettes – short and stubby and almost seedless. The skin is quite bitter, so they are usually peeled, or partially peeled, before eating. One of the most refreshing street snacks is a freshly peeled cucumber dipped in salt. Strips of cucumber sprinkled with salt is also a popular meze dish. When not being devoured on their own, cucumbers are sliced or chopped and added to salads, such as the cooling yogurt and mint dish, *cacık*

**Lamb's lettuce (semiz otu)** | The Turkish lamb's lettuce (or mâche) is fairly thick and fleshy. Its principal role is in a simple salad dressed with garlic-spiked yogurt, *semiz otu salatası*, which is served as a meze dish or as an accompaniment to grilled meat and savoury pastries. Otherwise, it is braised with minced meat, or sautéed with beans.

**Leeks (pirasa)** | In Turkish markets, the leeks are as long as hockey sticks and feature in the expression '*pırasa bıyıklı*', which means 'whiskered like a leek' in reference to the Turkish men with long, bushy moustaches that droop down the sides of their chins. Leeks have been used in cooking since the Turks migrated from Central Asia and remain very popular to this day. They are employed in a range of soups, stews, patties and savoury pastries. They are also cooked on their own in olive oil, *zeytinyağlı pırasa*, and are stuffed with rice and minced meat in *pırasa dolması*, which is usually served with an elegant egg and lemon sauce.

**Okra (bamya)** | Fresh okra is cooked on its own, lightly sautéed with lemon, or added to meat, poultry and vegetable stews. It is usually widely available in Middle Eastern, African and Asian stores, as well as many supermarkets. When choosing okra, look for pods that are firm, unblemished and bright green in colour. The tiny dried okra pods are grey-green and slightly hairy. They need to be rubbed in a cloth to remove the hairs before using. They are used primarily in soups and stews originating from the south-eastern region of Turkey, where the dried pods are enjoyed for the tart flavour they impart to the dish. Strings of dried okra hang in the markets alongside strings of dried aubergines and bell peppers.

Top left **Runner beans are often cooked with tomato and dill and in a *zeytinyağlı*, olive oil, dish.**

Top right **A wide variety of onions are grown, and are key ingredients in many Turkish dishes.**

Bottom left **Borlotti beans (sometimes known as cranberry beans) are satisfyingly meaty and are particularly delicious prepared as a *zeytinyağlı* meze dish.**

Bottom right **Broad beans are sought after to make the popular purée, *fava*.**

**Onions (soğan)** | All types of onion are usually available in the markets in Turkey, from the round and bulbous varieties in their varying shades of red, purple and gold, to the pearly, white onions, pink shallots and long, mild-tasting spring onions (scallions). Large white onions are often hollowed out and then stuffed with an aromatic mixture of rice and minced lamb before being baked in the oven. Golden onions are used for making a popular cumin-flavoured marinade for meat and fish. First, the peeled onion is grated and crushed to a pulp, which is sprinkled with salt and left to weep; the pulp is then pressed in a sieve to extract the onion juice, which is generally mixed with crushed cumin seeds and spread over the meat or fish.

Purple and red onions are particularly favoured for salads and meze dishes, as they are slightly sweet, and shallots are used in stews or threaded on to kebabs. The long onion tops are specially cut to sauté in butter with a squeeze of lemon, or to use in an omelette.

**Peppers (biber)** | The most common peppers used in Turkish cooking are small and green. These slightly tart peppers are the immature fruit of the capsicum pepper plants, and they are often favoured for use in stuffed dishes such as *zeytinyağlı biber*, and for slicing raw into salads.

The more mature, sweet, red capsicum peppers are used in vegetable or meat stews or they are grilled, skinned and marinated in olive oil. They are also dried in the sun, threaded on to long strings and sold in the markets. These dried peppers might be ground to a fruity powder, which we know as paprika; softened in a bowl of warm water to be stuffed with rice or bulgur wheat in the winter; or pounded with hot red pepper, olive oil and salt to form a thick paste, which is used in some meze dishes, soups and stews, and is also enjoyed simply spread thinly on a piece of bread.

The other commonly used pepper in Turkey is the long, thin, twisted, light-green variety, *çarliston biber*, which resembles a Turkish slipper. Mildly perfumed and sometimes slightly hot, these pretty peppers are generally grilled or fried and served whole as a meze dish or as an accompaniment to kebabs.

**Hot peppers and chillies** | Alongside the slipper-shaped peppers in the market, you will also find a darker-green, thinner, twisted pepper, which is – make no mistake – a hot chilli. Rarely cooked in dishes, it is often chopped or sliced and used raw in salads and meze dishes, such as the 'gypsy rice', *çingene pilavı*, and the fresh, fiery relish, *taze ezmesi*. Even hotter are the tiny, green matchstick chillies, which occasionally appear in meat dishes, but are more often preserved in vinegar to make a fiery pickle. The other hot pepper used in the Turkish kitchen is the red, horn-shaped chilli, which is generally dried and used as the ubiquitous spice, *pul biber* or *kırmızı biber*, in many dishes.

Top left **Leeks can be large, even to the length of a man's forearm.**

Top right **Okra, or ladies' fingers, are often tossed in lemon juice to retain their colour and cooked with tomatoes in stews.**

Bottom left **The mildly perfumed green *çarliston biber*.**

Bottom right **Vine leaves are traditionally used to make *dolma*, little hot or cold parcels stuffed with rice or minced meat, and are often used to wrap around fish and to add to jars of pickles.**

Top **Globe artichokes are sold on their stems so they can be kept fresh in a jug of water.**

Bottom **Street sellers and market stalls will prepare artichoke bottoms for the seasonal *zeytinyağlı* dishes.**

**Pumpkins (bal kabaği)** | Autumn, the season of pumpkins, heralds the arrival of the pumpkin-seller in the streets of villages and cities, his cart laden with the bright orange, gourd-like fruits. These he skilfully peels and cuts for the traditional syrupy dessert, *bal kabağı tatlısı*, in which succulent blocks of pumpkin are poached in a clove-scented syrup. Other pumpkin dishes include soup, stews, pilaff, savoury pastry, jam and baklava, but the most impressive of all is baked pumpkin stuffed with a jewelled pilaff, which consists of pine nuts, pistachio nuts, currants, orange peel, and apricots, or with an aromatic lamb pilaff. In some Anatolian villages, the hollowed-out pumpkin is used as a cooking vessel for soups and stews (although it can only be used once). Pumpkin seeds are roasted and eaten as a snack wherever you go in Turkey.

**Spinach (ispanak)** | Medieval records show that spinach was originally used as a herb and was not regarded as a vegetable until the Arabs introduced it into the Turkish cuisine. In Turkey it features in a number of vegetable or meat stews, but its most popular role is when it is combined with butter or a cheese sauce and used as a filling for savoury pastries and flat breads. It is also very popular as a meze dish, served warm or cold, with garlic-flavoured yogurt. The spinach roots are often sautéed in butter with beans or poached in lemon juice.

**Tomatoes (domate)** | One of the 16th-century New World arrivals in the region, tomatoes are so entrenched in the cuisine of Turkey that it is difficult to imagine how the Turks and other tribal peoples of Anatolia managed without them. The tomato harvests are abundant and the bright-red fruit come in a variety of shapes and sizes, all exceedingly tasty, as they benefit from being ripened in the sun. Generally, tomatoes are skinned and seeded before being added raw to salads or cooked in infinite ways. Whole tomatoes are stuffed with rice, bulgur wheat, or minced meat, in the same manner as bell peppers. Ripe tomatoes are crushed to a pulp, which is poured into trays and thickened in the sun to form a paste, whereas the unripe, green fruit is pickled.

Firm plum tomatoes are also poached in syrup to make a delicious jam that is spooned on to fresh, crusty bread. Turkey is one of the largest producers of tomatoes and exports them fresh, as well as dried and in cans of commercial paste.

**Vine leaves (yaprak)** | Fresh vine leaves are usually sold stacked in piles in the markets, as well as being preserved in brine in packets, jars and cans. The leaves have a slightly malted taste and are used for wrapping around poached or grilled fish, cheese and stuffed artichokes. Their most famous role, though, is the *dolma*, in which the leaves are filled with an aromatic rice mixture, or one made with minced meat and rice, and then rolled into logs and poached.

If you are using fresh vine leaves, plunge them into boiling water for 1 minute to soften, then drain and refresh them in cold water. Preserved vine leaves, on the other hand, have already been softened, but do need to be soaked to rid them of salt. Place the leaves in a bowl and pour boiling water over them, making sure it gets between the layers. Leave them to soak for about 15 minutes, drain and repeat. Make sure the leaves are thoroughly drained before use.

## Special cooking methods

There are several traditional cooking methods for vegetables. Dipped in batter; deep-fried in sunflower oil; grilled over charcoal – these are popular for meze and street dishes. When a variety of different vegetables are cooked together, they are often baked in an earthenware dish (*güveç*). Sometimes they are packed tightly in layers with meat and cooked gently to make *bastı*, which is usually tipped upside down on a plate so that the bottom layer of meat in the pan lies on top of the vegetables on the serving plate.

Some vegetables lend themselves to being hollowed out, then stuffed with minced meat or rice, or a mixture of the two, called *dolma* or *orturtma*, but the most unique of all is the *zeytinyağlı* dish, in which the vegetables are poached gently in olive oil.

**Zeytinyağlı** | The *zeytinyağlı* (olive oil) dishes are an exquisite legacy of the Palace kitchens. The traditional method involves poaching the vegetables, some of which may be stuffed, in a generous quantity of olive oil combined with a little lemon juice so that they are deliciously moist and tender, silky and melt-in-the-mouth. The vegetables are then left to cool in the oil and are served at room temperature. The flavoured oil at the base of the pan is very much part of the dish and is spooned over and around the vegetables on the serving plate.

**Dolma** | The word *dolma* is used for vegetables that are stuffed. In fact, it is used for anything that is stuffed, such as fruit and fish, and the famous *dolmuş*, the Turkish taxi stuffed with people! If there isn't a natural cavity to stuff, the Turks will create one, even in an aubergine without splitting it open – a great deal of gentle bashing and massaging expertly forces the aubergine to spit out its innards through a hole at one end, so that the skin can be stuffed.

Fruits, such as apples, plums and prunes, are stuffed and served as a vegetable dish, and vine leaves and cabbage leaves are wrapped around rice fillings to make *dolma*. The most traditional fillings for log-shaped *dolma* consist of an aromatic rice with pine nuts and currants, or minced beef or lamb with rice and herbs.

Top **Cooking vegetables in olive oil is known as *zeytinyağlı*.**

Bottom **Vine leaf *dolma* being prepared.**

# Fruit

I try to time my trips to Turkey with the cherry season. Sweet, juicy and plump, the ripe purple cherries are piled so high in the crates and barrows at the markets, it's a wonder they don't all topple to the ground. The season is short – mid June to mid July – so they are in huge demand. But when the cherry season is over, there are still plums, peaches, figs, grapes, apricots, quinces and pomegranates to look forward to and there are always honey-sweet melons and large juicy watermelons. Most of the seasonal fruit is enjoyed fresh but there is such an abundance that there is plenty to preserve in jams, pickles and juices; in puddings like *ayva tatlısı*, fresh quince poached in a clove-scented syrup; and to dry in the sun for refreshing winter compôtes like the classic *hoşaf*. Apricots, plums and figs, both in their dried and fresh forms, are often filled with cream or nuts and soaked in syrup, and fresh sour cherries are cooked with sugar and poured over baked bread to make *vişne tiridi*, also known as *vişneli ekmek tatlısı*. Other seasonal fresh fruits include mulberries, apples, oranges, green plums, persimmons and loquats.

Apricots (kayısı) | Although the soft-skinned, sun-ripened fresh apricots are often eaten fresh, many will be dried on the flat roofs of central Anatolian villages, destined for all kinds of inspired dishes. Fresh apricots are also poached in sugar to make a delicious, scented jam, while dried apricots are poached in syrup so that they are soft enough to stuff with almond paste or clotted cream, as in the delectable dessert *kaymaklı kayısı*. Dried apricots might be stuffed with a savoury rice and minced lamb filling or added to lamb and chicken stews, and they are combined with other dried fruits and nuts in pilaffs and fruit compôtes, such as *hoşaf*. Naturally sun-dried apricots are coffee-coloured with a hint of caramel in their intense flavour, whereas the commercially dried fruit is treated with sulphur dioxide to retain its bright orange colour.

Cherries, sweet (kiraz) and sour (vişne) | The height of the season for the sweet cherry is relatively short so the juicy, ripe fruits are passionately devoured in quantity for breakfast, for a little refreshment at any time of day, and for dessert. The sour cherry, however, has a number of culinary uses. Poached with sugar, they can be easily transformed into a delicious jam, *vişne reçeli*; a popular summer dessert, *vişne tiridi*; and a wonderful purple syrup that is used as the basis of a refreshing sherbet drink. Sour cherries are also puréed and dried to make 'leathers', and they are dried whole to preserve them for stews and pilaffs. The kernels of the black malep cherries are ground to a powder (also called *malep*), which is used for flavouring biscuits and cakes.

Top **Grapes are harvested in Anatolia for eating fresh as well as for pressing to make sweet, fruity molasses, fruit leathers, and a variety of good quality wines.**

Bottom **The pomegranate harvest on a small farm in Anatolia, where the women extract the seeds of the fruit to press for the juice, which is boiled down to make a sour molasses.**

Top left **There are several types of pomegranate (*nar*), sweet and sour, but the jewel-like seeds symbolise beauty and fertility.**

Top right **Ripe, fragrant quinces (*ayva*) are more usually cooked than eaten raw.**

Bottom left **Compared to fruits like figs and pomegranates, lemons may be relatively new to the Turkish table but they are served with everything.**

Bottom right **Grapes are eaten as dessert, as a snack, dried, juiced, and of course used for wine.**

Figs (incir) | Fresh figs really need to mature on the tree under a hot sun to be at their best: moist and very sweet. A variety of figs grow in Turkey, where they are enjoyed fresh – when ripe, the skin of the most common fig should be slate-grey tinged with purple, and the fruit plump and tender, as if it is about to burst open to reveal its vermilion or pink seeds. However, figs are also picked when small and green, as they are perfect for a delectable jam, *yeşil incir reçeli*, which resembles gleaming jewels floating in syrup, and tastes like honey. With huge harvests every year, figs are also dried in the sun until the skin hardens and lightens in colour. These have a chewy texture and crunchy golden seeds. Turkey is one of the largest exporters of dried figs, along with dried apricots.

Grapes (üzüm) | The grape vine and its fruit have had many culinary uses since ancient times. Turkey is one of the principal producers of the table grape, but there are many other varieties, too – some of which are specially grown to produce dried fruits, others for making wine. In general, the table grapes are green or reddish-purple, very sweet and juicy, and enjoyed just as they are. Tart green grapes are sometimes added to stews, but can be substituted with the sour green plums (*erik*). Fresh grapes are also puréed and dried to make popular 'leathers' and they are pressed for their juice, which is boiled and reduced to form a useful fruit molasses called *pekmez*.

The dried fruits, in the form of raisins and sultanas (golden raisins), are used in sweet dishes, such as Noah's dessert, *aşure*, and the tiny black currants, which are known as *kuş üzümü* (bird grape), are used in many savoury dishes, such as pilaffs and *köfte*, as well as in sweet dishes. Raisins and currants are also used in the production of *rakı*, the distilled aniseed-flavoured, alcoholic drink that many Turks prefer to wine.

Lemons (limon) | Before the arrival of lemons in Turkey, the juice of sour pomegranates, the fermented juice of sour grapes, and ground sumac berries were used as souring agents. Nowadays, though, juicy, thin-skinned lemons are harvested in abundance and are used in dressings, marinades, sherbet drink, and the syrup for *baklava* and other sweet pastries and doughs.

Lemon wedges are served with practically every dish, not simply as a garnish, but to squeeze over the food to give it a refreshing lift and to enhance the flavour. This is particularly effective when the fresh juice is squeezed over fruit, such as sweet melon or watermelon, most vegetable and rice, bean or grain dishes, and the tasty liver dish, *arnavut ciğer*.

Melons (kavun) and watermelons (karpuz) | Although not of the same family, melon and watermelon are sold beside one another in the markets and are eaten fresh and ripe, when the juice dribbles down your chin with every bite. Both fruits are enjoyed as a snack at any time of

Top **Ripe fresh figs are sweet like honey and delicious with savoury and sweet dishes.**

Bottom **Sour cherries grow in abundance and many end up in the country's most popular juice.**

day, cut into cubes at the start of a meal, or sliced into wedges to be served at the end. Golden cubes of honeydew, Galia or Casaba melons are perhaps one of the most traditional forms of meze. A popular way to enjoy them is with cubes of feta, as the sweetness of the juicy melon perfectly complements the salty, firm texture of the cheese. In the southern regions of Turkey, where many unusual jams seem to be concocted, the unripe flesh of both the golden varieties and the watermelon is poached with sugar to make interesting conserves.

When choosing melons in the markets, the simplest test of ripeness is to press the end opposite to the stem to see if it yields, or to smell it for its perfume. The flesh of ripe watermelons should be a vibrant reddish-pink when cut open, with a sweet, fresh taste and not over-watery.

**Pomegranates (nar)** | With its leathery skin and jewel-like seeds, the pomegranate is believed to be a symbol of beauty and fertility, as well as beneficial to the soul, as it purges it of anger, hate and envy.

During the Ottoman period, there were white-skinned and purple-skinned pomegranates available, in addition to the more common red- and pink-skinned fruit that can be found in abundance in the markets today. Generally, the fruit stalls separate the sweet pomegranates for eating from the sour ones for cooking and marinating, although the latter are mainly used for sherbets and molasses (*pekmez*), as lemons have now taken over the 'souring' role of pomegranates.

Fresh pomegranates are mainly enjoyed as a dessert fruit, as they are so deliciously juicy and sweet when ripe. On occasion, a bowl of gleaming, ruby-red seeds may be presented as a dessert, or as a palate-cleanser, all laboriously separated from skin and pith and then chilled – an exquisite and refreshing treat that is sometimes enlivened with a few fresh mint leaves. The fresh seeds are also combined with other fresh or dried fruit in exotic compôtes sprinkled with rose water, or they are scattered over meze dishes, salads and pilaffs.

Pomegranate 'leathers' are dark in colour and slightly sour-tasting, as is the molasses that is used to flavour several stews and roasted poultry, as well as the medieval walnut and red pepper dip, *muhammara*.

**Quinces (ayva)** | Related to the apple and the pear, the quince is similar in appearance although larger and lemon-yellow in colour. The flesh is firm, mildly perfumed, and slightly tart. When consumed in any quantity, it has a tendency to stick your tongue to the roof of your mouth.

The fruit really comes to life though when cooked, as it emits a delightful floral fragrance and lends a honeyed taste to the dish. Although quince is often cooked with lamb or poultry and stuffed with rice and minced lamb, it is at its most flamboyant when it is shredded and transformed into a syrupy, golden jam, or when it is poached with sugar and cloves to make the stunning Palace dessert *ayva tatlısı*, in which the fruit turns a pretty shade of pink and the syrup becomes jelly-like because of the pectin in the fruit and pips. Topped with a rolled log of *kaymak* (a local clotted cream), this is a seasonal treat.

**Jams (reçel)** | Exquisite and colourful, the jams of Turkey are out of this world. Both ripe and unripe fruits are sought after for making jam. Even some unripe vegetables, such as tomatoes, are destined for the syrupy conserves that are such a feature in Turkish culinary life. The delicious jams are served for breakfast with warm bread and slabs of moist white cheese; drizzled over freshly baked cakes and doughs as a sweet snack; or spooned on top of creamy yogurt. They range from the delicate, scented taste of steeped rose petals, to the honey-tasting, whole green figs. Other conserves are made from quince, peach or apricot, mulberry and sour cherry, watermelon, plum tomato with almonds, and, quite remarkably, whole baby aubergines. Jars of genuine Turkish jam are usually available in most Turkish and Middle Eastern stores, some delicatessens and online. Remember that the consistency of Turkish jam is more akin to a syrupy conserve than a thick, spreadable jam, so a spoon rather than a knife is required to transfer it to your bread.

Top **Boiling fresh rose petals in sugared water for rose petal jam, one of the most traditional Turkish sweets.**

Bottom **Thick, syrupy *pekmez*, the popular grape molasses.**

**Fruit leathers (pestil, bastık)** | In the dried-fruit-and-nut sections of Turkish markets, you will usually come across long, coloured strips hanging from hooks like rigid ribbons. These are fruit leathers, which are primarily made from apricots, grapes, mulberries, pomegranates, apples and sour cherries. First, the fresh fruit is pounded and sieved or strained to a smooth purée, which is spread very thinly and evenly in flat trays and left to dry in the sun. Once the sun-dried purée is firm enough to lift out of the tray, it is cut into thin strips, which are hung in the markets or rolled up to store. These leathers are especially popular with children, who like to chew on them in the same way other children might enjoy sweets, and they can also be melted in a little water to be used as a concentrated purée in stews, sauces and desserts. You can find some fruit leathers in Turkish and Middle Eastern stores, or online.

**Fruit molasses (pekmez)** | To make a fruit molasses, the juice is first extracted from the fruit before it is boiled and reduced to create a dark, fruity syrup. In its crude form in some Anatolian villages, the *pekmez* is slightly fermented and is used in place of sugar or honey in many dishes. As it is of pouring consistency, *pekmez* lends itself for use as a natural sweetener in cooking, and can be drizzled over yogurt or flat breads. It is also used in some *helva* recipes, or is combined with sesame paste to make *tahin pekmez*, a sweet, nutty mixture that is enjoyed on bread. A variety of fruits, such as mulberries, sour cherries, sour pomegranates and carob pods can be used to make *pekmez*, but the most popular one in Turkey is made from the juice of grapes.

# Nuts and seeds

If, like me, you love nuts then you won't be disappointed with their frequent appearance on the Turkish table – roasted and served as a nibble with a drink, pounded into sauces and dressings, stuffed into savoury and sweet dishes, and crushed and ground in between layers of syrupy pastry. Nuts and seeds are healthy, nourishing and a symbol of prosperity, and they play an important role in both the Palace and Anatolian culinary traditions, as well as in religious festivals and feasts. Hazelnuts grow along the Black Sea coast, pistachio nuts flourish in the Mediterranean and south-eastern regions of Turkey, chestnuts grow in abundance around Bursa, almond and walnut trees thrive wild and in orchards all over the country, and sesame and sunflower seeds are harvested in central Anatolia.

Almonds (badem) | In the spring, unripe almonds are picked while still green and velvety, to be dipped in salt and eaten as a snack. Ripe almonds are blanched or roasted, then find their way into numerous pilaffs and meat or poultry dishes, as well as desserts and sweetmeats, such as *keşkül*, a traditional Palace milk dessert made with almonds and marzipan. Blanched almonds are also coated in sugar and bought as gifts to celebrate births and circumcisions, and they are sold at the sweet festival, Şeker Bayramı. Blanched almonds are also bound in muslin and poached to extract their creamy milk, which is used to make a delicate syrup for a refreshing sherbet drink.

Chestnuts (kestane) | Dried and roasted chestnuts are used in a variety of lamb and vegetable stews, as they often take the place of potatoes. However, the best time to enjoy chestnuts in Turkey is in the winter when they are roasted in the street at makeshift stalls and sold piping hot in a funnel of newspaper, or when they are tender and succulent, having been poached in sugar syrup as a delectable sweet treat, *kestane şekeri*, which is often taken as a gift when visiting someone's home.

Top **Almond trees in blossom on the Datca peninsula. Almond trees have been regarded as a symbol of beauty since ancient times and are often depicted on Turkish ceramic tiles and crockery.**

Bottom **Picking hazelnuts in Ordu in the Black Sea region where the majority of the country's hazelnuts grow.**

Hazelnuts (fındık) | If you drive along the Black Sea coast in September, you will see carpets of freshly picked hazelnuts drying in the sun by the roadside. Destined for many Turkish biscuits and sweetmeats, such as *helva* and *lokum*, tons are also sent abroad, as Turkey is one of the largest exporters. Hazelnuts are pounded to make *tarator*, the popular garlicky nut sauce that can also be made with almonds, pine nuts or walnuts. They are roasted and crushed for use in several savoury dishes and, as they contain high levels of protein, children are encouraged to eat them, so they appear in many types of chocolate.

**Pine nuts (çam fıstık)** | Creamy pine nuts are perhaps the most popular of all, finding their way into numerous dishes. For both visual and gastronomic appeal, they are scattered over everything – meze, sweet and savoury pastries, pilaffs, and puddings – and are an important component of fish and meat *köfte* as well as the rice filling that is stuffed into every dolma. The versatility of their flavour and texture seems never-ending as they are also poached or soaked with fruit, such as in the traditional dessert, *hoşaf*, and they are added to a variety of sweetmeats, in particular the celebratory *helva* dishes: *un helvası*, prepared for births and marriages, and *irmik helvası*, which is offered at funerals.

**Pistachio nuts (antep fıstık)** | Freshly roasted pistachio nuts, still warm from the pan, are absolutely delicious and are often consumed on their own as a snack. They are also used in many sweet pastries and sweetmeats, such as *kadayıf*, the delectable shredded pastry filled with pistachio nuts and bathed in syrup, and pistachio marzipan, which is a lovely deep shade of green. They grow profusely in the southern region around Gaziantep and are, therefore, known as *antep fıstık*. A speciality from this region is a minced meat kebab containing a nest of whole pistachio nuts in the middle .

**Sesame seeds (sesam)** | Tiny, but flavoursome, sesame seeds are sprinkled over savoury pastries and breads, particularly *simit*, the ubiquitous bread rings you often see being sold at markets or carried through the streets on long poles and, occasionally, artfully balanced in a pile on top of a young boy's head. The seeds are also ground for their distinct oil, and to make the fine creamy paste called *tahin*, or tahini. This is used in many traditional sweet and savoury recipes and is combined with grape *pekmez* (a fruit molasses) to make a thick sweet mixture that is enjoyed on chunks of bread for breakfast, or for a quick snack.

**Sunflower seeds (günebakan)** | Bright yellow sunflowers grow all over Turkey, and the heads are gathered and left to dry in the hot sun, either in wooden carts or by the side of the road, until the small seeds burst out of the pods. The seeds, which are contained in black, or black-and-white striped, edible husks, are often roasted and eaten as a snack, or they are added to *köfte* and pilaffs instead of pine nuts. The light oil obtained from pressing the seeds is popular for cooking and deep-frying.

**Walnuts (ceviz)** | Regarded as the king of nuts, walnuts are used in many savoury and sweet dishes, such as *muhammara*, and in the moist walnut sponges soaked in syrup, called *kalburabastı*. The walnut is the most traditional nut to be used in the Palace cuisine of Istanbul, epitomised in the classic *baklava*, and the classic Istanbul version of *tarator* served with shellfish, such as deep-fried mussels, *midye tavası*.

Top left **Pistachios are added to rice and bulgur wheat pilaffs, and slivers are used to decorate a number of desserts because of their pretty colour.**

Top right **Pine nuts or kernels emit a subtle smell of pine and have a mild resinous taste, and, when they are roasted and golden, they are both nutty and pretty to look at.**

Bottom left **Sunflower seeds are often roasted and eaten as a snack and appear in many recipes.**

Bottom right **Walnuts add richness and texture to dishes. The trees typically live to a ripe old age yet still produce a good crop.**

# Fish and shellfish

There are so many delicious ways to enjoy fish and shellfish in Turkey but two of my favourite are grilled red mullet, and squid fried in batter with a garlicky sauce. Bounded by seas on three sides – the Mediterranean, Aegean and the Black Sea, the Sea of Marmara and its waterways, the Bosphorus and Dardanelles – Turkey has over 7,000km (4,350 miles) of coastline. The plentiful fishing waters provide daily catches of bluefish, red and grey mullet, swordfish, sea bass, tuna, bonito, turbot, plaice, mackerel, sardines, anchovies and all manner of shellfish. The Black Sea region is well known for its revered anchovies which pop up in everything – savoury dishes, puddings and jam, song and poetry. Inland, in the fast-flowing rivers of Anatolia, various species of carp are grilled or baked.

Traditionally regarded as a symbol of fertility, fish is treated with respect. It is cheaper than meat and always bought fresh straight off the boats or at the daily fish market where the smaller ones swim around in buckets, and the larger ones are beautifully arranged on ice, with bright eyes and gleaming skins. Sloshing about in rubber boots, the fish sellers will usually help to select and prepare the fish for your chosen dish, such as swordfish for your kebabs, mackerel for stuffing, and bonito for stews.

## Cooking methods

The *pilâki* recipes are the most distinctive of the Turkish fish dishes. These are made by sautéing onion, garlic, carrot and celery (or celeriac) in olive oil. The fish is then added with salt, water and sugar, and cooked until tender (all *pilâki* dishes, including those made with beans or mussels, are cooked the same way). One dish that seems to have nearly disappeared from the culinary scene is oyster *pilâki*, an old Ottoman favourite. Chunks of firm-fleshed fish are sometimes cooked in earthenware pots with vegetables, spices or herbs to make a stew, or they are marinated and threaded on to kebab sticks and chargrilled. Along the Black Sea coast, the concave roof tiles are often used as cooking vessels for baking, as they are perfectly shaped for a whole fish.

Small fish, such as anchovies and sardines, are gutted and cleaned, then salted and dipped in flour before being fried on both sides until golden brown. The joy of these little fish is that they can be popped straight into your mouth and eaten whole. Generally, most fish are grilled over charcoal, or fried. Prior to grilling or frying, the fish is marinated in onion juice and, once cooked, it is invariably garnished with parsley, dill or rocket (arugula) leaves.

Top **Fishing off the bridge over the Golden Horn is a popular thing to do at any time of day.**

Bottom **Fresh fish on sale in one of the busy fish markets along the Golden Horn and the Bosphorus in Istanbul.**

YERLI
TON
65

**Anchovies (hamsi)** | The Black Sea coast differs from the rest of Turkey in that it has its own unique fish cuisine, mainly revolving around the anchovy. This small, oily fish is celebrated in song and poetry as well as in many recipes, such as *hamsi sarması*, in which the anchovies are poached in vine leaves; *hamsi pilavı*, an impressive-looking mound of rice encased in anchovy fillets; in a bread baked with anchovies; and there is even an anchovy pudding and anchovy jam! A common sight along the Black Sea coast, where the fish is abundant, is anchovies hanging like washing on a line left in the sun to dry, to be used later in soups and stews. Pickled anchovies are a particular feature of the region too.

**Bonito (palamut)** | Another firm-fleshed fish, bonito is enjoyed baked whole with bay leaves, or with freshly squeezed lemon and a variety of fresh, leafy herbs. Its most traditional role, though, is in the classic *pilâki*, where the fish is baked, or poached, with diced carrots, potatoes and celeriac.

**Mackerel (uskumru)** | Rich and oily, mackerel is a very popular fish in the recipes of Istanbul and Izmir, where it is often cooked in olive oil and served at room temperature, but its moist flesh lends itself particularly well to grilling and baking and a number of stews.

The grandest role of the mackerel though is in a rather decadent dish, *uskumru dolması*, that originated in the Palace kitchens. In this classic Ottoman dish, the fresh mackerel is pummelled and massaged to loosen the flesh from the skin so that the flesh can be squeezed out of an opening whilst keeping the whole skin intact. The flesh is then fried with nuts and spices before being stuffed back into the skin. Baked or grilled, this stuffed mackerel dish is very impressive and can sometimes be found as a 'special' on traditional fish restaurant menus in Istanbul.

**Red mullet (barbunya)** | Once the favoured fish of the Romans, red mullet could be said to be one of the most prized among the Turks, too. It is a beautiful fish to look at, with its dappled pink skin. Since it is quite a meaty fish for its size, it is very rarely tampered with and is generally served fairly plain so that its natural sweet flavour can be appreciated. Grilled or fried, sometimes rubbed with garlic and served with lemon, is the best way to enjoy the sweet flesh of red mullet.

**Sardines (sardalya)** | Small sardines are often wrapped in vine leaves and poached or grilled or, like anchovies, they are dipped in flour and deep-fried. The large, fleshy sardines are juicy and lend themselves to being cooked whole over charcoal, baked with tomatoes and herbs, or to being stuffed with herbs and spices and grilled. Like anchovies, they are also dried and used in soups, stews and stocks, and preserved whole in vinegar or brine.

Top left **A favourite fish on Istanbul tables, red mullet is both pleasing to the eye and to the palate.**

Top right **Mackerel is enjoyed grilled and in stews and salads, particularly in the Aegean region.**

Bottom left **Fresh anchovies are grilled, fried and wrapped in vine leaves but are also dried and pickled.**

Bottom right **Sardines are, like anchovies, enjoyed fresh but are also dried and preserved whole in vinegar, brine or oil.**

Top **Large prawns (*karides*) are often grilled.**

Bottom **Prepared squid (*kalamar*) ready for stuffing or deep-frying.**

**Sea bass (levrek)** | Like sea perch, sea bass is extremely versatile as the tender flesh is firm and sweet and suited to being cooked in a number of ways. Popular among these is to bake the fish whole, encased in salt, or on a concave tile with a simple sauce of tomatoes and herbs. It is also used in stews and fish *köfte*, and sea bass fillets are often chopped into chunks and threaded on to kebab skewers with tomatoes and peppers, for the grill or barbecue.

**Sea perch (lüfer)** | This fish, also known as blue fish, is firm-fleshed and extremely versatile. It is one of the most popular fish for grilling, broiling and baking, and is often used in stews, such as the classic *lüfer yahnisi*, which is flavoured with cinnamon and a dash of vinegar.

**Swordfish (kiliç)** | The traditional way of cooking swordfish is to grill it on a skewer, as in *kiliç şiş*, a much-loved dish in fish restaurants. The firm meaty flesh lends itself well to marinades and the smoky flavour from grilling over charcoal.

**Tuna (orkinos)** | Generally, tuna fish is seared and served with dill, or the raw flesh is marinated in lemon juice and served as a cold meze dish. Like swordfish the meaty flesh of tuna lends itself to grilling over charcoal. Although it is native to the surrounding waters, tuna is a victim of overfishing and export, and has become quite expensive and more difficult to find in the local markets.

**Shellfish and cephalopods** | Istanbul, Izmir and the towns and coastal resorts of the Aegean and the Mediterranean are the main areas where shellfish, squid and octopus are generally enjoyed. Prawns (*karides*) are frequently stir-fried with garlic and cumin, or baked with peppers and onions. Some restaurants offer prawn kebabs, and prawns are added to many rice dishes.

Whole mussels stuffed with rice are a favourite street and café food in Istanbul and Izmir, and they also feature in a delicious *pilâki* dish. Squid rings (*kalamar*) and mussels are deep-fried in batter and often served with a garlicky sauce. Baby squid are typically stuffed with rice and herbs, and octopus is grilled and served with olives and bell peppers.

**To prepare fresh squid** First hold the body of the squid in one hand and grasp the head with the other. Tug off the head, taking most of the innards with it. Take out the backbone and then remove any remaining innards. Peel off the thin outer membrane by gripping one end firmly and pulling hard with the other hand. Rinse the sac inside and out, and pat dry. Trim the head of the squid by severing the tentacles just above the eyes; discard the eyes but keep the top of the head with the tentacles attached.

# Meat and poultry

There is more to Turkish meat than the kebab and there are more kebabs in Turkey than the infamous *döner*! In fact every region has its own kebab and not all kebabs are cooked on skewers or a spit. Meat dishes perhaps form the largest culinary group in Turkish cuisine as there seems to be no end to the number of stews, meatballs and kebabs throughout the country. Ever since the early Turks of Central Asia herded sheep to new grazing grounds, lamb or mutton has traditionally formed part of their daily diet. The fat-tailed sheep are the most highly prized, as the fat stored in the tail acts as an emergency supply for the beast in arid conditions, but also provides many Anatolian Turks with their favourite cooking fat.

In the early history of Anatolia, beef was rarely eaten, as the cattle were raised for milk and for tilling the fields, but, in modern Turkey, beef is available for those who can afford it and is often cooked in stews and minced for fillings and *köfte* in place of lamb. Wild game, such as rabbit, deer and bear, featured in the diet of the early hunters and was also sought after by various Ottoman sultans, but it rarely turns up on the modern Turkish table.

Apart from on festive occasions, when a whole sheep or large joint of lamb are roasted, meat is seldom cooked on its own. Instead the Turks cube or mince tender cuts of meat and combine it with herbs, spices and vegetables. This adds flavour and stretches the meat further. The Turks prefer their meat well-done, with no trace of blood, which can result in some of the grilled and seared dishes appearing rather dry to the taste.

Beef (dana) | The beef sold in most markets is obtained from animals that are under two years old. As the calves have been reared naturally, the well-hung meat is pinkish-red and very lean. Beef, or veal, is generally used in stews, or in grilled and seared dishes, such as *dana pirzola*, a dish of seared veal chops with oregano and lemon.

Beef is also combined with onions, parsley and spices for use in lean *köfte* for which the meat is passed through the mincer twice. The spicy tartare meatballs, *çiğ köfte*, from the south-east of Turkey, are generally made from beef and are reputed to contain thirty different spices. They are so well-kneaded that the raw meat is almost undetectable and the spice is cut by the bunches of leafy parsley eaten with each mouthful. In eastern Anatolia, the tradition of eating bull's testes still exists. Invariably grilled and sprinkled with Turkish red pepper, the village men gather around the *mangal* to devour the tender testes with *rakı*, or a locally brewed spirit, in the belief that their virility will be enhanced!

Top **Lamb is the most commonly eaten meat in Turkey.**

Bottom **Cooking chicken in stock for *çerkez tavuğu*.**

**Lamb (kuzu)** | When Turks talk about meat, they are often referring to lamb and mutton. It is the meat required for all religious and celebratory events, such as Kurban Bayramı, the festival to mark the near-sacrifice of Isaac, for which the whole sheep is ritually sacrificed. At this event, every part of the sheep is used in a variety of dishes – some of the meat will be prepared in a stew with fruit, while some will be simply fried in its own juices, known as the *kavurma* method. The podgy tail will be boiled and eaten with bread, and the intestines will be simmered in a soup, *işkembe çorbası*, or stuffed with a mixture of chopped offal, onions and spices and grilled in a traditional dish called *kokoreç*. When a ram is sacrificed, the testes are also usually consumed, often grilled or cooked in a stew.

A whole lamb or, sometimes, a kid goat, is spit-roasted for communal feasts. The most traditional method is to suspend the spit over the hot embers in a pit dug in the ground. In some regions, several lambs are roasted at once, hung lengthways from a spit. Other forms of spit-roasting include a brick-lined pit, *biryan*, into which the lambs are lowered on a spit and then sealed in with an iron lid, so that the meat roasts and steams at the same time.

In eastern Anatolia, the use of the *tandır* is widepread. Related to the Indian tandouri and the Persian tennur, the *tandır* can be a fairly primitive affair, made out of earth or clay and sealed with an earthenware or stone lid, with a pipe at the bottom or a chimney on top to control the air flow. The cooked lamb from the *biryan* and *tandır* is tasty, moist and tender.

**Chicken (tavuk or piliç)** | Chicken is the most widespread kind of poultry consumed in Turkey, although wild duck and quails are also found in some areas. Eaten almost as often as lamb, chicken can be cooked in many different ways, including spit-roasted whole, cut into chunks, threaded on to skewers and grilled as kebabs, or stewed with vegetables. Chicken can also be used in *köfte* and soups, or oven-roasted.

When it is roasted, the cavity of the chicken is often stuffed with almonds and apricots. It even appears finely shredded in the classical pudding, *tavuk göğsu*, a creation originating from the Ottoman Palace kitchens. Chicken livers are also enjoyed, sautéed with garlic and served with lemon, or combined with aromatic rice and pine nuts in a delicious dish called *iç pilavı*, which is particularly popular in Istanbul.

**Duck (ördek) and quails (bildircin)** | Medieval recipes include lavish dishes of duck stuffed with olives and figs, or even aubergines stuffed with quails, but neither of these dishes makes a frequent appearance on modern Turkish menus. Wild duck is still enjoyed in some rural regions, where it is generally roasted in the oven with herbs and honey, and some modern kebab houses offer duck kebabs. Roasted, stuffed quails are a feature of some kebab houses, but the most common venue for spit-roasted quails is at countryside picnics.

Top **Mountain goats at dawn in the Seven Capes region of Mugla.**

Bottom **Sheep are seen grazing everywhere in Turkey.**

Top **Minced meat *şis kebab* ready for the grill.**

Bottom **There are many types of *köfte*, some fried or grilled, others stuffed or poached.**

Kebabs | Kebabs are perhaps the best-known meat dish from Turkey, the most famous being *döner* and *şis*. Some kebabs are grilled, others roasted or baked in paper or earthenware pots. This is because they evolved out of a practical need to cook small chunks of meat simply and quickly while retaining their moisture.

Many popular kebabs are served on *pide*, bread, with yogurt or tomato sauce, and the fiery kebabs from the *güney* kitchen are often made of minced meat and plenty of Turkish red pepper (*pul biber* or *kırmızı biber*). Many of the kebabs on skewers are distinguishable by the types of vegetables used or by the region they have originated from, such as *Adana kebab* and *Tokat kebab*.

Köfte | Meatballs are an economical way of using minced meat as it is combined with breadcrumbs, onions, herbs and spices, so a small amount of meat goes a long way. The meatballs are kneaded to bind them and moulded into a variety of shapes; you will see them as little patties or burgers, as balls, and small cylinders. The exception is the Palace dish, *kadınbudu*, the descriptively named 'ladies' thighs', as the meat is combined with rice and then flattened and dipped in batter before frying. Generally, most meatballs can be grilled or fried, although the classic *kuru köfte* are always fried in olive oil, as they are designed to be eaten cold while travelling or on picnics.

Offal/innards | Apart from chicken livers, the offal in Turkish cooking is generally extracted from the sheep, although ox liver is sold in some areas. Lambs' liver is popular sautéed and served with lemon, tossed in a pilaf, or cooked in a special sausage called *bumbar dolması*; the intestines are cooked in soup or stuffed and grilled; and the brain is poached in water and vinegar and served sliced as a cold meze dish.

In addition to these more commonly consumed innards, there are a couple of specialities that fall into this category of ingredient: sheep's head and hooves. The sheep's head is often cooked in a soup with the hooves, or it is slow-roasted or baked on its own and served either hot or cold. Once all the meaty parts of the head have been eaten, the prized brain is released from the skull and then offered to a guest, or to the head of a household. When the earthy sheep's hooves are prepared on their own, they are simmered in water for a number of hours and then the tender meat is placed on lightly toasted bread and covered in a yogurt sauce.

During the Ottoman period, street vendors specialised in selling offal in both its cooked and its raw form. Some of these offal vendors still exist today, and the distinct aroma of grilled stuffed intestine, *kokoreç*, draws the hungry Turks from their roadside perches or shaded doorways. In most markets and urban butchers, offal is still sold separately from other meats.

**Cured meats** | There are two types of cured meats in Turkey: *pastırma*, the cured fillet of beef, and *sucuk*, the spicy sausages that resemble salami. Both hang in bunches at the markets and can be bought whole or sliced. The *pastırma* can be eaten just as it is or cooked with other ingredients, but the *sucuk* is usually cooked first.

**Pastırma** This is a cured, air-dried fillet of veal or beef coated in a thick paste known as *çemen*, which is made from ground cumin, fenugreek, *pul biber*, and garlic. Generally, *pastırma* is finely sliced and eaten on its own with bread, or with olives and pickles, as a meze. It is also cooked with pulses and eggs, and is used as a filling in savoury pastries.

**Sucuk** Shaped like a horseshoe, *sucuk* is a cured sausage made with lamb or beef and flavoured with garlic and cumin. In rural areas, people make their own *sucuk* with a variety of spices and hang them outside to cure. Clusters of *sucuk* horseshoes are easy to recognise at markets and most families buy several sucuk at once. When cooked they impart their wonderful flavour to pulses and eggs, or they are grilled on the *mangal* and enjoyed with slices of bread.

Top **The air-dried fillet of beef, *pastırma*, cured in a coating of *pul biber*, fenugreek, cumin and garlic, is generally served finely sliced.**

Bottom **Meat skewers sizzling enticingly over a charcoal stove are a frequent sight in streets and homes.**

## Cooking methods

There is a wide range of cooking methods when it comes to meat. Spit-roasting, grilling, stewing, frying, steaming, stuffing, sautéing and pressing minced meat into balls (*köfte*), are all popular techniques. Traditionally, meat is cooked in small pieces combined with other ingredients, as is clearly demonstrated in the many stews and kebabs on offer in Turkey.

Cooking whole cuts of meat is a rare event and usually reserved for a celebratory occasion. Traditional spit-roasting is a communal activity, as it requires a fire pit to be dug in the ground, over which a whole lamb or goat, rubbed with salt and spices, is cooked slowly over the glowing embers, producing an extremely tasty meat. *Yahni* is a classic meat stew with onions, but the stew can also incorporate fruit, such as green plums or apricots. The Anatolian *güveç* method refers to meat or poultry cooked with vegetables or pulses in earthenware pots or curved tiles, resulting in a wonderfully moist dish, such as the chicken and okra dish *güveçte piliçli bamya*.

In the Anatolian villages, large cuts of meat are usually cooked in the *tandır*, the communal clay oven, and throughout Turkey everyone has a *mangal*, a small outdoor charcoal stove – ideal for grilling small cuts of meat, fish, corn on the cob and chicken – which can be conveniently set up on a city balcony or transported to the beach or the woods for a countryside picnic.

# Dairy produce

Top **White cheese, *beyaz peynir*, varies from region to region but it is always served for breakfast.**

Bottom **Turkish clotted cream, *kaymak*, is enjoyed as a treat by itself and adds richness to many dishes.**

You can start the day with a couple of chunks of salty white cheese, accompanied by olives, bread and honey, and then move on to thick, creamy yogurt for the rest of the day as it is served with just about everything. The existence of dairy products in the diets of the Turks can be traced right back to the first millennium BCE. At this time, the milk of mares was regarded as superior to the milk from other animals and was used to make yogurt and cheese and a fermented drink, *kımız*. Milk from ewes was used to make a rancid-tasting butter, as well as yogurt and cheese. Fresh milk was rarely drunk; instead it was usually curdled in order to preserve it. It is thought that this may have led to the discovery of how to make yogurt, and how to use it for curative purposes. For a nation that claims to have a low tolerance for flowing milk, the Turks gain plenty of minerals and vitamins through their vast consumption of yogurt (*yoğurt*), cheese (*peynir*), and a delicious selection of milky puddings. In Turkey there are many varieties of white cheese, most of which are made from cow's or sheep's milk.

Beyaz peynir | The principal, everyday white cheese, *beyaz peynir* is fairly solid and is sold in blocks, which are often stacked like building bricks in the market stalls. Stored in brine, the cheese ranges in colour from pearly white to a pale yellow. The salt content varies from cheese to cheese, so the first thing a Turkish cook does is to immerse it in water to draw out the salt, and keep it in a cool place.

*Beyaz peynir*, which can be substituted with feta cheese in the recipes in this book, is eaten for breakfast with olives, bread and jam. It is used in salads and savoury pastries and is also served by itself as a meze dish, cut into cubes and drizzled with olive oil and a sprinkling of dried oregano and Turkish red pepper (*pul biber* or *kırmızı biber*), or paprika.

*Beyaz peynir* is made in blocks, which are left to dry out. These are then stored in salty water for at least six months to mature. The correct amount of salt is determined by a simple egg test: a pan containing enough water to submerge the cheese is brought to the boil and an estimated amount of salt is added. An egg is then cracked into the water – if it starts to sink more salt is required but, if it floats, the salt content is deemed accurate. The salty water is then left to cool before it is poured over the cheese in a container which must be kept in a cool place. During the maturing process, the cheese will slowly harden and absorb the salt.

When choosing one of these cheeses at the market, the women often try a nibble from several blocks to determine which one suits their palate in both salt content and texture.

**Clotted cream (kaymak)** | One of the delights of a traditional *muhallebici* (a milk-pudding shop) is *kaymak*, a particularly thick clotted cream made from the milk of water buffalo. *Kaymak* is left to set in a flat tray before it is cut and rolled into neat, spectacular-looking logs. These gleaming rolls of pearly white cream are piled on top of sticky desserts, stuffed into poached fruit and pastries, or eaten on their own with a dusting of icing (confectioner's) sugar.

Nowadays, *kaymak* is also often made from cow's milk and is sold unceremoniously in tubs and cans at supermarkets – and this type can be substituted with a thick, commercial clotted cream – but the traditional pudding shops prefer to stick to the original method, created by the Palace chefs, using buffalo milk to which a little *mastika* is also sometimes added for texture.

**Dil peyniri** | A mild-tasting cheese, *dil peyniri* is pulled apart in stringy strips and enjoyed with pickles as a snack. When cooking with *dil peyniri*, particularly in the traditional dessert *künefe*, you can use Italian mozzarella as a substitute, if necessary, as it is mild-tasting and melts with the same stringy consistency.

**Kaşar peyniri** | The hard and tangy *kaşar peyniri* is used in cooking and grated on top of dishes. (A strong Cheddar with no added colouring or Italian Pecorino and Parmesan can be used as substitutes in the recipes, if you can't find *kaşar peyniri*.)

**Köy peyniri** | A slightly softer, creamier white cheese, *köy peyniri* (village cheese) is made every week in rural areas. Regional variations are much sought after in the markets. Eat with bread, or combine with herbs and use as a meze dip.

**Making köy peyniri** To make about 350g/12oz, use 2 litres/3½ pints full-fat (whole) or semi-skimmed (low-fat) milk, 15ml/1 tbsp salt and 60ml/4 tbsp rennet or lemon juice.

**1** Pour the milk into a deep, heavy pan and heat it gently. Stir in the salt and rennet or lemon juice, and continue to heat until just below boiling point – don't bring the milk to the boil.

**2** Turn off the heat, cover the pan with a clean dish towel and leave it overnight, or for at least 6 hours, to separate into curds and whey. (If using lemon juice, this will happen immediately, so you don't need to leave it to separate.)

**3** Line a colander with a piece of muslin, and place it in a bowl. Pour the mixture into the middle, gather up the edges of the muslin and tie it to a rod suspended over the sink or a bowl.

**4** Leave the curds to drain overnight, or for at least 6 hours, so that you are left with a ball of soft, creamy cheese.

Top ***Mihaliç peyniri*, an aged sheep's milk curd cheese, slightly elastic in texture, and stored in brine so it is also a little salty.**

Bottom ***Kaşar peyniri* is a firm and slightly chewy strong-tasting cheese, traditionally made from sheep's milk.**

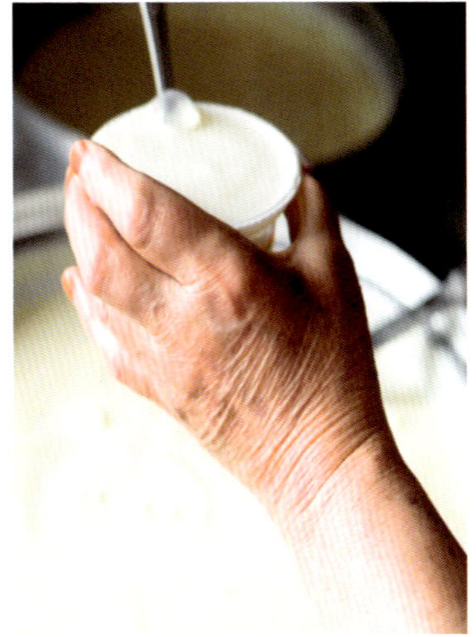

Top **Making batches of yogurt to sell.**

Bottom **Yogurt is hung in a muslin cloth to drain for at least six hours to produce *süzme*, which is thick and creamy and ideal for savoury dips and for filling poached fruit.**

**Yogurt (yoğurt)** | The Turks are one of the world's largest consumers of yogurt made from the milk of ewes and cows. In rural parts of Anatolia today, ancient methods of curdling milk and yogurt making are still used. These techniques include using a fig branch to curdle milk in the mountains, as the sap from the branch separates the curds from the whey; and some of the nomadic communities elsewhere collect the eggs of a particular kind of ant, which they then crush and use as a yogurt culture. Once a staple of their ancestors in Central Asia, the Turks love yogurt so much that it is served with almost everything, providing an easily digestible source of calcium and antibiotic properties, as well as numerous vitamins and minerals.

Eaten on its own as a snack, thick, creamy yogurt is often dusted with icing sugar, or drizzled with a generous spoonful of amber honey. It is served in dollops with many vegetable and kebab dishes, or mixed with the mashed or grated pulp of cooked vegetables to make soothing dips. Beaten with crushed garlic and a splash of lemon juice or vinegar, it is spooned over deep-fried or grilled vegetables and poached eggs.

The standard, everyday yogurt, *sıvı tas*, is thick, light and creamy, whereas the solid yogurt, *süzme*, which is required for particular dips and desserts, is strained through a piece of muslin or cheesecloth for about six hours, so that it is so thick you can stand a spoon in it. This is called *labna* in Arab cultures. For the recipes in this book you can choose the live, set yogurts generally available, or of course make your own.

Everyday yogurt recipes include *cacık*, a bowl of diced cucumber, yogurt, garlic and dill, which is often served as an appetiser or as an accompaniment to savoury pastries and kebabs; *haydari*, a strained yogurt dip spiked with garlic and fresh or dried mint; and *ayran*, the cooling, national yogurt drink, enjoyed with spicy food or as a thirst-quencher on a hot day.

**Making sıvı tas** When making yogurt you need to use live yogurt to start off the process. The standard ratio for yogurt to milk is 30ml/2 tbsp live yogurt to 600ml/1 pint full-fat (whole) or semi-skimmed (low-fat) milk. To make a thicker yogurt, you can add 15–30ml/1–2 tbsp powdered milk to the milk that is boiling in the pan.

**1** First, bring the milk to the boil in a large, heavy pan. When it starts to boil, reduce the heat and leave it to simmer for 2–3 minutes.

**2** Turn off the heat and allow the milk to cool to a temperature that is bearable to dip your finger into and leave there for a count of ten.

**3** Beat the yogurt with a wooden spoon in a large, deep bowl and strain a little of the milk into it, beating all the time. Strain the remainder of the milk into the bowl and beat well until everything is thoroughly combined.

**4** Cover the bowl with clear film or plastic wrap and cover the whole bowl with a piece of blanket or a thick cloth, tucking the edges around it to keep it warm.

**5** Place the wrapped bowl in a warm place overnight, or for at least 6 hours –the yogurt should have fermented and thickened a little during this time.
**6** Unwrap the bowl and place it in the refrigerator for 2–3 hours, or until it has set. This yogurt can be used in many dishes, for instance spiked with garlic and spooned over vegetables, or mixed with finely sliced cucumber to make *cacık*.

**Making süzme** This extra-thick strained yogurt makes a good dip or can be used for making Turkish desserts.
**1** Line a colander with a piece of muslin and tip the freshly made *sıvı tas* into the middle.
**2** Gather together the corners of the muslin and tie them around a rod, or a long wooden spoon, placed over the sink, a wide bowl or a bucket to catch the fluid.
**3** Leave the yogurt to drain for 4–6 hours, or until it is the consistency of cream cheese.

**Making ayran** Serve this refreshing drink with spicy food or as a cooler for a hot day. This serves two.
**1** In a jug, combine 300ml/½ pint each of thick, creamy yogurt and water, whisking the mixture until it becomes foamy. Season with a little salt to suit your taste.
**2** Pour the mixture into glasses and scatter the surface with a little dried mint. If it's a very hot day, add extra salt and some ice cubes.

## Eggs (yumurta)

Many villagers keep chickens for their eggs, and there are several egg dishes in modern Turkish cuisine that are worth mentioning, such as *menemen*, a ragout of bell peppers and tomatoes topped with eggs; *cilbur*, poached eggs served with garlic-flavoured yogurt; and eggs cooked with spinach, *pastırma*, the cured fillet of beef, or *sucuk*, the spicy cured sausage. A popular egg recipe is *yumurtali ispanak kavurmasi*, a dish of sautéed spinach and onions with an egg cooked in the middle.

*Menemen* is often regarded as street food as it is cooked on small stoves at bus stations and markets, but it makes a good supper dish. *Cilbir* is another classic. Traditionally, the eggs are poached in water that is boiling with a gentle roll and a dash of vinegar, but some cooks take a short-cut and fry the eggs lightly so that the yolks are still soft. It is often topped with melted butter that sometimes contains *pul biber* or *kırmızı biber*, the Turkish red pepper, or dried sage.

During the Ottoman period, eggs were stuffed in the same way as many vegetables, including aubergines and peppers, and poached eggs were frequently served with a dressing of olive oil and lemon juice, but these dishes rarely appear on menus any more.

Top **Thick, creamy yogurt is enjoyed every day in Turkish households.**

Bottom **Iced water is added to the diluted yogurt for a refreshing drink, *ayran*. Salt and dried mint is usually added.**

# Grains and pulses

Rice, bulgur wheat, chickpeas, beans and lentils appear on the table every day in Turkey but it has not always been that way. Bulgur wheat and beans were already established crops in the early history of Anatolia where it is still the staple grain. Rice (*pirinç*) is relatively new, as it was the grain of the nobility during the Ottoman period; it continues to play second fiddle in the wheat regions of Anatolia, but it is now the principal grain used in Ankara, Istanbul, Izmir and much of western Turkey.

The word *bakliyat*, meaning 'pulses' in Turkish, derives from the Arabic word *bakli*, which means vegetable. The main pulses in Turkish cuisine are dried haricot (navy), soya and borlotti beans, chickpeas, red and green lentils, black-eyed beans, split peas, and fresh and dried broad beans. Regarded as vegetables, pulse dishes are popular in Turkish cookery, served as snacks, meze dishes, or as meals on their own with bread. In the poor rural areas, pulses are often cooked as the main staple in place of meat. Considered to be 'food of heaven', beans are held in such high regard that there is a Turkish saying, "He thinks he is as blessed as a bean", meaning that he puts on airs.

If you are using dried pulses you will need to soak them before cooking. Rinse them well under cold, running water and then transfer them to a bowl. Cover with plenty of cold water and leave to soak overnight. During the soaking period, they will double in size (black-eyed beans and lentils do not need to be soaked before cooking).

**Broad beans/fava beans (fava)** | Like chickpeas, broad beans are also regarded as a staple of the poor, as they are so meaty and versatile. The season of the fresh green broad bean is short, so it is enjoyed in summery pilaffs, tossed in salads, and poached with artichokes. Fresh ones really need to be eaten on the day of purchase as the sugars in the beans alter the taste and texture after a few days. Dried broad beans are added to stews and soups. One of the specialities of Turkey is the meze dish *fava* (named after the bean), a purée of broad beans dressed in olive oil and fresh dill.

**Bulgur wheat (bulgur)** | Bulgur wheat is the freshly harvested wheat that is parboiled, drained and rubbed to remove the bran. The wheat is then crushed into coarse, medium or fine grains. The most commonly used are the coarse and medium – the fine grains are mainly used in fillings for stuffed vegetables, such as the dried aubergine shells, and for making the south-east Anatolian version of *kısır*, a bulgur wheat, tomato and herb salad. Mostly bulgur wheat is prepared as a pilaff, such as *arap pilavı*, or it is served plain. One of the most popular snacks in eastern

Top **Growing wheat in Bilecik, mid-western Turkey.**

Bottom **Harvesting wheat in traditional costume, in the Black Sea highlands region.**

Anatolia is a bowl of bulgur wheat, which is tipped on to a plate and then has a hole made in the centre, into which yogurt is spooned, and then melted ghee is poured over the top. Everyone takes a spoon and dips in.

**Chickpeas (humus)** | Often referred to as the 'food of the poor', chickpeas are cultivated in Turkey and the Middle East to be used in a variety of stews and soups, as well is in the garlicky purée, *humus*. The Turks also cook them in pilaffs and in an unusual Armenian dish, *topik*, in which puréed chickpeas are bound with mashed potato to make a parcel that is filled with a spicy currant and nut mixture. Earthy and meaty, they are ideal for cooking with strong flavours and they fill the belly in households where there is not much meat on the table. Roasted chickpeas are tossed in salt and served as a nibble, or they are coated in sugar and enjoyed as a sweet snack.

**Lentils (mercimek)** | Legumes of antiquity, lentils are regarded as a cheerful food. The most common varieties in Turkey are the tiny red ones, which are sometimes referred to as Egyptian lentils, and the larger matt-green ones. A little soaking in water helps to soften the bigger lentils before cooking, but the smaller ones don't need this.

Cooked lentils have a sprout-like taste and a good bite to them, unless they are cooked to a pulp for soup or a purée. Filling and nourishing, they are packed with protein and cheap to buy.

**Rice (pirinç** | Migrating Turkic tribes would have taken rice to Persia from China and India, but it did not really make an impact on Anatolia and Constantinople until the Ottoman era, when the wealthy imported large quantities from Egypt. Long grain rice from Iran, Syria and Turkey itself is preferred; shorter grains are reserved for the aromatic savoury fillings that are stuffed into vegetables and fruits, and for sweet desserts, such as the popular *sütlaç*. The Turkish concept of *pilav* is thought to have originated from the Persian tradition of *pulaw* dishes.

The cooking of rice is regarded as an art. The grains must be soft but still have a bite to them, as well as having absorbed the flavours in the dish. As a rule, the grains and other ingredients are cooked in a little butter, ghee or oil before adding the water. Once the water has been absorbed, a clean cloth, followed by the lid, is placed on top of the pan and the rice is left to steam off the heat, until cooked but still firm.

Fine, powdery white rice flour, slaked with a little water, is a necessary component of the much-loved traditional milk puddings, as it thickens and sets them. Traditionally, this was achieved by first soaking rice in water and then grinding it to extract a milky substance called *sübye*, which was a vital tool for the *muhallebici*, the maker of milk puddings. Rice flour works as a substitute, but some traditionalists stick to the more subtle method of their Ottoman ancestors.

Top left **There are three grades of bulgur wheat – fine, medium and coarse.**

Top right **Usually medium or long grain rice is used for pilaff dishes, whereas short grain or pudding rice is used for savoury stuffings and rice puddings.**

Bottom left **Dried broad beans feature in *fava*, a purée served as a meze dish.**

Bottom right **Dried chickpeas are the key component in the ubiquitous *humus*, which is the name of the dish as well as the pulse.**

Above **A boy selling freshly baked *simit*, the popular round bread rings coated in sesame seeds.**

Opposite top **Bread is indispensable at every meal, where it serves as a scoop or a mop for all the tasty flavours and juices, enhancing the pleasure of each mouthful. In many households, a meal without bread is unthinkable.**

Opposite bottom **The ancient Turkish dumplings, *mantı*, come in a variety of shapes; these tiny homemade ones are particularly fiddly but utterly delicious.**

# Bread, pastries and pasta

You can't enjoy Turkish food without bread – delicious freshly baked loaves or toasted flat breads – they just go in hand in hand. The tradition of breadmaking is one of the oldest, with records of cereal crops dating back to 7000BCE in Anatolia. Flat breads and layered breads emerged at this time but it wasn't really until the Ottoman period that more sophisticated bread and pastry doughs were developed. The industrious experimentation in the Palace kitchens resulted in wondrous creations that employed layers of thin flat bread dough to make divine pastries such as *baklava*. Noodle dough, on the other hand, is known to have come from China, as records of this dough can be traced along the route travelled by the early, nomadic Turkish ancestors.

**Bread loaves (ekmek)** | Regarded as the food of friendship and a gift from God, bread is treated with great respect in Turkey. In traditional households, bread is broken into pieces by hand, as the act of cutting it with a knife would be like raising a sword against God's blessing. The Turks buy bread daily, straight from the baker's hot oven. Torn apart with fingers, it is shared among friends and family and eaten with practically every meal. Day-old bread is used in soups, *köfte*, garlicky nut *tarator*, and it is soaked in syrup and poached fruits to make popular puddings. If bread is dropped on the ground or has to be thrown away, it is first kissed and held to the forehead as a mark of respect.

Generally, the harvested grains are ground between two heavy, flat stones to obtain flour. You can see this in rural villages and remote homesteads, as the country people very often grind small quantities of wheat or barley for basic flat breads and pancakes. As the dough for flat bread simply consists of ground flour and water, sometimes with the addition of a little ghee, it is easy to prepare and cooks quickly on a flat stone or metal sheet placed directly over a wood fire.

The standard crusty leavened loaves, similar to French baguettes in texture but shaped like kayaks, are found in every village and town throughout the country. In the rural villages leavened bread is cooked in the communal oven, the *fırın*, which can also be used for some flat breads by sticking the dough to the inside or outside walls of the hot oven. In small villages, where there may only be one *fırın*, certain days will be allocated for the communal baking.

In the larger villages and small towns, there are neighbourhood bakers, who often bake batches of bread twice a day – in the early morning and again in the evening. The tempting aroma of freshly baked bread lures you to the door, whether you were intending to buy bread or not. In the cities, there are many types of leavened loaves and specialist bakers that

Top ***Pide* for Ramazan.**

Bottom **Griddled flat breads are delicious served with honey for breakfast or plain to accompany meze dishes.**

cater for their own communities, such as the Jews and Armenians. In these bakeries, you will find a variety of wholemeal and rye loaves and rolls, sweet buns, and bread made with egg-based dough. There are several types of savoury and sweet buns, but the most popular are the sesame covered rings, *simit*, which are sold by street-sellers who carry them through the crowds stacked on long poles, or on wide, circular trays balanced on their heads.

Flat breads | The principal flat breads are the paper-thin sheets of *yufka* and the soft, spongy *pide*, with or without a hollow pouch. The local *yufkacı* is greatly valued for its daily supplies of freshly prepared *yufka*, ready for layering or wrapping around fillings to make savoury pastries. Making *yufka* is an art, since each tiny ball of dough is rolled out using a long thin rolling pin called an *oklava* until it resembles a large wheel that is as thin as paper. As the genuine article is difficult to obtain outside Turkey, it has been substituted in the recipes with filo pastry.

There are many types of pide available at the local *fırın*, such as the delicious, sweet *helva pide*, which melts in your mouth, and the sesame-sprinkled *Ramazan pide*, which is eaten to break the fast during the month of Ramazan. In some of the recipes, pitta breads, which are available in supermarkets and Middle Eastern stores, can be substituted, but if you have time to make fresh *pide* it is worth it.

**Making pide** This is an easy recipe for a tasty and very practical *pide* that can be enjoyed with any savoury dish in this book. Hot from the oven, it is also wonderful drizzled in honey. The charred flavour and aroma of the tiny, black nigella seeds scattered over the surface of the *pide* give it its unique taste. Makes 2 medium-sized *pide*, or 1 large.

**15g/½ oz fresh yeast, or 7g/¼ oz dried yeast**

**2.5ml/½ tsp sugar**

**about 150ml/¼ pint/⅔ cup lukewarm water**

**450g/1lb/4 cups unbleached strong white bread flour**

**5ml/1 tsp salt**

**30ml/2 tbsp olive oil, plus extra for greasing**

**30ml/2 tbsp thick, set natural (plain) yogurt**

**1 egg, beaten**

**15ml/1 tbsp nigella or sesame seeds**

**1** Preheat the oven to 220°C/425°F/Gas 7. Put the yeast and the sugar into a small bowl with 45ml/3 tbsp of the lukewarm water. Set aside for about 15 minutes, or until it froths.

**2** Sift the flour with the salt into a large bowl. Make a well in the centre and pour in the creamed yeast with the oil, yogurt and the remaining water. Using your hands, draw in the flour and work into a dough, until it leaves the side of the bowl – add more water if necessary; the dough should be sticky but pliable. Knead the dough on a lightly floured surface until it is smooth and light. Punch the dough flat, then gather up the edges into the middle, then flip it over.

**3** Splash a few drops of oil in the base of a large bowl, roll the ball of dough in it, and cover with a clean, damp dish towel. Leave to rise in a warm place for a few hours, or overnight, until it has doubled in size.

**4** Knock back (punch down) the dough to release the air, and knead it again for a few minutes. Lightly oil one large circular, or rectangular, baking tray, or two smaller ones, and place in the oven for 2 minutes.

**5** Place the dough on a floured surface, divide it into two pieces if you like, and flatten with the heel of your hand. Use your fingers to stretch it from the middle, creating a thick lip at the edges. Indent the dough with your fingertips and place it on the baking tray. Brush with a little beaten egg and scatter the nigella or sesame seeds over the top.

**6** Bake the dough in the hot oven for about 20 minutes, until the surface is crispy and golden. Transfer the *pide* to a wire rack and serve warm.

## Pasta

Pasta or noodle dough is thought to have arrived in Anatolia with some of the migrating Turks who came all the way from the northern borders of China. Early records show that a variety of pasta-style dishes were prepared with the meat of sheep and horses. In central and eastern Anatolia today, the most popular pasta is *mantı* (derived from Chinese *mantu*), which is rather like a cross between Italian ravioli and a Chinese dumpling. The Tartar Turks who settled around Kayseri are renowned for their skills at making *mantı*, and today the ancient dish has become fashionable in the restaurants of Istanbul and Ankara. Another popular pasta-style dish is *erişte*, a ribbon-shaped pasta that can be combined with various ingredients, such as spinach, tomatoes, herbs, spices or minced meat.

## Pastries

The Ottomans left a wonderful legacy of savoury and sweet pastry-making in Istanbul. During the reign of Sultan Mehmet II, the Palace chefs took their role very seriously and the pastry cooks of the city had to adhere to their recipes and methods, otherwise they risked being punished. Today, both savoury and sweet pastries form a large category of dishes that are popular in Turkish cuisine. Some pastries are made using *yufka*, others employ specially made doughs that resemble flaky and puff pastries, and then there is *kadayıf*, long, finely shredded strands of pastry used for desserts. *Börek* is a category of pastry that varies in shape and size with regional variations on the fillings. The most common fillings found throughout Turkey include mashed white cheese with fresh herbs; spinach and onions; and one made with finely minced lamb or beef and onions. Regional specialities include puréed pumpkin or potato; baked aubergine and cheese; or fish mixed with herbs.

Top **A rolled stack of paper-thin sheets of *yufka*, ready to be used to make various sweet and savoury pastries. Filo pastry can be substituted.**

Bottom **Thin strands of *kadayıf* pastry are used to make many desserts.**

Above **Olive oil.**

Opposite top **An olive grove in spring.**

Opposite bottom **Young black olives being harvested.**

# Olives and oils

Turks never stray too far from a bowl of olives, and olives are also, of course, pressed for their valuable fruity oil.

**Olives (zeytin)** | The Turks enjoy olives throughout the day, kicking off with a handful for breakfast to accompany *beyaz peynir*, the ubiquitous white cheese, followed by a few plucked from the market stall while shopping, to a bowlful of marinated, plump ones as a snack or meze dish in the middle of the day, and again in the evening. As a meze dish, olives are often served with lemon to squeeze over to enhance their flavour.

The hardy olive tree manages to grow in poor soil in varied climates, which means that olives are grown all over Turkey. The trees are indigenous to the region and live up to a great age; some are reputed to be more than a thousand years old, yet they still bear fruit. The western region of Anatolia is particularly rich in its variety of olives ranging in shades of purple, red, green, brown and black. The most common way to serve them is simply with a squeeze of lemon. To harvest, the trees are shaken so that the olives fall on to sheets placed on the ground. When the young black olives are harvested, they are immersed in salt for a week, so that the skin crinkles and the flesh softens. Rinsed of salt and stored in olive oil, these wrinkled black olives are the most popular for breakfast and for snacking on. Even the olive stones have a purpose: once they have been cleaned and polished, they are threaded on to string to make the prayer beads, *tespih*.

**Cooking oils** | Olive oil, sunflower oil, butter, ghee (clarified butter), and sheep's tail fat (*kuyrukyağı*) are the principal cooking fats employed. Olive oil has only been used in Turkish cooking since the Ottoman period – prior to that it was used as a lighting fuel in the mosques. Nowadays, olive and sunflower oils are used interchangeably, or together, for cooking. Olive oil is almost always used where the flavour of the oil contributes to the flavour of the dish, particularly in the *zeytinyağlı* dishes – the most famous these is the aubergine speciality, *imam bayıldı*, meaning that the Imam swooned, possibly because of the quantity of olive oil or because of the melt-in-the-mouth texture of the dish. Depending on the region, olive oil is used in most salads, as well as for marinating and basting meat, poultry and fish.

Ghee and sheep's tail fat are the oldest and most traditional of the fats used for cooking in Anatolia. Sheep's tail fat, literally the fat from the podgy tail of the sheep, is enjoyed in the eastern region but an acquired taste, as it never quite loses the odour of the animal; the tail is burned to release the fat, which is collected in a jar and stored for use.

Above **A fresh green pickle combination of cucumber, peppers, and herbs.**

Opposite **A stack of jars in a pickle-shop window makes a colourful display.**

# Pickles

The pickles (*turşu*) of Turkey are like no other. Both extraordinary in their variety and in their creativity, they are not just things to tuck into a sandwich or to snack on. A kaleidoscope of colour, the jars stacked in pickle shop windows beckon people to stop and buy their favourites by the kilo, or to quench their thirst with a glass of *turşu suyu*, pickle juice. In the autumn, the market stalls are stocked with rock salt, bushels of garlic and bunches of celery stalks – the chief elements for pickle making. Small, unripe vegetables and fruit are destined for pickling, as their acidity contributes to the fermentation process and they retain the desired crunchiness. Brine and wine vinegar are the standard pickling agents but in the past fresh grape juice was used, which inevitably turned to vinegar during fermentation. Yeast, provided by a few chickpeas or mustard seeds, or by a slice of stale bread wrapped in muslin, is sometimes added to speed up the process.

Some recipes like *patlıcan turşusu*, stuffed aubergine pickle, are unchanged in method since the 15th century. Other traditional pickles include white or red cabbage leaves; firm, green tomatoes; turnip with a little beetroot to colour it pink; long, twisted green chilli peppers, as well as the tiny, fiery ones and vast quantities of pungent garlic; and unripe fruit, such as apricots, melons and pears, combined with immature, green almonds. A recipe for pear pickle is given here.

**Making armut turşusu** Most Turkish pickles are sour or piquant to taste, but there are several sweet-and-sour ones that are delicious served with roasted or grilled meat, and with cheese. This recipe for pickled pears with saffron, honey and spices is popular in the agricultural regions around Bursa, where the orchards provide plentiful harvests every year.

**400ml/14fl oz/1¾ cup white wine or cider vinegar**

**175g/6oz aromatic honey (rosemary, lavender or pine forest)**

**2 cinnamon sticks**

**8 allspice berries**

**a fingerful of saffron threads**

**4 firm pears, cut in half lengthways with the stalks intact, or 8 small, firm pears left whole**

**1** Heat the vinegar in a large heavy pan with 120ml/4fl oz water, the honey, cinnamon, allspice and saffron. Bring the liquid to the boil, stirring all the time, until the honey has dissolved. Lower the heat, slip in the pears and poach gently for 15–20 minutes until tender but still firm.
**2** Lift the pears out of the pickling liquid and arrange them in a sterilised jar or crock. Pour over the hot liquid and leave to cool. Cover and store.

# Spices, herbs and flavourings

I can spend hours in the spice markets, admiring the mounds of coloured powders and selecting pungent seeds and bark, all with a story to tell of long journeys from their indigenous lands as well as their culinary and medicinal uses. During the Golden Age of Islam, between the 8th and 12th centuries, with Mecca as the religious centre and Baghdad as its capital, the cooking of the Middle East flourished as Arab ships sailed to China for silk and porcelain and to the East Indies for spices. Once the spices arrived in the ports and markets of Egypt and Constantinople, they influenced the cooking of the whole region. As the ancient yin and yang theories of China filtered through to the Seljuk Empire, a belief in balancing the warming and cooling properties of certain foods developed and set the course for many dishes. Warming spices such as cumin, cinnamon, allspice, cloves and Turkish red pepper (*pul biber* or *kırmızı biber*) are believed to induce the appetite and aid digestion, to cure colds and curb flatulence, and to contribute to physical and mental well-being; generous quantities of fresh herbs, particularly mint, dill and flat leaf parsley, are often mixed together as a warming triad to balance the cooling properties of some vegetable dishes and salads; and garlic is believed to be beneficial for the healthy circulation of the blood. This philosophy of food as a healer with a focus on the digestion and the gut is at the root of many traditional Turkish dishes.

Allspice (yeni bahar) | Dried reddish-brown allspice berries originally came to Constantinople from the New World during the Ottoman-Spanish alliance and are, therefore, known as *yeni bahar*, 'new spice'. They are used whole in marinades and pickles, and crushed for some stews, but their principal role is to flavour the aromatic rice that is used to stuff vegetables, fruit, mussels and small poultry. Sold ready-ground for this purpose, the ground spice is commonly known as *dolma bahar* (dolma refers to any dish that is stuffed). The spice, with a taste reminiscent of cloves and cinnamon, also features in many ready-prepared mixtures.

Cinnamon (tarçin) | Brought from the Spice Islands by Arab traders, cinnamon quickly became absorbed into the Turkish culinary culture. Sold in bark or ground form, the spice is pungent and warming, and lends itself to sweet and savoury dishes. The Turks use ground cinnamon in a number of minced lamb dishes, such as *köfte* and *musakka*, and in several Anatolian fish and vegetable stews. It is used to flavour rice dishes, such as *iç pilavı*, and is one of the warming spices in ready-made mixtures. A principal spice in many sweetmeats, pastries and breads, cinnamon is also sprinkled over milk puddings and the hot orchid-root drink, *salep*.

Top left **The aromatic rose flavours many dishes, typically in the use of rose flower water, but the petals are used for garnishing and in the delicious syrupy jam *gül reçeli*.**

Top right **Various types of runny, set and comb honey are found in the different regions of Turkey.**

Bottom left **Dried sage is used in preference to fresh in some stews and soups, and for a healing tisane.**

Bottom right **Mastic crystals are the aromatic gum from a tree indigenous to the Turkish Mediterranean, and are used to impart a distinctive resinous flavour and chewy tang to dishes.**

Top **Fresh dill is a key part of many classic olive oil vegetable dishes such as *zeytinyağlı taze fasulye*.**

Bottom **Fresh flat-leaf parsley is used constantly in the Turkish kitchen as an ingredient, garnish and palate cleanser.**

**Coriander seeds (kişniş)** | Fresh coriander (cilantro) seldom features in the cooking of Turkey, apart from in some traditional Circassian dishes, such as *çerkez tavuğu*. The dried seeds, however, are used to flavour a number of stews, soups and pickles, though tend to feature more in the cooking of central eastern Anatolia than in the Palace cuisine of Istanbul. Along with cumin and cinnamon, ground coriander is one of the spices incorporated in the ready-made spice mixtures that are mainly used for flavouring *köfte* and some pilaff dishes.

**Cumin (kimyon)** | When roasted, cumin seeds emit a nutty aroma, and they have a distinctive taste. They are best stored in seed form and then ground when needed, as the ready-ground spice loses its pungency fairly quickly. Believed to aid digestion, cumin is used in a number of dishes that might cause a degree of indigestion or flatulence, such as pulse dishes and some vegetable stews. Cumin is also one of the principal flavourings of *sucuk*, the cured sausage, and it is combined with fenugreek and *pul biber* in *çemen*, the paste that coats the cured beef fillet, *pastırma*.

**Dill (dereotu)** | With long feathery fronds, fresh dill is used both as a garnish and a flavouring in many Turkish dishes. Chopped, it is added to a number of meze and vegetable dishes, such as the Palace *zeytinyağlı* dishes in which various vegetables, such as artichokes, are poached in olive oil and served at room temperature.

Dill is often combined with mint and flat leaf parsley in the traditional herb triad used in many vegetable and pulse dishes, as well as in the cheese filling for savoury pastries. It is also the most popular herbal flavouring for grilled fish and shellfish, either by adding it to the marinade or dressing, or by scattering the chopped fresh leaves over the fish as a garnish.

**Flat leaf parsley (maydanoz)** | Large bunches of flat leaf parsley are stacked high at the Turkish market stalls, since it is the most ubiquitous herb of all. It is sold in big bunches and it keeps well at home if the stalks are put into a jug of water – just like flowers. Coarsely chopped, parsley is added to numerous meze dishes and salads, such as the popular shepherd's salad, *çoban salatası*, and it is often served on its own with fish or meat kebabs, particularly *çöp şiş*, where it plays an integral role. Garnishes of parsley are often served to heighten the appetite, to cleanse the palate or to temper the flavours, and small bunches of parsley always accompany fiery dishes with the idea that you chew on the leaves to cut the spice. Parsley is married with dill and mint in the classic herb trio.

Curly parsley does not have the same intensity of flavour, nor is it as juicy and refreshing.

**Garlic (sarmısak)** | Garlic is used liberally in the cooking of Anatolia but sparingly in the Palace cuisine. One of its key roles is to flavour thick creamy yogurt in the ubiquitous and delicious garlic-yogurt that goes so well with so many dishes. Garlic also adds a pungent kick to the various *tarator* sauces that are made with pounded nuts and served with deep-fried shellfish and fried or steamed vegetables, and it is the principal flavouring in the bread-based sauce *sarmısaklı sos*, a popular accompaniment to the deep-fried mussels in Istanbul and Izmir. Jars of pickled garlic bulbs are a common sight in the markets and pickle shops and whole bulbs are often threaded on to kebab skewers and grilled with sheep's tail fat in central and eastern Anatolia. Garlic is well known for its healing properties and it is also hung in doorways as it is believed to ward off the evil eye.

**Honey (bal)** | Ranging in colour from black coffee to muddy-river brown, sparkling gold, amber yellow and frothy white, there are so many different honeys to choose from. The dark, fragrant honey from the pine forests of the Aegean and Mediterranean regions is much sought after in its runny or comb form, as is the pungent chestnut honey from the Black Sea region, but there is one extraordinary honey – the *deli bal*, 'silly honey' – of the Kars region, where opium poppies grow naturally and the honey drives you wild as it momentarily grips the back of your throat with a fiery blast that brings with it mild hallucinatory sensations. It is the most bizarre honey I have ever had.

**Pul biber** | This is the most useful spice in my kitchen. I sprinkle it on everything. Also known as *kırmızı biber*, it is finely chopped dried red chilli, a medium-hot, fruity variety that came originally from the New World, but so intertwined in modern Turkish cuisine that you would think it was indigenous to the region. It ranges in colour from vermilion to a deep blood-red, and is almost black when roasted. The best quality is sold ready-oiled (*yağlı*) so that it imparts its flavour immediately, even in uncooked dishes. Whole dried red chilli peppers are threaded together and hung up on balconies, in courtyards, and in the markets. The spice is inseparable from the *güney* cuisine, the cooking of southern Turkey, and is used liberally in Gaziantep and Antakya. As substitutes for both the oiled and roasted versions you can use Aleppo or Urfa chillies, both of which are available in Middle Eastern stores and online. For ease, you can turn to paprika but it won't give you the same heat and flavour.

**Mastic (mastika)** | This is the aromatic gum from a tree (Pistacia lentiscus) that grows wild in the Mediterranean region of Turkey. The blobs of sticky gum turn hard when exposed to air, and are sold in their crystallised form. Traditionally, the gum was used in a number of savoury and sweet dishes but, nowadays, it is mainly used in the Ottoman Palace

Top **In parts of Anatolia, cumin and coriander seeds are dry-roasted to enhance their flavour and aroma.**

Bottom **Dried chilli is the essential Turkish spice, whole, flaked or ground.**

Top **Fresh mint leaves are sold in large bunches, and used in liberal quantities for their distinctly refreshing taste.**

Bottom **Saffron is a highly prized spice. It requires roughly 10,000 crocus flowers to yield only 50g (2oz) of saffron threads – hence the high price. There are substandard versions using wild flower filaments that claim to be saffron.**

milk puddings and in the famous snowy-white, chewy ice cream from Istanbul. The gum crystals can be chewed but, when using them for culinary purposes, they must first be pulverised with a little sugar, using a mortar and pestle, to impart their delicious resinous flavour and chewy tang. Mastic crystals can be found in Turkish, Greek and Middle Eastern stores and are available to order online.

Mint (nane) | Both the fresh and dried leaves of mint are used in meze dishes, salads, vegetable dishes and pilaffs, such as *Sultan Reşat pilavı*, the delicious aubergine rice dish with cinnamon and lots of mint. One of the 'warming' herbal trio, along with flat leaf parsley and dill, fresh mint leaves are sold and used in large quantities. The dried leaves are used in tea, in the traditional soup, *yayla çorbası*, and in several thick meze dips such as *haydari*, a popular yogurt, mint and garlic dip; and *tahin tarama*, a mixture of sesame paste and grape syrup.

Nigella (çöreotu) | In Turkey, nigella is most commonly associated with *çörek* (hence the name *çöreotu*), a sweet bun that is eaten during the Sweet Festival, Şeker Bayramı. The little black seeds look like tiny charcoal teardrops and have an aromatic, peppery flavour, which gives a lift to many breads and buns, such as *pide*. Due to their distinctive flavour, nigella seeds are occasionally tossed in salads and sprinkled over cheese.

Oregano (kekik) | Fresh oregano leaves are sometimes scattered over white cheese or tossed in salads but, generally, the herb is sun-dried and crumbled or finely chopped. It is the favourite herb to scatter over roasted or grilled lamb, and bowls of dried oregano are a frequent sight at kebab houses, where they are placed on the tables alongside bowls of sumac and *pul biber*, the three traditional grilled meat condiments. Both dried oregano and thyme are popular herbs for flavouring the marinades prepared for olives, as they retain their flavour and texture in the olive oil, and they are also scattered over savoury breads.

Saffron (safron) | Worth its weight in gold, saffron is the only spice in the world to be measured by the carat. It is the dye contained in the dried stigmas of the purple crocus (Crocus sativus), which flowers for only two weeks in October. The dried stigmas are generally sold in small quantities and resemble a tangle of burnt-orangey-red threads – the deeper the colour the better the quality. Although only mildly perfumed at this stage, the stigmas come into life when soaked in water, as they impart a magnificent yellow dye and a floral hint to their flavour. Most of Turkey's saffron comes from neighbouring Iran and is used mainly in milk puddings, ice cream and *zerde*, a special jelly-like rice dessert that is often prepared for wedding feasts.

**Sage (adı)** | The hillsides of the Mediterranean and Aegean regions of Turkey emit a delicious herby aroma as the sun-kissed wild sage bushes produce the most wonderfully perfumed and tasty leaves. The fresh leaves are added to a variety of salads, vegetable dishes, and grilled or lightly fried shellfish. The dried leaves are used in stews and soups, and are often added to melted butter that is drizzled over poached eggs, the Anatolian noodle dumplings, *mantı*, and the Circassian chicken and walnut dish, *çerkez tavüğü*. In the markets throughout Turkey, stalks of dried sage leaves are strung up at spice stalls, destined for an aromatic winter tea that is believed to be healing and cleansing.

**Scented waters** | The perfumed blossoms of the bitter orange tree and roses are distilled to make the clear scented waters – *portakal suyu* and *gül suyu* – which have been employed in the kitchen since medieval times. The origins and uses of rose petals can be traced back to the bathing habits of the ancient Egyptians and the wine traditions of the Romans, but the invention of a distilled rose water for culinary purposes is attributed to the Persians. Adopted by the Ottomans, the scenting of dishes with rose and orange blossom waters became popular in the Palace kitchens, where they were used in syrupy pastries and milk desserts, such as *güllaç* and *muhallebi*.

**Sumac (sumak)** | Sumac is a deep-red, slightly sour-tasting spice prepared by crushing and grinding the dried berries of a wild bush (Rhus coriaria) that grows prolifically in Anatolia and parts of the Middle East. The ground spice has a fruity flavour but it was the sour taste that was originally sought after. Long before the arrival of lemons in Turkey and the Middle East, sumac was used as one of the principal souring agents, along with the juice of sour pomegranates, to season, flavour and preserve a wide variety of foods.

**Thyme (dağı kekik)** | Thyme comes from the same family as oregano, and is also known as 'mountain oregano', as it grows further up the hillsides. The fresh sprigs are used to flavour roasted meats and poultry, such as *ördek fırında*, roast duck with honey, thyme and almonds. In central and eastern Anatolia, fresh thyme is used to flavour dishes prepared with sheep's tail fat, as the herb is believed to cut the fat and aid digestion. The dried sprigs, on the other hand, are brewed in a herbal tea to aid digestion but was traditionally prepared as an aphrodisiac.

**Vanilla (vanilya)** | The majority of the vanilla pods that arrive at the Mısır Çarşısı, the famous Egyptian spice bazaar in Istanbul, come from Madagascar, but as the flavour of vanilla is mainly confined to baking and desserts, little bottles of vanilla extract are more commonly sold than the moist, plump pods. Vanilla is mainly seen in the Palace desserts.

Top **Dried mint, oregano and sage are frequently used for meat marinades and seasonings.**

Bottom **Wonderfully fragrant orange blossom is used to scent water, like rose petals, and incorporated in many cordials, syrups and sweets.**

# Drinks

Tea rules in Turkey. It is without doubt the king of drinks. Everywhere you go, you will be offered a glass – a mark of hospitality, or simply to quench your thirst. Coffee is surrounded by tradition and ritual, but tea is the national drink. For hot days there are a number of refreshing fruity sherbet drinks and in the winter there is nothing more welcoming than a cup of sweet milky *salep*, prepared with ground orchid root.

Coffee (kahve) | For those who can afford it, the first small cup of *kahve* is enjoyed on rising, the second cup is drunk mid-morning, and a third may be drunk after a long meal. As it is more expensive, and more prestigious, than tea, coffee is not available to all on a daily basis. In some Anatolian communities, where it is reserved for special occasions, there still exists the tradition of selecting a suitable bride partially based on her ability to prepare and serve coffee, while the prospective mother-in-law and her son inspect the young girl's beauty and grace.

The traditional cooking vessel for Turkish coffee is a *cezve*, a slim, deep pot, often made from tin-lined copper, with a long handle. Generally, medium-roast arabica coffee beans are passed through a very fine grinder until almost powdery. A wide selection of suitable coffee beans are available, but the Turkish setting on grinding machines usually doesn't grind the beans fine enough for the desired effect, so make sure it is passed through the grinder twice. Most Turks drink their coffee sweet, but you can drink it *sade* (black), *orta şekerli* (medium sweet), or *şekerli* (sweet). There is an art to making an acceptable cup of Turkish coffee.

**Making Turkish coffee** To make the thick, strong coffee, measure the water by the coffee cup (a standard, small cylindrical cup) and the coffee by the teaspoon. The general rule allows for one coffee cup of water to 5ml/1 tsp coffee and 5ml/1 tsp sugar per person.

**1** Tip the water into the *cezve* and spoon the coffee and sugar on the top. Use a teaspoon to stir the sugar and coffee quickly into the surface of the water to give the desired froth a good kick-start.

**2** Put the pan over a medium heat and, using the teaspoon, gradually scrape the outer edges of the surface into the middle to create an island of froth. The key to achieving the perfect froth is always to work at the surface; never touch the bottom of the pot with the spoon.

**3** Once the coffee is hot, pour about one-third of it into the coffee cup to warm it and return the pan to the heat. Continue to gather the froth into the middle and, just as the coffee begins to bubble up, take it off the heat and pour it into the cup. Leave the coffee cup to stand for 1 minute to let the coffee grains settle and then drink it while it is hot.

Top **Tulip-shaped glasses of tea – the national drink of Turkey.**

Bottom **Traditional Ottoman-style coffee cups have a metal outer, holding the porcelain cup, and lid.**

Top ***Salep* is a drink made from a flour ground from orchid tubers.**

Bottom **Making *boza*, the traditional fermented drink made from bulgur.**

**Tea (çay)** The drinking of tea, *çay*, is big business in Turkey. It is also an enjoyable pastime. There are *çay* houses, stalls and gardens in every village, in every city street, at ports and stations, and near busy office buildings. You will often see young boys or men carrying trays of tea glasses through crowds or across busy roads as tea is served throughout the day to passers-by, gatherings of friends, and thirsty staff in the buildings. Tea is offered to you in banks while you wait, in shops and markets as you browse, in meetings of any description, and in houses when you are welcomed. It is a drink of friendship and hospitality and it is polite to accept.

Invariably, tea is served in tulip-shaped glasses, a legacy of Sultan Ahmet III (1703–30), who encouraged the design of tulips on tiles and other artefacts. Traditionally, it was made in a bulky copper samovar, but nowadays it is made in a modern tin or aluminium version consisting of a small teapot, containing the tea, resting on a larger teapot, containing the water.

Generally, the tea leaves are home-grown, mainly from plantations at Rize on the Black Sea coast, and the tea is made strong. It is never drunk with milk and is served with lumps of sugar, which some people stir in, whereas others place them in their mouths and suck the tea through them. Packets of Turkish tea are available to buy in Turkish stores and online but you can make a similar pot of fragrant tea using a combination of loose Assam and Earl Grey leaves.

**Herbal and fruit teas** Alternative teas are often put in the category of 'healing' teas, as most Turks would only abandon their regular tea for a herbal one if suffering from an ailment. These herbal and aromatic infusions range from rose petals, camomile (*papatya*), and lemon, to orange blossom, rosemary and mint. The dried leaves and blossom of the linden tree are sold as a medicinal tea, *ıhlamur çayı*, which is believed to aid the digestive system and clear up colds. An invigorating tea, *adı çayı*, is made from the steeped branches of wild, sun-dried sage, and there are several complex herbal tea mixes that combine a variety of wild herbs with wild flowers, sticks of bark and spices, for different seasons and ailments. Fruit, such as apples and oranges, are dried, too, and used to make tea, but there is also a commercial apple tea, *elma çayı*, which consists of sugar and apple-flavoured granules.

**Salep** I love this drink. It's thick, milky, nourishing and warming with a dusting of cinnamon – perfect for a cold winter's day. Prepared from finely ground orchid root, *salep* is traditionally made in large copper or brass urns, some of which are still in use in specialist pudding shops, but there are also sachets of instant salep available in Turkish and Middle Eastern stores.

**Boza** | In the winter, one of the traditional drinks is *boza*, a thick mixture made from fermented bulgur wheat and sprinkled with cinnamon. Glasses of the pale yellow liquid are lined up in pudding shop windows. The village *boza* seller pulls his cart through the streets, laden with copper jugs filled with the beverage, and shouting "bozacı" to alert people to his presence so that they stop for a glass of the unusual, but popular, drink.

**Sherbet (şerbet)** | The most common cold drink in Turkey is *şerbet*, which is a cool, refreshing drink made from fruit syrups, such as lemon, cherry or pomegranate, as well as syrups made with rose petals, orange blossom, honey, almonds and tamarind. Preparing syrups with seasonal fruits or petals was part of traditional kitchen life and still is in some households. Sugar and water are simmered until the former is dissolved, and the mixture thickened and syrupy, then the floral essence or other flavouring is added and simmered for a few minutes. The cordial is diluted with iced water to serve.

**Alcoholic drinks** | Prior to the influence of Islam, the Turks enjoyed a variety of alcoholic drinks, such as crude beers and local wines and the fermented milk of mares, *kımız*, all of which were collectively known as *çakır* (*çakırkeyif* means 'tipsy') and were usually accompanied by meze dishes to soak up the spirits. With the conversion to Islam, however, alcoholic drinks were prohibited. In Turkey today, many devout Muslims still adhere to the strict Islamic rules but, with the influence of Europe, tourism and diverse religions within the country, there are many people who do drink alcohol and there are several good Turkish beers, wines and spirits.

The best-known beer is called Efes but there is a growing number of local beers. Many Turkish wines have been rather unpredictable in the past and benefited from being decanted and aired, but there are now several recognised wines on a par with French and Italian wines. The two leading wine producers have quite a good range of wines, such as Dikmen (red) and Cankaya (white), but my favourite bottle of red is called Yakut.

The best-known spirit is the aniseed-flavoured *rakı*, which turns cloudy when water is added and is often referred to as 'lion's milk'. *Rakı* can be drunk in three ways: neat as a shot; served in a tall glass with ice to which water is added; or served in two glasses, one containing a measure of *rakı*, the other filled with water, both glasses being drunk alternately with ice. *Rakı* is the favoured drink to enjoy with meze and fish dishes in particular. A liquid form of *mastika* is sometimes added to the bottle to give it a chewy twang. Top-of-the-range bottlings of *rakı* are Atinbas and Yeni, which can be found outside Turkey.

Top **Grape sherbet, a sweet and refreshing drink.**

Bottom ***Rakı* and water on the café table.**

# Meze and salads

The tradition of meze may be ancient but it symbolises modern eating – small portions, healthy ingredients, food to share. I've enjoyed wonderful spreads of meze dishes at the family table, at the beach, on a city balcony and in the countryside under the shade of a fig tree. Time just floats away as you embrace the philosophy that a selection of tasty dishes, dips and salads can bring people together.

# Humus

This is one of those dishes to make according to your personal taste. Some people like humus strongly flavoured with garlic or thickened with an intense sesame flavour from additional tahini; some like it smooth, others coarse. I like mine light and lemony, fairly garlicky and smooth, served with toasted flat breads or crudités, succulent olives, pickles and feta salad.

## Serves four to six

**225g/8oz dried chickpeas, soaked in cold water for at least 6 hours or overnight, or 2 x 400g/14oz cans of chickpeas, rinsed and drained**

**juice of 1–2 lemons**

**2 garlic cloves, crushed**

**5ml/1 tsp cumin seeds**

**60–75ml/4–5 tbsp olive oil, plus extra to drizzle**

**salt and ground black pepper**

**a sprinkling of *pul biber* or paprika, to garnish**

Drain the chickpeas and place them in a pan with plenty of water. Bring to the boil, reduce the heat and simmer, covered, for about 1½ hours or until they are very soft. Drain then remove any loose skins by rubbing the chickpeas in a clean kitchen towel. If you are using canned chickpeas, rinse and drain before using.

Tip the chickpeas into a blender. Add the lemon juice, garlic and cumin seeds and blend thoroughly. Gradually drizzle in the olive oil as you blend. Season well and adjust the consistency and flavour to your taste by adding a little more lemon or olive oil and continuing to blend.

Transfer the humus to a serving bowl and drizzle a little oil over the surface to keep it moist. Sprinkle a little *pul biber* or paprika over the top and serve with warm bread or crudités of your choice.

# Smoked aubergine and yogurt purée

The smoky flavour of chargrilled aubergines features in many Turkish dishes. This dish, *patlıcan ezmesi*, is one of the simplest and most popular ways of enjoying the puréed, smoky flesh but there are many variations on the theme. Serve with fresh crusty bread.

## Serves four

**2 large, plump aubergines (eggplants)**

**30ml/2 tbsp olive oil, plus extra for drizzling**

**juice of 1 lemon**

**2–3 garlic cloves, crushed**

**225g/8oz thick and creamy natural (plain) yogurt**

**salt and ground black pepper**

**a few fresh dill fronds, to garnish**

**lemon wedges, to serve**

Gripping them firmly between tongs, place the aubergines directly on the gas flame on top of the stove, or under a conventional grill or broiler, and turn them from time to time until the skin is charred on all sides and the flesh feels soft to the touch. Place the aubergines in a plastic bag and leave for a few minutes.

Hold each aubergine by the stalk under cold running water and peel off the charred skin until you are left with just the flesh. Squeeze the flesh to get rid of any excess water and place it on a chopping board. Chop the aubergine flesh to a pulp, discarding the stalks.

Or if you have a barbecue, lay them on the rack over hot charcoal and cook for 15–20 minutes, turning them from time to time until they are soft. Split lengthways on a chopping board and scoop out the flesh.

Put the smoked flesh in a bowl with the olive oil, lemon juice and garlic. Beat well to mix, then beat in the yogurt and season with salt and pepper. Transfer to a small bowl, drizzle with extra olive oil and garnish with dill. Serve at room temperature, with lemon wedges for squeezing.

## Variation

To make *patlıcan salatası*, toss the smoked aubergine flesh with the oil and lemon juice, some sliced spring onion, chopped tomato, parsley and dill.

Left **Tahini and lemon dip** Right **Carrot and caraway purée with yogurt**

# Tahini and lemon dip

I first had this delightful tangy dip, *tahin tarama*, in central Anatolia in one of the simple outdoor kebab houses – plastic tables and chairs arranged under trees with an outdoor grill and a stove for making tea. It was just brought to the table – a sort of whetting of the appetite – while you waited for the rest of your order to be grilled. You will often see a group of old men drinking tea, sharing a plate of *tahin tarama* and a bowl of roasted chickpeas while they play a game of backgammon.

## Serves two

**45ml/3 tbsp tahini or sesame paste**

**juice of 1 lemon**

**15–30ml/1–2 tbsp clear honey**

**5–10ml/1–2 tsp dried mint**

**lemon wedges, to serve**

Beat the sesame paste and lemon juice together in a bowl. Add the honey and mint and beat again until thick and creamy – thin with a little water if you need to – then spoon into a small dish. Serve the dip with warm bread or crudités.

## Cook's tip

Popular for breakfast or as a sweet snack is *tahin pekmez*. Combine 30–45ml/2–3 tbsp light tahini or sesame paste with 30ml/2 tbsp grape *pekmez* to form a sweet paste, then scoop up with chunks of fresh crusty bread. If you can't find grape molasses, use the date one which is easily available online and in Middle Eastern stores.

# Carrot and caraway purée with yogurt

You can make this dish, *havuz ezmesi*, with the standard sweet orange carrots or the more tangy red and purple ones available in the Turkish markets between November and March. I often make this dish as part of a meze spread as it adds such a lovely touch of colour to the table as well as balance to some of the stronger-flavour dishes. Steam, don't boil, the carrots for the best results.

## Serves four

**6 large carrots, thickly sliced**

**5ml/1 tsp caraway seeds**

**30–45ml/2–3 tbsp olive oil**

**juice of 1 lemon**

**225g/8oz thick and creamy natural (plain) yogurt**

**1–2 garlic cloves, crushed**

**salt and ground black pepper**

**a few fresh mint leaves, to garnish**

Steam the carrots for 25 minutes, until they are very soft. While they are still warm, mash them to a smooth purée, or blend them in a processor.

Beat the caraway seeds into the carrot purée, followed by the oil and lemon juice. Season with salt and pepper.

Beat the yogurt and garlic in a separate bowl, and season to taste.

Spoon the warm carrot purée around the edge of a serving dish, or pile into a mound and make a well in the middle. Spoon the yogurt into the middle, and garnish with mint. Try serving it warm, with chunks of crusty bread or warm *pide* to scoop it up.

# Hot humus with pine nuts and melted butter

I came across this delectable baked humus in 1985 in Kars in eastern Anatolia and I have been waxing lyrical about it ever since. It was years before I found it served anywhere else – none of my Turkish friends had ever had it – but now it crops up in many places. I make my version with yogurt to inject a mousse-like quality into the consistency, which just begs to be scooped up with a chunk of *ekmek*, fresh crusty bread.

## Serves four

**225g/8oz dried chickpeas, soaked in cold water for at least 6 hours or overnight, or 2 x 400g/14oz cans of chickpeas, rinsed and drained**

**about 50ml/2fl oz/¼ cup olive oil**

**juice of 2 lemons**

**3–4 garlic cloves, crushed**

**5–10ml/1–2 tsp cumin seeds**

**30–45ml/2–3 tbsp tahini or light sesame paste**

**60–75ml/4–5 heaped tbsp thick and creamy natural (plain) yogurt**

**30ml/2 tbsp pine nuts**

**45g/1½ oz/3 tbsp butter**

**5–10ml/1–2 tsp oiled or roasted Turkish red pepper, *pul biber* or paprika**

**salt and ground black pepper**

Drain the chickpeas and place them in a pan with plenty of water. Bring to the boil, reduce the heat and simmer, covered, for about 1½ hours or until they are very soft. Drain then remove any loose skins by rubbing the chickpeas in a clean kitchen towel. If you are using canned chickpeas, rinse and drain before using.

Preheat the oven to 200°C/400°F/Gas 6.

Tip the chickpeas into a blender with the olive oil, lemon juice, garlic, cumin seeds and tahini. Whizz to a thick paste. Add the yogurt and whizz until light and creamy. Season well with salt and pepper and tip the humus into an oven dish.

Dry-roast the pine nuts in a small, heavy-based pan over a medium heat until golden brown. Stir in the butter until it melts, then stir in the red pepper or paprika.

Spoon the butter over the humus and bake for about 25 minutes, until it has risen slightly and the butter has been absorbed. Serve straight from the oven.

# Fiery cheese and parsley dip

Reputed to be fit for a *paşa* (a nobleman), this Anatolian dish is called *paşa ezmesi*, perhaps because it combines two of the grand ingredients of the Ottoman period: white cheese, *beyaz peynir*, and thick, creamy strained yogurt, *süzme*. Spiked with *pul biber*, it is often served to whet the appetite for the dishes to follow. To cut the spice, you can drizzle a little honey over the top or serve it village-style with a bowl of leafy parsley stalks to chew on.

## Serves three to four

**250g/9oz *beyaz peynir*, or feta cheese**

**15–30ml/1–2 tbsp *süzme*, or strained yogurt**

**5–10ml/1–2 tsp *pul biber*, or hot paprika or chilli powder**

**1 small bunch of flat leaf parsley, leaves finely chopped**

**salt, to taste**

**lemon wedges, a small bunch of flat leaf parsley, honey and *pide*, to serve**

In a bowl, mash the cheese with a fork, or process it in a food processor or blender. Beat in the yogurt, again using the fork or the blender, until the mixture is fairly smooth and creamy.

Add the *pul biber* and the parsley. Taste the dip to see if you need to add any salt – often the cheese is sufficiently salty.

Spoon the cheese dip into a dish and serve as part of a meze spread with warm flat bread, such as pitta pouches or Turkish *pide*, wedges of lemon to squeeze over each mouthful, or a drizzle of honey and leafy stalks of flat leaf parsley to chew on.

## Variations

✻ Crushed walnuts can be mixed into the dip, or sprinkled over the top, to add some texture.

✻ Finely chopped fresh mint can be added to the parsley to give a refreshing lift to the dish.

# Smoked cod's roe dip

Traditionally, this dish (*tarama*) is made with the smoked roe of grey mullet, a popular fish in Turkey. However, the smoked roe of other fish, such as cod, can also be used, Like *humus*, this a dish that you can make according to your taste, adjusting the oil and lemon and the density of the purée. Chunks of warm, crusty bread and strips of cucumber sprinkled with salt or a selection of tangy pickles are ideal accompaniments to this dip.

## Serves four to six

**2 slices of white bread, with the crusts removed**

**about 105ml/7 tbsp milk or water**

**225g/8oz smoked cod's roe, skin removed**

**2–3 garlic cloves, crushed**

**45–60ml/3–4 tbsp olive oil, or a mixture of olive and sunflower oil**

**juice of 2 lemons**

**salt and ground black pepper**

**finely chopped flat leaf parsley, to garnish**

First soak the bread in a little milk or water (the quantity of liquid will vary according to the size and type of bread). Squeeze the bread to remove the excess liquid.

Using a mortar and pestle, or an electric blender, pound the cod's roe to a smooth paste. Add the bread and garlic, and gradually pour in the olive oil and lemon juice, until the purée is light and creamy – adjust the quantity of oil and lemon juice to your taste.

Season the purée with salt and a generous grinding of black pepper, and transfer it to a serving bowl.

Garnish the dip with a little chopped parsley and serve.

## Variation

Some of my Turkish friends prefer to make a delicious warm version of *tarama* by using mashed potato instead of the soaked bread. Simply mix the smoked roe with freshly made hot mashed potato and garnish it with chopped parsley. Using this method makes the purée a little heavier when left to stand.

# Tangy charred pepper and smoked aubergine

Arab in origin, this dish of charred peppers and smoked aubergine is popular in the southern part of Turkey. Traditionally served warm with lemon wedges to squeeze over it, *acvar* is delicious served with toasted flat breads and a dollop of yogurt, or as an accompaniment to grilled meats.

## Serves four

**2 red bell peppers**

**1 fat aubergine (eggplant)**

**30–45ml/2–3 tbsp olive oil**

**1 red onion, cut in half lengthways and finely sliced along the grain**

**1 fresh red chilli, deseeded and finely sliced**

**2 garlic cloves, chopped**

**5–10ml/1–2 tsp sugar**

**juice of 1 lemon**

**dash of white wine vinegar**

**a big handful of fresh flat leaf parsley, roughly chopped**

**salt and ground black pepper**

**lemon wedges and toasted flat bread, to serve**

Place the peppers and aubergine directly on the gas flame on top of the stove, under a conventional grill or broiler, or on a rack over the hot coals of a barbecue. Turn from time to time until the skin is charred on all sides and the flesh feels soft. Place in a plastic bag and leave for a few minutes.

One at a time, hold the charred vegetables under cold running water and peel off the skins. Place them on a chopping board and remove the stalks. Halve the peppers lengthways and scoop out the seeds, then chop the flesh to a pulp. Chop the aubergine flesh to a pulp.

Pour the oil into a wide, heavy pan and toss in the onion, chilli, garlic and sugar. Cook over a medium heat for 2–3 minutes, until they begin to colour. Toss in the pulped peppers and aubergine, stir in the lemon juice and vinegar, and season to taste with salt and pepper. Toss in the parsley and serve with lemon wedges and toasted flat bread.

# Spicy walnut and red pepper dip

*Muhammara* is one of my favourite dishes from the southern part of Turkey, particularly in the Antakya region close to the Syrian border where it is often served as a dish of hospitality. Traditional recipes include the local hot pepper paste, which lends a rich colour and texture to the dish but I often adapt the recipe at home by roasting bell peppers and adding chilli. You can pound all the ingredients together using a mortar and pestle or you can make your life easier by using an electric blender. Serve with strips of pitta bread.

## Serves four to six

**175g/6oz broken shelled walnuts, toasted in the oven**

**5ml/1 tsp cumin seeds, dry-roasted and ground**

**5–10ml/1–2 tsp *pul biber*, or 1–2 fresh red chillies, deseeded and finely chopped, or 5ml/1 tsp chilli powder**

**1–2 garlic cloves, chopped**

**2–3 red bell peppers, roasted in the oven, skinned, deseeded and roughly chopped**

**2–3 slices of day-old bread, soaked in the juice of 1 lemon**

**15–30ml/1–2 tsp tomato purée (paste)**

**5–10ml/1–2 tsp honey**

**30ml/2 tbsp pure sour pomegranate molasses, or lemon juice**

**120ml/4fl oz/½ cup olive oil, plus extra for serving**

**salt and ground black pepper**

**a few sprigs of fresh flat leaf parsley, to garnish**

Using a mortar and pestle, pound the walnuts with the cumin seeds, *pul biber* or chilli, and garlic.

Add the roasted peppers and soaked bread, and pound to a paste, then beat in the tomato purée, honey and pomegranate molasses.

Now slowly drizzle in the olive oil, beating all the time until the paste is thick and light. Season with salt and pepper, adjust the pomegranate molasses and honey according to your taste, and spoon into a bowl.

Splash a little olive oil over the top to keep it moist, and garnish with parsley leaves. Serve at room temperature.

## Cook's tip

If you have an electric blender you can whizz all the ingredients together but you still need to drizzle in the oil at the end. Many local cooks prefer the traditional mortar and pestle method as the pounding releases the natural oils and flavour of the nuts, and this contributes considerably to the finished taste and texture of the dish. There is a practical reason too as the electricity supply in many regions is not reliable.

# Stuffed vine leaves

Devised by the Ottomans, these stuffed vine leaves, *yalancı yaprak dolması*, are a popular meze dish throughout Turkey and the Middle East. They are called *yalancı*, which means 'false', because they contain no meat. This term applies to all vegetables that are stuffed solely with aromatic rice and then cooked in olive oil and served cold on their own or as part of a meze spread. Stacks of fresh vine leaves are available in season in some Middle Eastern, Greek and Italian stores but I use the jars of vine leaves preserved in brine.

## Serves six

**24–30 fresh or preserved vine leaves, plus extra for lining the pan**

**45ml/3 tbsp olive oil**

**2 onions, finely chopped**

**2–3 garlic cloves, finely chopped**

**30ml/2 tbsp pine nuts**

**5ml/1 tsp ground allspice**

**5ml/1 tsp ground cinnamon**

**15ml/3 tsp sugar**

**225g/8oz/generous 1 cup short grain rice, well rinsed and drained**

**a small bunch each of fresh parsley, mint and dill, leaves finely chopped**

**150ml/¼ pint/⅔ cup olive oil**

**150ml/¼ pint/⅔ cup water**

**juice of 1 lemon**

**salt and ground black pepper**

**2 lemons, thickly sliced, to serve**

Prepare the vine leaves. If using fresh leaves, bring a pan of water to the boil and plunge the leaves into it for 1–2 minutes. Drain and refresh under cold running water, then drain thoroughly. Trim off the stems. If using preserved leaves, place in a bowl and cover with boiling water. Soak for 15–20 minutes, using a fork to separate the leaves. Drain and then soak again in cold water for 2–3 minutes, then drain thoroughly. Stack the vine leaves on a plate and cover with a clean dish towel to keep them moist.

Heat the oil in a heavy pan and cook the onions and garlic until they begin to colour. Stir in the pine nuts, spices and 10ml/2 tsp of the sugar. Cook, stirring, for 1 minute. Add the rice, mix well, and season. Pour in enough water to just cover the rice and bring to the boil, then reduce the heat and simmer for 10 minutes, or until all the water has been absorbed. The rice should have a bite to it. Toss in the herbs and leave the rice to cool.

Place a vine leaf on a board and put a heaped teaspoon of rice at the base. Fold the stem edge over the filling, then bring both of the side edges in towards the middle of the leaf, so that the filling is sealed in. Now roll the leaf up like a small, fat cigar. Place in the palm of your hand and squeeze it lightly. Repeat with the remaining leaves and rice.

In a small bowl, mix together the olive oil, water, lemon juice and remaining teaspoon of sugar. Line the base of a shallow pan with the extra vine leaves, then place the stuffed vine leaves on top, tightly packed side by side. Pour the olive oil mixture over and place a plate on top of the rolls to prevent them from unravelling during cooking. Cover the pan and simmer gently for about 1 hour, topping up the cooking liquid if necessary. Leave the stuffed leaves to cool in the pan, then lift them out and arrange on a plate with slices of lemon.

# Tomato, pepper and chilli salsa

The Turkish word *taze* means fresh, which is exactly what this dish is – a kind of fresh salsa, often called *taze ezmesi*. Along with cubes of honey-sweet melon and feta, or plump, juicy olives spiked with red pepper and oregano, this is meze food at its simplest and best. Popular in kebab houses, *taze ezmesi* is brought to the table as a tasty snack or appetiser, served with chunks of warm or toasted *pide*, to enjoy while the meat is grilling.

## Serves four

**2 large tomatoes, skinned, deseeded and finely chopped**

**2 Turkish green peppers or 1 green bell pepper, deseeded and finely chopped**

**1 onion, finely chopped**

**1 green chilli, deseeded and finely chopped**

**a small bunch of fresh flat leaf parsley, finely chopped**

**a few fresh mint leaves, finely chopped**

**a small bunch of coriander (cilantro) leaves, finely chopped**

**a sprinkling of sugar**

**juice of 1 lemon**

**15–30ml/1–2 tbsp olive oil**

**sea salt and ground black pepper**

**toasted flat or pitta bread, to serve**

Put the finely chopped tomatoes, peppers, onion, green chilli, parsley, mint, coriander and sugar into a bowl and mix well together. Toss in the lemon juice and olive oil and season with salt and pepper.

To toast the bread, place on a hot griddle for 1–2 minutes, turn, and toast for a further 1 minute. (If using pittas, split in half using a sharp knife before toasting separately.)

Serve the salsa with pieces of toasted bread.

## Variation

To turn this salsa into a dip or a tangy paste for spreading on bread, just add 30ml/2 tbsp tomato purée with a little extra sugar, chilli and olive oil. Also called *taze ezmesi*, this is often served to whet the appetite in specialist kebab houses or as a condiment with grilled meats.

# Fresh bulgur salad with mint and lemon

If you go to the south of Turkey, in particular the region of the *güney* cuisine, you will most likely be offered this dish as a symbol of hospitality. Combining fine bulgur (cracked wheat) with lots of fresh mint and parsley, *kısır* is both sustaining and refreshing – be liberal with the lemon, herbs and chilli. I often serve it as part of a meze spread or as a fabulous addition to a barbecue. When it is served in Turkish households as a welcome dish, it is often spooned into little vine or lettuce leaves and garnished with a slice of tomato or pickles on the side.

## Serves four to six

**175g/6oz/scant 1 cup fine bulgur wheat, rinsed and drained**

**45–60ml/3–4 tbsp olive oil**

**juice of 1–2 lemons**

**30ml/2 tbsp tomato purée (paste)**

**10ml/2 tsp sugar**

**1 large or 2 small red onions, cut in half lengthways, in half again crossways, and sliced along the grain**

**10ml/2 tsp *pul biber*, or 1–2 fresh red chillies, deseeded and finely chopped**

**5–10ml/1–2 tsp dried mint**

**a large bunch each of fresh mint and flat leaf parsley, finely chopped, plus a few leaves to garnish**

**salt and ground black pepper**

**lemon wedges, to serve**

Put the bulgur wheat into a wide bowl, pour over enough boiling water to cover it by about 2.5cm/1in, and give it a quick stir. Cover the bowl with a plate or a pan lid and leave the bulgur wheat to steam for about 25 minutes, until it has soaked up the water and doubled in quantity.

Pour the olive oil over the bulgur and squeeze on the lemon juice, and toss to mix. Add the tomato purée and toss the mixture again until everything is combined and the bulgur is well coated.

Add the sugar, sliced onions, *pul biber* or chillies, dried mint and the chopped fresh herbs. Season with salt and pepper and mix well to combine.

Serve at room temperature, garnished with a little mint and parsley and with wedges of lemon to squeeze over it.

## Variation

In the south-east of Turkey, the juice of sour pomegranates is often used instead of lemons and hot red pepper is added liberally; this fiery *kısır* is moulded into small balls and served in lettuce-leaf wrappings.

# Fried vegetables with garlic yogurt

Frying vegetables and serving them with a garlicky yogurt as a meze dish, *yoğurtlu sebze*, is hugely popular in Turkey. A street food, served in top-class restaurants, cooked at home – wherever you go, seasonal vegetables will often be served this way. At home, I prefer to roast the vegetables instead of frying but both ways are delicious. Accompany with chunks of fresh, crusty bread to scoop and mop up the cool yogurt.

## Serves four

**1 large aubergine (eggplant)**

**1 courgette (zucchini)**

**1 red bell pepper**

**4 Turkish *çarliston* peppers, kept whole with stalk**

**sunflower oil, for deep-frying**

**500g/1¼lb thick and creamy natural (plain) yogurt**

**2–3 garlic cloves, crushed**

**salt and ground black pepper**

**seeds of half a pomegranate**

Using a vegetable peeler, partially peel the aubergine in stripes – a bit like the markings of a zebra. Cut the aubergine in half lengthways and then cut each half into thick slices. Drop the slices into a bowl of salted water to prevent them discolouring. Drain and squeeze them dry before frying, otherwise the excess water will cause the hot oil to spatter everywhere.

Cut the courgette in half lengthways and then cut it widthways into thick slices. Deseed the pepper and cut it into large pieces.

Heat enough oil for deep-frying in a wide pan. Fry the vegetables, including the whole Turkish peppers, in batches, until they are golden brown. Lift them out of the oil with tongs or a slotted spoon and drain on kitchen paper.

In a bowl, beat the yogurt with the garlic, and season to taste with salt and pepper. Pile the hot vegetables on to a serving dish and spoon dollops of the yogurt over the top – you can serve the rest of the yogurt in a bowl to accompany the dish. Garnish with pomegranate seeds and serve immediately, while the vegetables are still warm.

## Cook's tip

To extract the seeds from a pomegranate, cut the fruit into quarters and bend each one backwards so that the seeds are pushed upwards – some will fall out; the rest you can flick out with your thumbs.

# Warm aubergine salad with pepper and tomatoes

Smoky and fresh tasting, I associate this dish with summer holidays in the south of Turkey. Many an evening we would place the aubergines on the charcoal grill and watch the sun set with a glass of wine. The Turkish name for the dish is *patlican salatası* but it is really more of a purée than a salad and is best served while the aubergine flesh is still warm, however you can only do that if you smoke the aubergines over a charcoal grill. Scoop up with flat bread.

## Serves four to six

**2 tomatoes**

**2 large aubergines (eggplants)**

**1 red bell pepper**

**4–6 spring onions (scallions), trimmed and finely chopped**

**1 green chilli, deseeded and finely sliced**

**a good-sized bunch of flat leaf parsley, leaves chopped**

**a small bunch of mint, chopped**

**2–4 garlic cloves, crushed**

**45–60ml/3–4 tbsp olive oil**

**30–45ml/2–3 tbsp pure sour pomegranate molasses**

**juice of 1 lemon**

**a sprinkling of sumac**

**salt and ground black pepper**

**dill sprigs, to garnish**

Plunge the tomatoes into boiling water for 30 seconds, then refresh in cold water. Peel away the skins. Remove the seeds and chop the flesh.

Place the aubergines and red pepper directly over the gas flame or over a charcoal grill.

When the skin of the pepper has buckled and browned, hold it immediately under cold running water and peel off the skin. Remove the stalk and seeds, roughly chop the softened flesh, and set aside.

When the aubergines are charred and soft, hold them by the stalk under running cold water and carefully peel off the skin. Squeeze out the excess water, place the flesh on a board and roughly chop it in big clumps. (If you have smoked the aubergine over a charcoal grill, the skin toughens so all you need to do is place them on a board, slit them open and scoop out the warm flesh.)

Place the clumps of aubergine flesh in a wide bowl. Add the pepper, spring onions, tomatoes, green chilli, parsley, mint and garlic. Add the olive oil, pomegranate molasses and lemon juice and toss well.

Season to taste, sprinkle with sumac, garnish with dill and serve.

# Spinach with currants, pine nuts and yogurt

This, *ıspanak salatası*, is a lovely way to enjoy spinach – simple, tangy and creamy. When I prepare it for a meze spread I like to serve it warm with cooling garlicky yogurt and toasted flat bread. Remember you need a lot of spinach as it wilts down so much you wonder where it has all gone.

## Serves three to four

**450g/1lb fresh spinach leaves, thoroughly washed and drained**

**about 400g/14oz thick and creamy natural (plain) yogurt**

**2 garlic cloves, crushed**

**30–45ml/2–3 tbsp olive oil**

**1 red onion, cut in half lengthways, in half again crossways, and sliced along the grain**

**15–30ml/1–2 tbsp currants, soaked in warm water for 5–10 minutes and drained**

**30ml/2 tbsp pine nuts**

**5–10ml/1–2 tsp *pul biber*, or 1 fresh red chilli, deseeded and finely chopped**

**5–10ml/1–2 tsp runny honey**

**juice of 1 lemon**

**salt and ground black pepper**

**a pinch of paprika, to garnish**

Steam the spinach for 3–4 minutes, until wilted and soft. Drain off any excess water and chop the spinach.

In a bowl, beat the yogurt with the garlic. Season and set aside.

Heat the olive oil in a heavy pan and gently sauté the onion until it begins to colour. Toss in the currants and pine nuts. When the currants plump up and the pine nuts begin to colour, stir in the *pul biber* or fresh chilli and the honey.

Add the chopped spinach, tossing it around the pan until everything is well mixed, then stir in the lemon juice and season well with salt and pepper.

Tip the spinach onto a serving dish and spoon the yogurt on top, or in a well in the middle. Sprinkle with a little paprika, and tuck in while the spinach is still warm.

## Variations

✻ To make a very simple spinach and yogurt dish, steam the spinach until soft, then chop it to a pulp. Mix the yogurt with a finely chopped clove of garlic and beat in the spinach. Season and serve.

✻ Drizzle a little tahini (light sesame paste) over the salad if you like.

# Haricot bean salad with eggs and anchovies

Salads made with haricot, soya, borlotti or black-eyed beans are popular as meze dishes, or as accompaniments to grilled or barbecued meats. Often, the salads are simply made from beans, onions and flat leaf parsley tossed in olive oil. Others, such as this, *fasulye piyazı*, are more elaborate, and make a tasty, healthy and delicious lunch dish. You can use canned beans if you like but I prefer a bite to mine so I soak and simmer dried ones.

## Serves four

**225g/8oz/1¼ cups dried haricot (navy), soya or black-eyed beans, soaked in cold water for at least 6 hours or overnight**

**1 red onion, cut in half lengthways, in half again crossways, and sliced along the grain**

**45–60ml/3–4 tbsp black olives**

**a bunch of fresh flat leaf parsley, roughly chopped**

**60ml/4 tbsp olive oil**

**juice of 1 lemon**

**3–4 eggs, boiled until just firm, shelled and quartered**

**12 canned or bottled anchovy fillets, rinsed and drained**

**salt and ground black pepper**

**lemon wedges, to serve**

Drain the beans, transfer them to a pan and fill the pan with plenty of cold water. Bring the water to the boil and boil the beans for 1 minute, then lower the heat and partially cover the pan. Simmer for about 45 minutes, until the beans are cooked but still firm – they should have a bite to them, and not be soft and mushy.

Drain the beans, rinse well under cold running water and remove any skins.

Mix the beans in a wide, shallow bowl with the onion, olives and most of the parsley. Toss in the oil and lemon juice, and season with salt and pepper.

Place the eggs and anchovy fillets on top of the salad and add the remaining parsley. Serve with lemon wedges to squeeze over.

# Orange and onion salad with olives

This zingy salad, called *portakal salatası*, is popular in the western region of Turkey and along the Mediterranean coast from Izmir to Marmaris and Adana to Antakya. There are many variations of the salad, some of which include chillies and are quite fiery, others including tangy slices of lemon or sweet grapefruit. It is a refreshing accompaniment to spicy stews and kebabs.

## Serves four

**3-4 sweet, juicy oranges**

**1 red onion, finely sliced in rings**

**10–12 plump black olives, such as Kalamata**

**5ml/1 tsp cumin seeds, crushed**

**5ml/1 tsp ground sumac**

**5ml/1 tsp dried thyme**

**30ml/2 tbsp pure sour pomegranate molasses**

**salt**

**a few fresh mint leaves, torn or roughly chopped, to garnish**

Place each orange on a board and, using a small, sharp knife, carefully cut away the peel and pith, making sure that no pith remains.

Thinly slice the orange into rings and then either keep the rings whole or cut them into half-moon shapes. Do the same with the onion rings.

Arrange the orangesand onion slices in a shallow bowl or a serving dish and add the olives. Sprinkle the cumin, sumac and thyme over and drizzle with the pomegranate molasses. Leave to sit for about half an hour before serving to allow the flavours to mingle.

Just before serving, sprinkle over the mint leaves to garnish.

## Variations

✻ You can add finely sliced beetroot to this salad, which lends a pretty pinkish-purple hue to the orange slices.
✻ You can use slices of pink grapefruit instead of orange.

# Salad with feta, chillies and parsley

There are two common salads eaten as meze, or served as accompaniments to meat and fish dishes in Turkey: Shepherds' Salad (*çoban salatası*), made with chopped cucumber, tomatoes, peppers, onion and flat leaf parsley, and this Gypsy Salad (*çingene salatası*) which uses crumbled cheese rather than rice, and added chilli for a fiery kick. Rice used to be an expensive and less obtainable ingredient, and the cheese represented it visually.

## Serves three to four

**2 red onions, cut in half lengthways and finely sliced along the grain**

**1 green bell pepper, deseeded and finely sliced**

**1 fresh green chilli, deseeded and chopped**

**2–3 garlic cloves, chopped**

**a bunch of fresh flat leaf parsley, roughly chopped**

**225g/8oz *beyaz peynir*, or firm feta cheese, rinsed and crumbled**

**2 large tomatoes, skinned, deseeded and finely chopped or sliced**

**30–45ml/2–3 tbsp olive oil**

**30ml/2 tbsp pure sour pomegranate molasses**

**scant 5ml/1 tsp *pul biber*, or paprika**

**scant 5ml/1 tsp ground sumac**

**salt and ground black pepper**

Place the sliced red onions in a small bowl and sprinkle with a little salt. Leave for 10 minutes to draw out the onion juices, then transfer the onions to a sieve and rinse under cold running water. Pat the slices dry with kitchen paper.

Mix the onions and green pepper in a bowl with the chilli, garlic, parsley, cheese and tomatoes.

Add the olive oil and pomegranate molasses and season with salt and pepper to taste. Toss well to combine everything thoroughly.

Transfer the salad to a large serving dish and sprinkle with the *pul biber* or paprika, and sumac.

# Melon and feta salad with pastırma

One of my go-to nibbles to have with a drink is the combination of little cubes of juicy sweet melon with cubes of salty *beyaz peynir* or feta. It is such a perfect flavour match if your melon is ripe – that is the key. To extend the idea I created a little salad with fine strips of cured beef, *pastırma*, and fresh basil – *kavun ve peynir salatası*, a simple meze dish with a modern twist.

## Serves four to six

**1 ripe juicy melon, such as Galia, Honeydew or Cantaloupe**

**200g/7oz *beyaz peynir*, or feta cheese**

**115g/4oz *pastırma*, very finely sliced with the coating (*çemen*) removed**

**a small bunch of fresh green or purple basil leaves**

**15–30ml/1–2 tbsp olive oil**

**15–30ml/1–2 tbsp pure sour pomegranate molasses**

**freshly ground black pepper**

Cut the melon in half and scoop out the seeds with a spoon. Cut in half again and, using a sharp knife, remove the flesh from the skin and cut it into bitesize cubes. Cut the *beyaz peynir* or feta into bitesize cubes. Slice the *pastırma* into thin strips.

Put the melon and cheese cubes into a shallow bowl or the serving dish, and add the strips of *pastırma* and most of the basil leaves. Cover and leave to sit until ready to serve.

Drizzle the olive oil and pomegranate molasses over the salad and grind a little black pepper over the top (you are unlikely to need salt). Garnish with the remaining basil leaves and toss gently as you serve.

## Cook's tip

Don't dress the salad too far in advance or the melon will emit a lot of juice and the basil leaves will wilt.

Left **Lamb's lettuce salad** Right **Cucumber and mint salad**

# Lamb's lettuce salad

The lamb's lettuce in Turkey and the Middle East is a slightly thicker, meatier version of the plant that is generally available elsewhere. Quick and easy, this popular summer salad, *semiz otu salatası*, is delicious as part of a meze spread but it goes with just about everything.

## Serves four

**450g/1lb thick and creamy natural (plain) yogurt**

**juice of 1 lemon**

**1–2 garlic cloves, crushed**

**225g/8oz fresh lamb's lettuce, well rinsed and drained**

**salt and freshly ground black pepper**

**sumac, for sprinkling**

In a wide serving bowl, beat the yogurt with the lemon juice and garlic. Season to taste with salt and pepper.

Toss the lamb's lettuce into the dressing, making sure it is thoroughly coated with the yogurt.

Sprinkle with sumac and serve immeciately while the leaves are still fresh and crisp with a little crunch.

## Cook's tip

There is no rule regarding the ratio of yogurt to lamb's lettuce, as some households enjoy this salad packed with leaves, whereas others like it with double the amount of yogurt.

# Cucumber and mint salad

Traditionally this salad, *cacık*, is served as meze dish or as a yogurt accompaniment to meat dishes. A thinner version, diluted with a little water, is served in some fashionable restaurants as a cold soup with cubes of ice in it. For the salad you can slice or chop the cucumber, cut it in thin strips or grate it – everyone has their own way and a personal preference for fresh or dried mint, or with fresh dill, to flavour it. Serve with chunks of fresh bread.

## Serves four

**1 large cucumber or 2 small ones**

**salt**

**500g/1¼lb thick and creamy natural (plain) yogurt**

**2 garlic cloves, crushed**

**a bunch of fresh mint leaves, finely chopped**

**olive oil, for drizzling**

**freshly ground black pepper**

Using a vegetable peeler, partially peel the cucumber skin in stripes. Cut the cucumber in half lengthways and slice it very finely.

Place the slices in a colander and sprinkle with salt. Leave to weep for 5–10 minutes. Rinse the sliced cucumber, drain well and gently squeeze out any excess water.

In a wide bowl, beat the yogurt with the garlic and most of the mint. Add the sliced cucumber and season with black pepper and a little salt to taste.

Transfer to a serving bowl if required, drizzle a little olive oil over the top and garnish with the remaining chopped mint.

# Celery and coconut salad with lime and yogurt dressing

Although fresh coconut is not often employed in Turkish dishes, this juicy and refreshing salad, *kereviz salatasıdt*, is welcome on a summer's day in the heat of the Mediterranean. Perhaps North African in origin, I've only come across it in a few kebab and meze houses specialising in the *güney* cuisine, which has Arab influence in its roots.

## Serves three to four

**45–60ml/3–4 tbsp thick and creamy natural (plain) yogurt**

**2 garlic cloves, crushed**

**5ml/1 tsp grated lime zest**

**juice of 2 limes**

**8 long celery sticks, grated (leaves reserved for the garnish), with stringy bits trimmed off**

**flesh of ½ fresh coconut, grated**

**salt and ground black pepper**

**a few sprigs of fresh flat leaf parsley, to garnish**

Mix the yogurt and garlic in a bowl, add the lime rind and juice, and season with salt and pepper.

Fold in the celery and coconut. Set aside for about an hour to let the celery weep a little into the dressing. Spoon the salad into a bowl and garnish with celery leaves and parsley.

## Variation

A medieval meze still found in some old-fashioned drinking haunts in Istanbul features a bowl of gleaming ruby-red pomegranate seeds tossed with shavings of fresh coconut and a squeeze of lemon or lime – a delight to the eye and very refreshing.

# Grated beetroot and yogurt salad

One of the joys of this salad is the colour – a beautiful pinkish purple – a wonderful bright splash in any meze spread. The beetroot can be boiled, steamed or roasted for this dish and some versions opt for it to be grated raw. I prefer to steam or roast for flavour and texture, but the choice is yours. Serve *pancar salatası* with warm bread.

## Serves four

**500g/1¼lb thick and creamy natural (plain) yogurt**

**2 garlic cloves, crushed**

**4 good-sized beetroot (beet), cooked until tender**

**5–10ml/1–2 tsp poppy seeds**

**salt and ground black pepper**

**pure sour pomegranate molasses, for drizzling**

**a few fresh mint leaves, finely shredded, to garnish**

In a bowl, beat the yogurt with the garlic and season with salt and pepper.

Grate, finely slice or dice the beetroot and fold it into the yogurt. Tip the salad into a shallow serving dish.

Dry-roast the poppy seeds in a small heavy-based pan until they begin to pop, and scatter them over the salad.

Drizzle a little pomegranate molasses over the top and garnish with the shredded mint.

## Variations

✻ To make a carrot version of this salad, cut four carrots into chunks and steam them for about 15 minutes, until they are tender but still retain some bite. Leave the carrot chunks until they are cool enough to handle, then grate and mix with the yogurt and garlic. Season to taste with salt and pepper and garnish with mint or dill.

✻ In some households, the beetroot is diced and stir-fried with coriander seeds, sugar and a splash of apple vinegar. Then it is served warm with the cooling garlic-flavoured yogurt and garnished with dill.

# Soups and hot snacks

In every village, town and city, soup stalls and soup houses do brisk business, serving customers at all hours. You can start the day in rural Anatolia with a bowl of thick, minty Meadow Soup or end it in Istanbul with Classic Tripe Soup laced with vinegar, a renowned pick-me-up for late-night revellers. During the day hot snacks cooked at street stalls range from juicy mussels fried in beer batter to Arab-style pizzas topped with spicy minced lamb.

# Sour pomegranate broth

With its origins in Persia and Azerbaijan, this fresh-tasting delicate broth, *nar çorbası*, is an ancient way of appreciating the colour and flavour of sour pomegranates. Clear, refreshing and sophisticated, it is pleasing to both the eye and the palate. Traditionally prepared with sour pomegranates – the same ones that are used to make the delectable molasses – it is designed to be appetising and cleansing so, if you can't find the sour fruits, use the more readily available sweet ones and stir in lemon juice to achieve the desired tartness.

## Serves four

**5–6 sour or sweet pomegranates, plus the seeds of 1 more pomegranate**

**1.2 litres/2 pints/5 cups clear chicken stock**

**juice of 1–2 lemons, if using sweet pomegranates**

**salt and ground black pepper**

**fresh mint leaves, to garnish**

For 150ml/¼ pint/⅔ cup juice, you will need 5–6 sour pomegranates. Cut these pomegranates in half and extract the juice with a stainless steel, glass or wooden lemon squeezer.

Pour the stock into a pan and bring to the boil. Lower the heat, stir in the pomegranate juice, and lemon juice if using sweet pomegranates, then bring the stock back to the boil. Lower the heat again and stir in half the pomegranate seeds. Season to taste and turn off the heat.

Ladle into warmed bowls. Sprinkle the remaining pomegranate seeds over the top and garnish with mint leaves.

## Cook's tip

Do not use any metal other than stainless steel for squeezing, or it will cause the juice to discolour and taste unpleasant.

# Fish broth with celeriac

With such an extensive coastline, there is a wide choice of fish for making this classic soup – *balık çorbası* – including sea bass, blue fish, scorpion fish, mackerel, bonito, turbot and red mullet. Along the Black Sea, the local soup invariably includes the beloved anchovy. In central Anatolia freshwater fish, such as carp, are occasionally used, whereas fish soup is unheard of in the east.

## Serves four to six

**500g/1¼lb fresh fish, such as trout, cod or sea bass**

**250g/9oz prawns (shrimp)**

**2 onions, quartered with their skins on**

**4–6 peppercorns**

**1 whole celeriac, peeled and diced and kept in a bowl of water until ready to use**

**2 potatoes, peeled and diced**

**2 carrots, peeled and diced**

**a small bunch of celery leaves, coarsely chopped**

**a small bunch of flat leaf parsley, leaves coarsely chopped**

**2 garlic cloves, crushed**

**15ml/1 tbsp vinegar**

**salt and ground black pepper**

**lemon wedges, to serve**

First prepare the stock. Skin and fillet the fish and shell the prawns. Cut the fillets into bitesize pieces and set them aside with the prawns.

Put the fish head and bones with the prawn shells into a large, heavy pan. Add the onions and peppercorns and about 2.5 litres/4 pints/10¼ cups of water.

Bring the water to the boil, reduce the heat and simmer for 25–30 minutes, skimming the top to remove any scum. Strain the stock into another pot and bring it to the boil.

Drain the celeriac and tip into the stock along with the diced potatoes and carrots. Bring the stock to back to the boil, reduce the heat and simmer for about 15 minutes, or until the vegetables are tender.

Stir in the celery leaves and parsley, and slip in the fish fillets and prawns. Simmer for about 5 minutes or until the fish and prawns are cooked.

Season with salt and pepper to taste, and stir in the garlic and vinegar to sharpen the flavours.

Ladle the broth into heated serving bowls and serve with wedges of lemon to squeeze into it to lend a sour note to every mouthful.

# Meadow soup with rice and mint

In every soup house, bus station and roadside café throughout Turkey, you will come across a traditional yogurt soup. Based on well-flavoured stock and yogurt, it usually contains a little rice, bulgur, chickpeas or barley, depending on which region you are in, and occasionally it is coloured with saffron or sprinkled with paprika. When it is flavoured with dried mint, it is called *yayla çorbası*, Meadow Soup.

## Serves four

**15ml/1 tbsp butter or sunflower oil**

**1 large onion, finely chopped**

**scant 15ml/1 tbsp plain (all-purpose) flour**

**1.2 litres/2 pints/5 cups lamb or chicken stock**

**75g/3oz long grain rice (wild or plain), well rinsed**

**15–30ml/1–2 tbsp dried mint**

**400ml/14fl oz thick and creamy natural (plain) yogurt, strained (see Cook's tip)**

**salt and ground black pepper**

Melt the butter or oil in a heavy pan, add the onion and cook until soft.

Take the pan off the heat and stir in the flour, then pour in the stock, stirring constantly. Return the pan to the heat and bring the stock to the boil, stirring often.

Stir in the rice and most of the mint, reserving a little for the garnish. Lower the heat, cover the pan and simmer for about 20 minutes, until the rice is cooked. Season with salt and pepper.

Beat the yogurt until smooth, then spoon almost all of it into the soup. Keep the heat low and stir vigorously to make sure the yogurt remains smooth and creamy and becomes well blended.

Ladle the soup into serving bowls, swirl in the remaining yogurt, and garnish with the rest of the mint.

## Cook's tip

If you can't get strained yogurt you can make it yourself. Line a sieve with a piece of muslin or cheesecloth, spoon thick and creamy natural yogurt into it and leave it to drain for 4–6 hours. By draining the yogurt, you prevent it from splitting when added to hot soup, and it helps to thicken it.

# Leek soup with feta, dill and paprika

A bowl of creamy leek soup is always satisfying and this Turkish version, *pırasa çorbası*, is no exception. Flavoured with dill and topped with crumbled white cheese, it is herby and salty at the same time. Serve with chunks of fresh, crusty bread as a snack or as a light meal on its own.

## Serves three to four

**30ml/2 tbsp olive or sunflower oil**

**3–4 large leeks, trimmed, roughly chopped and washed**

**1 onion, chopped**

**5ml/1 tsp sugar**

**a bunch of fresh dill, chopped, with a few fronds reserved for the garnish**

**1.2 litres/2 pints/5 cups chicken or vegetable stock**

**200ml/7fl oz double (heavy) cream**

**15ml/1 tbsp butter (optional)**

**115g/4oz *beyaz peynir* or feta cheese, crumbled**

**salt and freshly ground black pepper**

**paprika, to garnish**

Heat the oil in a heavy-based pot and stir in the chopped leeks and onion. Cook for about 15 minutes, or until the vegetables are soft.

Add the sugar and chopped dill, and pour in the stock. Bring to the boil, lower the heat and simmer for about 40 minutes. Leave the liquid to cool a little, then process in a blender until smooth.

Return the puréed soup to the pan and bring it back to the boil. Reduce the heat and stir in the cream (don't let it come to the boil).

Season to taste with salt and pepper. If using the butter, drop it on to the surface of the soup and let it melt.

Ladle the soup into bowls and top with the crumbled *peynir beynir* or feta. Serve immediately, garnished with a little paprika and the dill fronds.

# Pumpkin soup with yogurt and melted butter

This simple puréed soup – *bal kabağı çorbası* – is a great winter treat. Pumpkin sellers set up their stalls in the streets and deftly peel and seed huge wedges of pumpkin for the neighbourhood so all they have to do is go home and poach it in syrup for the sweet dessert, *bal kabağı tatlisi*, or transform it into this nourishing soup of pumpkin flesh and tart, creamy yogurt.

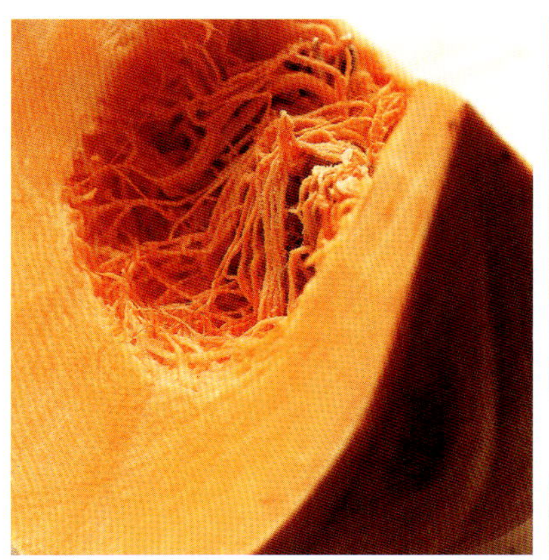

## Serves three to four

**1kg/2¼lb prepared pumpkin flesh, cut into cubes**

**1 litre/1¾ pints/4 cups chicken stock**

**10ml/2 tsp honey**

**30ml/2 tbsp butter, or ghee**

**5ml/1 tsp *pul biber*, or paprika**

**60–75ml/4–5 tbsp thick and creamy natural (plain) yogurt**

**salt and freshly ground black pepper**

Put the pumpkin cubes into a pan with the stock, and bring the liquid to the boil. Reduce the heat, cover the pan, and simmer for about 40 minutes, or until the pumpkin is tender. Liquidise the soup in a blender, or use a potato masher to mash the flesh.

Return the soup to the pan and bring it to the boil again. Stir in the honey and season to taste with salt and pepper. Keep the soup simmering over a low heat.

In a small pan melt the butter or ghee in a small over a low heat and stir in the *pul biber*, or paprika.

Pour the soup into a tureen, or ladle it into individual serving bowls. Swirl a little yogurt on to the surface of the soup and drizzle the melted butter over the top.

Serve immediately, offering extra yogurt so that you can enjoy the contrasting burst of sweet and tart in each mouthful.

## Cook's tip

If pumpkins are not in season, you can use butternut squash instead.

# Spicy red lentil soup with onion

Every region of Turkey has its own lentil soup – some smooth and creamy and lightly spiced, others chunky with tomato, mutton and herbs. Generally, these soups are prepared with red lentils and I have chosen to share a meatless village version in which the garnishings of chopped onion and parsley and a squeeze of lemon bring it to life.

## Serves four

**30–45ml/2–3 tbsp olive or vegetable oil**

**1 large onion, finely chopped**

**2 garlic cloves, finely chopped**

**1 fresh red chilli, deseeded and chopped**

**5–10ml/1–2 tsp cumin seeds**

**5–10ml/1–2 tsp coriander seeds**

**1 carrot, finely chopped**

**scant 5ml/1 tsp ground fenugreek**

**5ml/1 tsp sugar**

**15ml/1 tbsp tomato purée (paste)**

**250g/9oz/scant 1½ cups split red lentils**

**1.75 litres/3 pints/7½ cups chicken stock**

**salt and ground black pepper**

To serve

**1 small red onion, finely chopped**

**a large bunch of fresh flat leaf parsley, finely chopped**

**lemon wedges**

Heat the oil in a heavy pan and stir in the onion, garlic, chilli, cumin and coriander seeds.

When the onion begins to colour slightly, toss in the carrot and cook for 2–3 minutes.

Add the fenugreek, sugar and tomato purée and stir in the lentils.

Pour in the stock, stir well and bring to the boil. Lower the heat, partially cover the pan with a lid and simmer for 30–40 minutes, until the lentils have broken up.

If the soup is too thick for your preference, thin it down to the desired consistency with a little water. Season with salt and pepper to taste.

Serve the soup as it is or, if you prefer a smooth texture, leave it to cool slightly, then whizz it in a blender and reheat.

Ladle it into bowls and garnish with a little of the chopped onion and parsley – put the rest in small bowls on the table for people to help themselves to, and serve with wedges of lemon to squeeze into the soup.

# Lamb and yogurt soup

*Düğün çorbası* is the soup of Turkish weddings. Steeped in tradition, it is a genuine classic and varies little throughout the country, the only variant being the inclusion of cinnamon to flavour the lamb stock. This soup has a slightly sour taste from a liaison of lemon, egg and yogurt and is finished with a flourish of Turkey's signature melted butter with *pul biber*.

## Serves four to six

**500g/1¼lb lamb on the bone – neck, leg or shoulder**

**2 carrots, roughly chopped**

**2 potatoes, roughly chopped**

**1 cinnamon stick**

**45ml/3 tbsp thick and creamy (natural) plain yogurt**

**45ml/3 tbsp plain (all-purpose) flour**

**1 egg yolk**

**juice of ½ lemon**

**salt and ground black pepper**

To serve

**30ml/2 tbsp butter**

**1–2 garlic cloves, crushed**

**5ml/1 tsp *pul biber*, or paprika**

Place the lamb in a deep pan with the carrots, potatoes and cinnamon. Pour in 2 litres/3½ pints/8 cups of water and bring to the boil over a high heat, then skim any scum off the surface and lower the heat. Cover the pan and simmer the mixture gently for about 1½ hours, or until the meat is so tender that it almost falls off the bone.

Lift the lamb out of the pan using a slotted spoon, drain, and place it on a chopping board. Remove the meat from the bone and chop it into small pieces.

Strain (and retain) the stock, discarding the carrots and potatoes. Pour the stock back into the pan, season and bring to the boil.

In a deep bowl, beat the yogurt with the flour. Add the egg yolk and lemon juice and beat well again, then pour in about 250ml/8fl oz/1 cup of the hot stock, beating all the time so that the hot liquid doesn't cook the yolk.

Lower the heat under the pan and pour the yogurt mixture into the stock, beating constantly. Add the meat to the pan and warm gently, ensuring the meat heats through but the mixture doesn't boil.

Melt the butter in a small pan and fry the garlic for a few minutes then stir in the *pul biber* or paprika.

Ladle the soup into bowls and drizzle the pepper-garlic butter over the top before serving.

# Classic tripe soup

With its splash of nostril-tingling vinegar spiked with garlic, *terbiyeli işkembe çorbası* is regarded as a faithful pick-me-up and is in great demand late at night from the local *işkembeci* (a café that specialises in tripe dishes). It is one of the classic dishes prepared for the religious feast, Kurban Bayramı, when every part of the sacrificed sheep is used to mark the occasion.

## Serves four to six

**225g/8oz lamb tripe, washed**

**15ml/1 tbsp butter or ghee**

**25ml/1½ tbsp plain (all-purpose) flour**

**1 egg yolk**

**15ml/1 tbsp lemon juice**

**30ml/2 tbsp butter**

**5ml/1 tsp *pul biber*, or paprika**

**salt and ground black pepper**

To serve

**90ml/6 tbsp white wine vinegar**

**1–3 garlic cloves, crushed**

Put the tripe into a large, heavy pan and cover with 1.2 litres/2 pints/5 cups of water. Bring it to the boil and skim off any froth. Continue to boil for 20–25 minutes, until the tripe is tender. Drain and reserve the cooking liquid. Cut the tripe into fine strips.

Melt the butter or ghee in a heavy pan and stir in the flour to make a paste. Pour in the cooking liquid, stirring until it thickens. Stir in the tripe, increase the heat, and simmer for 15–20 minutes.

In a small bowl, beat the egg yolk with the lemon juice. Beat in two spoonfuls of the hot soup, then pour it back into the pan, stirring constantly to ensure the egg doesn't curdle. Season the soup with salt and pepper to taste.

Pour the vinegar into a small bowl and beat in the crushed garlic to taste and a little salt.

In a small pan, gently melt the butter and stir in the *pul biber* or paprika.

Ladle the soup into individual serving bowls and pour a little of the melted butter mixture over each one. Serve the soup immediately, passing around the spiked vinegar to drizzle over the top.

# Tomatoes and peppers with eggs

This is such a simple dish for breakfast, brunch or lunch. Called *menemen* in Turkish and *shakshuka* in Arabic, it is often cooked in the street on makeshift stoves at bus and train stations, ports and markets and it varies according to the cook – sometimes the eggs are scrambled through it, other times they are cracked into little pockets in the stewed vegetables. At home, we often eat it with garlic yogurt and chunks of warm crusty bread.

## Serves four

**15ml/1 tbsp olive oil**

**15ml/1 tbsp butter**

**2 red onions, cut in half lengthways and sliced along the grain**

**1 red or green bell pepper, halved lengthways, deseeded and sliced**

**2 garlic cloves, roughly chopped**

**5–10ml/1–2 tsp *pul biber*, or 1 fresh red chilli, deseeded and sliced**

**400g/14oz can of chopped tomatoes**

**5–10ml/1–2 tsp sugar**

**4 eggs**

**a handful of fresh flat leaf parsley, roughly chopped**

**salt and ground black pepper**

To serve

**90ml/6 tbsp thick and creamy natural (plain) yogurt**

**1–2 garlic cloves, crushed**

**salt and ground black pepper**

Heat the oil and butter in a frying pan. Stir in the onions, pepper, garlic and *pul biber* or chilli, and cook until they begin to soften but not brown.

Add the tomatoes and sugar to the pan and mix them in well. Cook for about 10 minutes, or until the liquid has reduced and the mixture is quite thick, then season with salt and pepper to taste.

Create little pockets in the mixture and crack the eggs into them. Cover the pan with a lid or aluminium foil and cook until the eggs are just done. Alternatively, scramble the eggs loosely through the mixture.

Meanwhile, beat the yogurt with the garlic in a bowl and season with salt and pepper.

Scatter the parsley over the eggs and serve hot with dollops of the garlic-flavoured yogurt.

## Cook's tips

✻ If you like, you can divide the tomato mixture between four small pans and crack an egg into each one, so that each person has their own serving.
✻ For breakfast, you will often be served the scrambled version of this dish which many people enjoy on top of buttered toast.

# Simple eggs with garlic yogurt

This dish, *çılbır*, is served as a hot meze dish or breakfast snack in Turkey, but we enjoy it for lunch or supper with a green salad. Hen's or duck's eggs can be used, and you can either poach or fry them. Served with toasted flat bread or chunks of a warm, crispy loaf, lashings of garlic yogurt and a good drizzle of melted butter, it is incredibly simple and satisfying.

## Serves two

**500g/1¼lb thick and creamy natural (plain) yogurt**

**2 garlic cloves, crushed**

**white wine vinegar, for poaching (optional)**

**4 large eggs**

**15–30ml/1–2 tbsp butter**

**5ml/1 tsp *pul biber*, or paprika**

**a few dried sage leaves, crumbled**

**salt and ground black pepper**

Beat the yogurt with the garlic and seasoning. Spoon into a serving dish or on to individual plates, spreading it flat to create a thick mattress for the eggs. Keep it at room temperature as a contrast to the hot eggs.

Fill a pan with water, add a dash of vinegar (to seal the egg whites), and bring to a rolling boil. Stir the water to create a whirlpool and crack in the first egg.

As the white of the egg sets around the yolk, stir the water ready for the next one. Poach each egg for 2–3 minutes so the yolk is still soft.

Lift the eggs out of the water with a slotted spoon and place them on the yogurt mattress.

Quickly melt the butter in a small pan. Stir in the *pul biber* or paprika and sage leaves, then spoon over the eggs. Serve immediately.

## Variation

Other popular egg recipes include *yumurtali ispanak kavurmasi*, a dish of sautéed spinach and onions with eggs cooked in the middle, and a classic Palace dish of eggs cooked with *pastırma*.

# Chickpea dumplings

## Serves four to six

**450g/1lb/4 cups plain (all-purpose) flour**

**2.5ml/½ tsp salt**

**1 whole egg, beaten with 1 egg yolk**

**50ml/2fl oz/¼ cup water**

**600ml/1 pint/2½ cups vegetable or chicken stock**

For the filling

**400g/14oz can of chickpeas, drained and thoroughly rinsed**

**5ml/1 tsp cumin seeds, crushed**

**5ml/1 tsp Turkish red pepper or paprika**

For the yogurt

**about 90ml/6 tbsp thick and creamy natural (plain) yogurt**

**2–3 garlic cloves, crushed**

**salt and ground black pepper**

For the sauce

**15ml/1 tbsp olive oil**

**15ml/1 tbsp butter**

**1 onion, finely chopped**

**2 garlic cloves, finely chopped**

**5ml/1 tsp *pul biber*, or 1 fresh red chilli, deseeded and finely chopped**

**5–10ml/1–2 tsp sugar**

**5–10ml/1–2 tsp dried mint**

**400g/14oz can of chopped tomatoes, drained of juice**

**a small bunch each of fresh flat leaf parsley and coriander (cilantro), roughly chopped**

I could sing about these fabulous dumplings, they are so delicious. Falling between Italian pasta and a Chinese dumpling, *mantı* is a dish from central and eastern Anatolia. Variously filled with spicy minced beef, lamb, vegetables, nuts or chickpeas, then swamped in creamy garlic yogurt and drizzled in melted butter or a tomato sauce, they come in many guises. Here, I am sharing with you the very traditional baked version with chickpeas.

Make the dough. Sift the flour and salt into a wide bowl and make a well in the middle. Pour in the beaten egg and water. Using your fingers, draw the flour into the liquid and mix to a dough. Knead for 10 minutes, cover with a damp towel and leave to rest for 1 hour.

Mash the chickpeas in a bowl with a fork. Beat in the cumin and *pul biber*. In another bowl, beat the yogurt with the garlic and seasoning.

To make the sauce, heat the oil and butter in a pan and gently fry the onion and garlic until soft. Add the *pul biber* or chilli, sugar and mint. Stir in the tomatoes and cook over a low heat for about 15 minutes, until thick. Season and remove from the heat.

Preheat the oven to 200°C/400°F/Gas 6. Roll out the dough as thinly as possible on a lightly floured surface. Using a sharp knife, cut the dough into small squares (roughly 2.5cm/1in).

Spoon a little chickpea mixture into the middle of each square and bunch together the corners to form a pouch. Place the filled parcels in a greased ovenproof dish, stacking them next to each other. Bake, uncovered, for 15–20 minutes, until golden brown.

Bring the stock to the boil in a pan. Take the parcels out of the oven and pour the stock over. Return the dish to the oven and bake for a further 15–20 minutes, until almost all the stock has been absorbed. Meanwhile, reheat the tomato sauce.

Transfer the parcels to a serving dish and spoon the yogurt over them. Top with the hot tomato sauce and sprinkle with fresh herbs.

## Cook's tip

*Mantı* can also be cooked in the same way as pasta – seal the parcels like ravioli and drop them into salted boiling water for a few minutes.

# Filo cigars filled with feta, parsley, mint and dill

I like to offer these classic cigar-shaped pastries, *sigara böreği*, as a nibble with a drink or as a hot meze dish, which is how they are served in Turkey. Here they are packed with a mixture of cheese and herbs, but other popular fillings include aromatic minced meat, baked aubergine and cheese, or mashed pumpkin, cheese and dill. They can be prepared in advance and kept under a damp dish towel in the refrigerator until you are ready to fry them.

## Serves three to four

**225g/8oz *beyaz peynir*, or feta cheese**

**1 large egg, lightly beaten**

**a small bunch each of fresh flat leaf parsley, mint and dill, finely chopped**

**4–5 sheets of filo pastry**

**sunflower oil, for deep-frying**

**dill fronds, to garnish**

In a bowl, mash the cheese. Beat in the egg and fold in the herbs.

Place the sheets of filo on a flat surface and cover with a damp dish towel to keep them moist. Working with one sheet at a time, cut the filo into strips about 10–13cm/4–5in wide, and pile them on top of each other. Keep the strips covered with another damp dish towel.

Lay one filo strip on the surface in front of you, making sure you re-cover the other strips with the dish towel. Place a heaped teaspoon of the cheese filling along one of the short ends. Roll the end of the pastry over the filling, quite tightly to keep it in place, then tuck in the sides to seal in the filling and continue to roll. As you reach the end, brush a little water over the end of the pastry to help seal the filo and prevent it unravelling during cooking.

Place the filled filo pastry cigar, join-side down, on a plate and cover with another damp dish towel to keep it moist. Continue with the remaining sheets of filo and filling until all the filling has been used.

Heat enough oil for deep-frying in a suitable pan, and fry the filo cigars in batches for 5–6 minutes until crisp and golden brown. Lift out of the oil with a slotted spoon and drain on kitchen paper. Serve immediately, garnished with dill if you like.

## Variation

To make a puff pastry log, roll out 400g/14oz puff pastry. Spoon on the filling. Roll into a log, tucking in the ends as you go, and place on an oiled baking tray. Cut diagonally into portions, keeping it intact at the base. Brush with a mixture of egg yolk and sunflower oil and bake in a preheated oven at 180°C/350°F/Gas 4 for 30 minutes, until crisp.

# Flat breads with spinach

These traditional flat breads from central Anatolia, called *gözleme*, are cooked quickly on a hot griddle or over the dome of an upside-down cauldron. They can be filled with various combinations of ingredients, including cheese and herbs; eggs and *pastırma*; minced beef with pine nuts; or with this creamy spinach and onion mixture. For breakfast they are often cooked plain and drizzled with a little honey.

## Serves two to four

**115g/4oz/1 cup strong unbleached white bread flour, plus extra for dusting**

**2.5ml/½ tsp salt**

**15ml/1 tbsp olive oil, melted butter or ghee**

**50ml/2fl oz/¼ cup water**

For the filling

**250g/9oz fresh spinach**

**15ml/1 tbsp butter**

**1 onion, chopped**

**pinch of freshly grated nutmeg**

**5ml/1 tsp *pul biber*, or paprika**

**7.5ml/1½ tsp plain (all-purpose) flour**

**120ml/4fl oz/½ cup milk**

**45ml/3 tbsp *kaşar peyniri*, or Parmesan cheese, grated**

**salt and ground black pepper**

Sift the flour with the salt into a bowl. Make a well in the centre and pour in the oil, butter or ghee, and the water. Using your hand, draw in the flour from the sides and work the mixture into a dough. Knead thoroughly. Divide the dough into four pieces, knead them and roll into balls. Place the balls on a floured surface, cover with a damp cloth, and leave them to rest for 30 minutes.

Meanwhile, prepare the filling. Place the spinach in a steamer, or in a colander set in a large pan with a lid, and steam the spinach until it wilts. Refresh the spinach under running cold water and drain well. Place the cooked spinach on a wooden board and chop it roughly.

Melt the butter in a heavy pan and soften the onion. Stir in the chopped spinach and add the nutmeg and *pul biber* or paprika. Stir in the flour and pour in the milk, stirring constantly until thickened. Beat in the cheese and seasoning. Cover the pan to keep it warm.

On a lightly floured surface, roll out each of the balls of dough with a rolling pin into thin, flat rounds, about 15–20cm/6–8in in diameter.

Heat a griddle, wipe it with a little oil, and place one of the rounds of dough on to it (if you have a wide griddle, as they do in Turkey, you can cook several at a time). Cook for about 1 minute on one side, then flip it over and spread a thin layer of the spinach filling over the cooked side. Cook the second side for 1–2 minutes, allowing it to buckle and brown, then lift it off and place on a piece of baking parchment. Roll up the *gözleme*, wrap the paper around it to make it easier to hold, and hand it to the first person waiting. Repeat.

## Variation

An alternative method is to spread the filling on one half of the cooking *gözleme* and fold the other half over to resemble a half moon. Make sure the edges are sealed, and serve immediately.

# Courgette fritters

Often served as a hot meze dish, *kabak kizartmasi* are delicious served with the ubiquitous garlic yogurt, sometimes flavoured with a little ketchup – a yogurt version of 'marie-rose' sauce. They are also tasty simply served with lemon wedges to squeeze over them.

## Serves four

**3–4 firm, fat courgettes (zucchini)**

**2 eggs**

**30ml/2 tbsp plain (all-purpose) flour**

**sunflower oil, for deep-frying**

**salt and ground black pepper**

To serve

**60ml/4 tbsp thick and creamy natural (plain) yogurt**

**1 garlic clove, crushed**

**juice of ½ lemon**

**salt and ground black pepper**

Cut the courgettes on the diagonal, crossways, into thin slices. If moist, pat them dry with a piece of kitchen paper, so that the batter will stick to them.

Beat the eggs in a bowl and add the flour. Beat until smooth and season with salt and pepper.

Heat enough oil for deep-frying in a wide, shallow pan. Dip the courgette slices into the batter and then drop them into the oil. Fry them in batches for 3–4 minutes, or until golden brown all over. Drain the fritters on kitchen paper and keep warm.

In a small bowl, quickly beat the yogurt with the garlic and lemon juice. Season to taste.

Arrange the warm fritters on a serving dish with the yogurt. Enjoy the juicy fritters dipped in the garlic yogurt as a snack or as a hot meze dish.

# Deep-fried mussels in beer batter

This is street food at its best and a wonderful Ottoman tradition at stalls and fish restaurants in Istanbul and Izmir. Fried in huge, curved pans, *midye tava* are skewered on sticks and sold in batches with a garlic-flavoured *tarator* sauce that can be made with pounded walnuts, almonds or pine nuts, or simply with day-old bread.

## Serves four to five

**sunflower oil, for deep-frying**

**about 50 fresh mussels, cleaned (discarding any that don't close when tapped), shelled and patted dry**

For the batter

**115g/4oz/1 cup plain (all-purpose) flour**

**5ml/1 tsp salt**

**2.5ml/½ tsp bicarbonate of soda (baking soda)**

**2 egg yolks**

**175–250ml/6–8fl oz/¾–1 cup beer or lager**

For the sauce

**75g/3oz/broken walnuts**

**2 slices of day-old bread, sprinkled with water and left for a few minutes, then squeezed dry**

**2–3 garlic cloves, crushed**

**45–60ml/3–4 tbsp olive oil**

**juice of 1 lemon**

**dash of white wine vinegar**

**salt and ground black pepper**

Make the batter. Sift the flour, salt and soda into a bowl. Make a well in the middle and drop in the egg yolks. Using a wooden spoon, slowly beat in the beer and draw in the flour from the sides until a smooth, thick batter is formed. Set aside for 30 minutes.

Meanwhile, make the sauce. Pound the walnuts to a paste using a mortar and pestle, or blend them in a processor. Add the bread and garlic, and pound again to a paste. Drizzle in the olive oil, stirring, and beat in the lemon juice and vinegar. The sauce should be smooth, with the consistency of thick cream – if it is too dry, stir in a little water. Season and set aside.

Heat sunflower oil for deep-frying in a suitable pan. Dip each mussel into the batter and drop into the hot oil. Fry in batches for a minute or two until golden brown. Lift out with a slotted spoon and drain well on kitchen paper. Thread the mussels on to wooden skewers, or spear them individually, and serve hot with the garlic-flavoured dipping sauce.

## Cook's tip

Raw mussels are prised from their shells with ease by street vendors, but it can be fiddly. An easier option is to steam them open for 3–4 minutes, then remove them from their shells (discarding any that don't open), or use ready-shelled mussels sold frozen in bags, defrosting before use.

# Deep-fried squid with garlic bread sauce

Wherever I go in the Mediterranean region, I will choose deep-fried squid if it's on the menu. When it's fresh and juicy with a bite to it but not too chewy, it is one of my favourite seafood dishes. All it needs is a little lemon, a herb mayonnaise, or a garlicky sauce. In Turkey, *kalamar* is often served as a hot meze dish in fish restaurants, and in some coastal areas it will be offered to you as a snack to accompany a chilled glass of beer or *rakı*.

## Serves two to four

**4 good-sized fresh squid, prepared (see Cook's tips), then cut into rings or strips**

**sunflower oil, for deep-frying**

**1 lemon, cut into wedges, to serve**

For the batter

**15g/½oz fresh yeast**

**300ml/½ pint/1¼ cups beer**

**225g/8oz/2 cups plain (all-purpose) flour**

**5ml/1 tsp salt**

For the sauce

**3 slices day-old white bread, with crusts removed**

**100ml/3½fl oz/scant ½ cup olive oil**

**juice of 1 lemon**

**2–3 garlic cloves, crushed**

**salt and ground black pepper**

To make the batter, cream the yeast with 30ml/2 tbsp of the beer in a small bowl. Gradually stir in the remainder of the beer. Sift the flour with the salt into a bowl. Make a well in the centre of the flour and pour in the beer and yeast mixture, beating constantly. Use a whisk to produce a smooth batter, then cover it and leave to stand for 1 hour.

To make the sauce, soak the bread in water for 10 minutes. Squeeze it dry and put it in a bowl. Using a fork or a wooden spoon, beat the oil and lemon juice with the bread until it resembles a thick sauce. Beat in the garlic and seasoning. Transfer to a serving bowl and set aside.

Heat enough oil for deep-frying in a pan. Dip the prepared squid rings in the batter and fry it in batches. When the batter turns crisp and golden brown lift the squid pieces out of the oil and place them on a trivet in the pan to keep them warm while you fry the remaining squid. When all of the squid has been cooked, drain on kitchen paper. Serve hot with the garlic sauce and lemon to squeeze over it.

## Cook's tips

✻ To prepare the squid, hold the body sac in one hand and pull the head off with the other. Most of the innards should come out, but reach inside the sac to remove any that remain. Remove the backbone and rinse the body sac inside and out. Pat the body dry and put it aside. Sever the tentacles just above the eyes, so that you have the top of the head and tentacles together. Discard everything else.

✻ To tenderise squid and enhance its naturally sweet taste, rub it in lemon juice, sprinkle over a little sugar and bicarbonate of soda, and chill in the fridge for an hour. Rinse and pat dry before cooking.

# Flat breads with spicy lamb and tomato

This Anatolian snack, *lahmacun*, is a great culinary creation. The thin crispy base is smeared with a layer of lightly spiced lamb with fresh parsley, sumac and a squeeze of lemon. Rolled into a cone to eat, it is the most perfect form of street food – hot, portable and delicious. In restaurants, miniature versions are often served as a hot meze dish.

## Serves two to four

**scant 5ml/1 tsp active dried yeast**

**2.5ml/½ tsp sugar**

**150ml/¼ pint/⅔ cup lukewarm water**

**350g/12oz/3 cups strong white bread flour**

**2.5ml/½ tsp salt**

**a few drops of sunflower oil**

For the topping

**15ml/1 tbsp olive oil**

**15ml/1 tbsp butter**

**1 onion, finely chopped**

**2 garlic cloves, finely chopped**

**225g/8oz finely minced (ground) lean lamb**

**30ml/2 tbsp tomato purée (paste)**

**15ml/1 tbsp sugar**

**5–10ml/1–2 tsp *pul biber*, or 1 fresh red chilli, finely chopped**

**5ml/1 tsp dried mint**

**5–10ml/1–2 tsp ground sumac**

**a bunch of fresh flat leaf parsley, roughly chopped**

**juice of 1 lemon**

**salt and ground black pepper**

Make the dough. Put the yeast and sugar into a small bowl with half the lukewarm water. Set aside for about 15 minutes until frothy. Sift the flour and salt into a large bowl, make a well in the middle and add the creamed yeast and the rest of the water. Using your hand, draw in the flour and work to a dough, adding more water if necessary.

Turn the dough on to a lightly floured surface and knead until smooth and elastic. Drip a few drops of sunflower oil into the base of the bowl and roll the dough in it. Cover with a damp dish towel and leave in a warm place for about 1 hour or until the dough has doubled in size.

Meanwhile, heat the oil and in a heavy pan and gently fry the onion and garlic until they soften. Leave to cool in the pan.

Put the lamb in a bowl, add the tomato purée, sugar, *pul biber* or chilli and mint, then the softened onion and garlic. Season with salt and pepper, and knead with your hands. Cover and keep in the refrigerator until you are ready to use.

Place two baking sheets in the oven, and preheat to 220°C/425°F/Gas 7. Punch down the risen dough, knead it on a lightly floured surface, then divide into two or four equal pieces. Roll each piece into a thin flat round, stretching the dough with your hands as you roll.

Oil the hot baking sheets and place the dough rounds on them, then cover with a thin layer of the meat mixture, spreading it right to the edges. Bake in the oven for 15–20 minutes, until the meat is nicely cooked. As soon as the *lahmacun* are ready, sprinkle them with the sumac and parsley. Squeeze a little lemon juice over the top. Roll them up while the dough is still pliable, or eat like a pizza – with your hands, or on plates with a knife and fork.

# Minced meat and pine nut pie

A *tepsi* is a deep round baking tray in which savoury and sweet pastries are baked. In this dish, *tepsi böreği*, the sheets of *yufka* are layered with a minced meat filling. Although not exactly the same, filo pastry, which is more readily available, works as a substitute for the large sheets of traditional *yufka*, but you may require twice as many sheets of filo, as they are usually smaller.

## Serves four to six

**2 eggs**

**300ml/½ pint/1¼ cups milk**

**150ml/¼ pint/⅔ cup sunflower oil or olive oil, plus 15ml/1 tbsp extra**

**5 sheets of *yufka* or 10–12 of filo pastry, thawed if frozen**

For the filling

**15ml/1 tbsp olive oil**

**15ml/1 tbsp butter**

**1 onion, finely chopped**

**2–3 garlic cloves, crushed**

**30–45ml/2–3 tbsp pine nuts**

**250g/9oz finely minced (ground) lean veal or beef**

**10ml/2 tsp ground cinnamon**

**10ml/2 tsp dried oregano**

**a small bunch of fresh parsley, leaves finely chopped**

**salt and ground black pepper**

To serve

**7.5ml/1½ tsp olive oil or butter**

**15ml/1 tbsp pine nuts**

Preheat the oven to 200°C/400°F/Gas 6 and grease an ovenproof dish (the size is not important, just vary the number of layers to fit the dish).

For the filling, heat the olive oil and butter in a heavy pan and stir in the onion. Cook for 1–2 minutes until softened. Add the garlic and pine nuts. Once the pine nuts begin to turn golden, add the meat. Cook the meat for 3–4 minutes, then stir in the cinnamon and herbs. Season with salt and pepper. Leave to cool.

In a bowl, beat the eggs with the milk and the oil. Lay a whole sheet of *yufka* in the base of the dish, with the sides overlapping the edge – this may require two to three sheets of filo pastry, overlapped in the base of the dish to prevent seepage. (If using filo, keep the unused pastry covered with a damp dish towel to prevent drying.) Pour a little of the egg and milk mixture into the centre and spread it to the sides.

Tear two sheets of *yufka* (or three to four of filo) into wide strips and layer them in the dish, brushing each layer with the milk mixture. Leave the last layer dry and spread the meat mixture over it. Tear the remaining two sheets of *yufka* (three to four of filo) and layer them up in the same way with the milk mixture. Reserve 15ml/1 tbsp of the mixture in the bowl and beat in the 15ml/1 tbsp of the oil.

Pull up the dangling flaps of *yufka* from the base sheet lining the dish and fold them over the top of the pie, sticking them down with the and oil mixture, which you can apply with a brush, but it is easier and more effective to smear it on with your fingers. Make sure the very top pieces are well oiled, and put the pie into the oven for about 45 minutes. The pie should puff up and turn golden brown.

Remove the pie from the oven (it will sink back down quite quickly) and cut it into rectangular, square or triangular wedges, to your preference.

To serve, heat the oil or butter in a small pan, add the pine nuts and cook until golden brown. Drain them on kitchen paper and sprinkle a few over each portion. Serve hot or at room temperature.

# Vegetable dishes

The Turks are absolute wizards with vegetables. They have such an abundance of seasonal produce to choose from and they genuinely follow the cycles. If you shop at a vegetable market or stop by the man selling artichokes, tomatoes or pumpkins from his barrow, you will enter into animated chatter about what to cook and the best way to do it – stuff your peppers with aromatic rice, turn your courgettes into feta and herb patties, or poach your aubergines in olive oil until you swoon like the Imam.

# Spinach with eggs and paprika

A much-loved vegetable in Turkey, spinach often finds its way into fillings for savoury pastries and flat breads, or is combined with yogurt in a number of delicious meze dishes. This simple spinach and egg dish, *yumurtalı ıspanak kavurması*, is an example of Turkish comfort food – everyone's mother and grandmother makes it .You can serve it with garlic yogurt and chunks of bread, or scatter grated cheese like *kaşar* (you can substitute with Parmesan) over the eggs and bake them in the oven – it's a dish to suit your mood.

## Serves two

**750g/1lb 10oz fresh spinach**
**15ml/1 tbsp butter**
**1 onion, finely chopped**
**1–2 garlic cloves, finely chopped**
**2.5ml/½ tsp freshly grated nutmeg**
**2 large eggs**
***pul biber*, or paprika, to sprinkle**
**salt and ground black pepper**

Place the spinach in a steamer, or in a colander set in a large pan with a lid, and steam the spinach until it wilts. Refresh the spinach under running cold water and drain well. Place the cooked spinach on a wooden board and chop it roughly.

Heat the butter in a shallow pan until it melts, then stir in the onion and garlic. Cook gently until softened. Toss in the spinach and mix well. Add the nutmeg, salt and pepper.

Make two hollows in the spinach mixture and drop in the eggs. Cover the pan and leave the eggs to cook in the steam, until the whites are firm but the yolk remains soft.

Sprinkle a little *pul biber* or paprika over the eggs. Serve immediately from the pan.

# Smoked aubergines in cheese sauce

In our family, this is real comfort food – the smoky flesh of aubergines bound in a creamy and tangy cheese sauce and baked in the oven. This recipe is for my version of *beğendi*, which was originally created for one of the Ottoman sultans. Invariably, the classic dish consists of lamb and tomato stew, or meatballs cooked in a tomato sauce, served on a bed of aubergine in a cheese sauce. This recipe is for my version which I serve as a main dish for lunch or supper with chunks of fresh, crusty bread and a juicy green salad.

## Serves four

**4 aubergines (eggplants)**

**50g/2oz butter**

**30ml/2 tbsp plain (all-purpose) flour**

**600ml/1 pint/2½ cups milk (you may need a little more)**

**225g/8oz Cheddar cheese, grated**

**salt and ground black pepper**

**finely grated Parmesan cheese, for the topping**

Preheat the oven to 200°C/400°F/Gas 6. Put the aubergines directly on the gas flame on top of the stove, or under a conventional grill or broiler, and turn them until the skin is charred on all sides and the flesh is soft. Place the charred aubergines in a plastic bag and leave for a few minutes. Hold each aubergine by the stalk under cold running water and gently peel off the charred skin. Squeeze the flesh with your fingers to get rid of any excess water and place on a chopping board. Remove the stalks and chop the flesh to a pulp.

Make the sauce. Melt the butter in a heavy pan, remove from the heat and stir in the flour. Slowly beat in the milk, then return the pan to a medium heat and cook, stirring constantly, until the sauce is smooth and thick. Gradually stir in the grated Cheddar cheese a little at a time, then beat in the aubergine pulp and season with salt and pepper.

Transfer the cheese and aubergine mixture to a baking dish and sprinkle a generous layer of Parmesan over the top. Bake in the oven for about 25 minutes, until the top is browned. Serve immediately.

# Stuffed poached aubergines

Whether the Imam fainted from shock or pleasure at the quantity of olive oil used in this dish, no one knows, but 'the Imam fainted' is the translation of *ımam bayıldı*. The aubergines are sometimes baked, but the more traditional method is gentle poaching on top of the stove – when cooked this way they melt in the mouth.

## Serves four

**2 large aubergines (eggplants)**

**sunflower oil, for shallow-frying**

**a bunch each of flat leaf parsley and dill**

**1 large onion, halved and finely sliced**

**3 tomatoes, skinned and finely chopped**

**2–3 garlic cloves, finely chopped**

**5ml/1 tsp salt**

**150ml/¼ pint/⅔ cup olive oil**

**50ml/2fl oz/¼ cup water**

**juice of ½ lemon**

**15ml/1 tbsp sugar**

**lemon wedges, to serve**

Using a vegetable peeler or a small, sharp knife, peel the aubergines lengthways in stripes like a zebra. Place the aubergines in a bowl of salted water and leave for 5 minutes, then drain and pat dry.

Heat about 1cm/½in sunflower oil in a suitable pan. Fry the aubergines quickly on all sides to soften them. This should take a total of 3–5 minutes. Lift the aubergines out on to a chopping board and slit them open lengthways to create pockets, keeping the bottoms and both ends intact so they look like canoes when stuffed.

Reserve a few herbs for the garnish, then chop the rest and mix them in a large bowl with the onion, tomatoes and garlic. Add the salt and a little of the olive oil. Spoon the mixture into the aubergine pockets, packing it in tightly so that all of it is used up.

Place the filled aubergines side by side in a deep, heavy pan. Mix the remaining olive oil with the water and the lemon juice, pour it over the aubergines, and sprinkle the sugar over the top.

Cover the pan with a lid and place over a medium heat to get the oil hot and create some steam. Then, lower the heat and cook the aubergines very gently for about 1 hour, basting from time to time. They should be soft and tender, with only a little oil left in the pan.

Leave to cool then carefully transfer the aubergines to a serving dish and spoon over the oil from the pan. Garnish with the reserved herbs and serve at room temperature, with lemon wedges for squeezing.

## Variation

Place the filled aubergines in an ovenproof dish instead of a pan, with the oil and lemon water, cover with foil and bake in the oven for about 45 minutes at 180°C/350°F/Gas 4. Remove the foil, sprinkle a little grated *kaşar peyniri* or Parmesan cheese over the top and return to the oven for about 15 minutes, until the aubergines are browned. Serve hot. Courgettes (zucchini) are often cooked in a similar way.

# Stuffed leeks with a sauce

The Turks are master stuffers! Anything with a cavity – fruit, vegetable, bird, fish or shell – gets stuffed and, if there isn't a natural cavity then one will be created, such as stuffed meatballs. Even the hollow tubes of leeks get stuffed and then served in a sophisticated egg and lemon sauce, an elegant finish to a household dish, called *pırasa dolması*. A little fiddly to prepare, but it is worth the effort.

## Serves four

**2–3 fat leeks, trimmed at both ends**

**25ml/1½ tbsp long grain rice, rinsed**

**225g/8oz finely minced (ground) beef**

**1 onion, finely chopped**

**a small bunch of flat leaf parsley, leaves finely chopped**

**5–10ml/1–2 tsp *pul biber*, or paprika**

**15ml/1 tbsp soft butter**

**15ml/1 tbsp tomato purée (paste)**

**salt and ground black pepper**

**mint leaves, to garnish**

For the sauce

**2 egg yolks**

**30ml/2 tbsp plain (all-purpose) flour**

**juice of ½ lemon**

**15ml/1 tbsp natural (plain) yogurt**

**250ml/9fl oz/1 cup water**

**a small bunch of mint, leaves finely chopped**

**salt and ground black pepper**

Cut the leeks into equal lengths, about 15cm/6in long, and remove the green outer layers. Place in a steamer basket and steam for 10 minutes to soften them. Refresh the leeks under cold running water and drain. Carefully, using your fingers, push out the inner layer of each leek to create a collection of soft tubes. Put to one side.

Bring a pan of water to the boil. Boil the rice for about 10 minutes, or until cooked but still firm. Drain and refresh under cold water.

In a large bowl, mix the meat with the onion, parsley and *pul biber*. Add the rice, and salt and pepper. Using your hands, bind the mixture with the butter so that it becomes pasty.

Take each leek tube in your hand, and gently push some of the meat filling into it, like stuffing a sausage. Don't pack too tightly as the rice will expand more on cooking, and you want the tubes to remain intact. Leave a little room at either end to use as flaps that can be tucked underneath. Place them, side by side, in a large, heavy pan.

Put the tomato purée in a bowl and stir in about 300ml/½ pint/1¼ cups water (add more if necessary – it should be the consistency of pouring cream). Season and pour over the stuffed leeks. Cover the pan and cook the leeks gently for about 30 minutes, or until the rice has expanded and the meat has cooked. Lift the stuffed leeks on to a serving dish and keep warm. Pour the cooking liquid into a small pan.

Just before serving, prepare the sauce. Put all the sauce ingredients in a bowl and beat with a wire whisk. Beat two spoonfuls of the cooking liquid into the bowl, then pour the whole lot into the pan with the remainder of the cooking liquid. Gently heat the sauce, beating constantly with a wooden spoon. Take it off the heat just as it is about to boil, stir in the chopped mint and check and adjust the seasoning.

Spoon the sauce over the stuffed leeks, garnish with the extra fresh mint leaves, and serve while hot.

# Peppers stuffed with aromatic rice

Throughout Turkey, small bright green peppers are stuffed with aromatic rice, poached in olive oil and served cold as the meze dish, *zeytinyağlı biber dolması*. In people's homes a variety of peppers are stuffed and cooked in the same way but might be served hot as an accompaniment to a meat or pastry dish. You can make an attractive arrangement by using red, yellow, orange and green all in one dish. Serve hot with thick, creamy yogurt spiked with a little garlic, or leave them to cool in the pan and eat cold with wedges of lemon to squeeze over.

## Serves four

**30ml/2 tbsp currants**

**30ml/2 tbsp olive oil**

**2 red onions, finely chopped**

**5ml/1 tsp sugar**

**45ml/3 tbsp pine nuts**

**10ml/2 tsp ground cinnamon**

**5ml/1 tsp dried mint**

**2.5ml/½ tsp ground allspice**

**175g/6oz/scant 1 cup short grain rice, washed and drained**

**a small bunch of flat leaf parsley, leaves finely chopped**

**a small bunch of dill, finely chopped**

**a small bunch of mint, leaves finely chopped**

**3 tomatoes**

**4–6 bell peppers, with stalks removed and deseeded, but kept whole**

**salt and ground black pepper**

For the cooking liquid

**50ml/2fl oz/¼ cup olive oil**

**juice of 1 lemon**

**about 250ml/9fl oz/1 cup water**

**about 2.5ml/½ tsp sugar**

Soak the currants in warm water for 15 minutes and then drain them thoroughly in a sieve or strainer. This will rehydrate the raisins, making them plump and juicy.

Heat the olive oil in a heavy pan and stir in the onions and sugar. When the onions begin to colour, stir in the pine nuts and currants. Cook, stirring, until the pine nuts turn golden brown in colour. Take care not to let them burn. Add the cinnamon, dried mint and allspice.

Stir in the rice, making sure it is coated in the spices. Pour in just enough water to cover the rice and season with a little salt and pepper. Give the rice a stir and bring the water to the boil. Reduce the heat and let it simmer, uncovered, until all the water has been absorbed. Turn off the heat and cover the rice with a clean dish towel. Leave it to steam for 10 minutes, then toss in the fresh herbs.

Slice off the ends of each tomato to use as lids for the peppers (you don't need the remainder of the tomatoes for this recipe, but they can be used in a salad to accompany the peppers).

Spoon the rice mixture into each pepper and seal them with their tomato lids. Place them upright, packed tightly, in a heavy pan.

To make the cooking liquid, mix together the olive and lemon juice in a bowl and pour in the water. Pour the mixture over and around the peppers in the pan and sprinkle a little sugar over the top. Bring the liquid to the boil, reduce the heat, cover the pan and cook gently for 25–30 minutes, or until the peppers are tender. Serve warm or cold.

# Baked stuffed apples

In the same manner that they stuff vegetables, the Turks also stuff fruit for savoury dishes. Apples, quinces, apricots and plums are great favourites for aromatic rice or minced meat stuffings. I enjoy making this dish, *elma dolması*, to serve as an accompaniment to roasted meat or chicken.

## Serves four

**4 cooking apples, or any firm, sour apple of your choice**

**100ml/3½fl oz/scant ½ cup water**

**30ml/2 tbsp olive oil**

**juice of ½ lemon**

**10ml/2 tsp sugar**

**a few fresh mint or basil leaves, to garnish**

**lemon wedges, to serve**

For the stuffing

**30ml/2 tbsp olive oil**

**a little butter**

**1 onion, finely chopped**

**2 garlic cloves**

**30ml/2 tbsp pine nuts**

**30ml/2 tbsp currants, soaked in warm water for 5–10 minutes and drained**

**5–10ml/1–2 tsp ground cinnamon**

**5–10ml/1–2 tsp ground allspice**

**5ml/1 tsp sugar**

**175g/6oz/scant 1 cup short grain rice, thoroughly rinsed and drained**

**a bunch each of flat leaf parsley and dill, finely chopped**

**salt and ground black pepper**

Make the filling. Heat the oil and butter in a heavy pan, stir in the onion and garlic and cook until they soften. Add the pine nuts and currants and cook until the nuts turn golden. Stir in the spices, sugar and rice, and stir to combine thoroughly.

Pour in enough water to cover the rice – roughly 1–2cm/½–¾in above the grains – and bring to the boil. Taste, then season the mixture with salt and pepper to taste and stir to combine. Lower the heat and simmer for about 10–12 minutes, until almost all the water has been absorbed.

Toss in the chopped herbs, stir to combine and turn off the heat. Cover the pan with a dry, clean dish towel and the lid, and leave the rice to steam for 5 minutes.

Preheat the oven to 200°C/400°F/Gas 6. Using a knife, cut the stalk ends off the apples and keep to use as lids.

Carefully core each apple, removing some of the flesh to create a cavity that is large enough to stuff. Take spoonfuls of the rice and pack it into the apples. Replace the lids and stand the apples, upright and tightly packed, in a small baking dish.

In a bowl, mix together the water with the oil, lemon juice and sugar. Pour over and around the apples, then bake for 30–40 minutes, until the apples are tender and the juices are caramelised. Serve garnished with a few fresh herbs.

## Variation

Long, slender aubergines (eggplants) are also good stuffed with this mixture. Roll the whole aubergine on the work surface and pummel it with your hand to separate the flesh from the skin. Now, using a knife, cut round the stalk without severing it, and pull the stalk out. If the innards have been sufficiently separated from the skin, they should come out with the stalk. The cavity is now ready to stuff.

# Aubergine stew

With over 200 dishes made with aubergines alone in Turkey, there are many ideas to choose from. This particular stew, *patlıcan bastisi*, is a popular village dish as it combines potatoes, aubergines and peppers, ingredients many people grow in their gardens or can pick up at the country markets. It is just as good hot as it is cold. Serve with plenty of crusty bread to mop up the garlicky sauce, and with a dollop of thick, creamy yogurt if you like.

## Serves four to six

**2 potatoes, peeled**

**2 slim aubergines (eggplants)**

**2 green Turkish *çarliston* peppers, or bell peppers, deseeded**

**60ml/4 tbsp olive oil**

**10ml/2 tsp coriander seeds, crushed**

**2–3 garlic cloves, chopped**

**400g/14oz can of chopped tomatoes**

**10ml/2 tsp tomato purée (paste)**

**15ml/1 tbsp sugar**

**a small bunch of flat leaf parsley, leaves chopped**

**a small bunch of dill, chopped**

**salt and ground black pepper**

Cut the potatoes, aubergines and peppers into small bitesize chunks.

Heat the oil in a wide, heavy pan and stir in the potato pieces. Fry them over a medium heat for about 5–6 minutes to soften. Stir in the coriander seeds and garlic.

Add the tomatoes, tomato purée and the sugar, followed by the aubergine and pepper pieces. Top up the liquid with enough water (about 150–175ml/5–6fl oz/¼–⅔ cup) to surround the vegetables. Bring the liquid to the boil, partially cover the pan, and cook gently for 15–20 minutes.

Remove the lid and cook for a further 5–10 minutes. Season with salt and pepper to taste, and stir in half the parsley and dill. Transfer the stew to a serving dish and garnish with the remainder of the herbs.

# Vegetable stew

I love the name of this dish as much as I enjoy eating it. *Türlü* is a seasonal vegetable stew made with winter or summer vegetables. Some versions contain lamb or chicken, but this one is made solely with vegetables. It can be served on its own, or as an accompaniment to grilled or roasted meats. Traditionally, *türlü* is cooked in an earthenware pot.

## Serves six

**60ml/4 tbsp olive oil**

**15ml/1 tbsp coriander seeds**

**2–3 cinnamon sticks**

**3–4 garlic cloves, bashed**

**3 red onions, cut into quarters lengthways**

**3 fresh artichoke hearts, cut into quarters (see page 200 for preparing artichokes)**

**150g/5oz green beans, trimmed and cut into bitesize pieces**

**1 aubergine (eggplant), halved lengthways and sliced, or cut into bitesize chunks**

**2 courgettes (zucchini), thickly sliced, or cut into bitesize chunks**

**6 red or green Turkish *çarliston* peppers, left whole, or 2 bell peppers, cut into bitesize chunks**

**400g/14oz can of chopped tomatoes**

**15ml/1 tbsp sugar**

**15ml/1 tbsp tomato purée (paste)**

**15ml/1 tbsp white wine vinegar**

**300ml/½ pint/1¼ cups water**

**a small bunch of flat leaf parsley, leaves roughly chopped**

**a small bunch of dill, chopped**

**salt and ground black pepper**

Heat the oil in a heavy pan, or flameproof earthenware pot. Stir in the coriander seeds, cinnamon sticks and garlic to flavour the oil.

Add the red onions, artichoke hearts and green beans, and fry them gently for 2–3 minutes. Add the aubergine, courgettes, and peppers. Cover the pan or pot with a lid and let the vegetables cook in the steam for 2–3 minutes.

Add the tomatoes, sugar, tomato purée, vinegar and water – add more water, if necessary. Cover the pan and cook gently for about 35 minutes, or until the vegetables are tender. Toss in the herbs and season with salt and pepper. Serve hot.

## Variation

A sustaining winter version of this stew is generally made with pumpkin, potato and a variety of pulses.

# Carrot and apricot rolls with mint yogurt

I was inspired to create this recipe, *havuç köftesi*, after enjoying a meze dish of plain carrot balls dipped in garlic yogurt somewhere in Istanbul. Delicious though they were, I felt I could adapt the idea to include a bit more flavour and texture with herbs and pine nuts. I often serve these as part of a meze spread or I serve miniature ones on sticks as a nibble to go with drinks, using the yogurt as a dip.

## Serves four

**8–10 carrots, cut into thick slices**

**2–3 slices of day-old bread, ground into crumbs**

**4 spring onions (scallions), finely sliced**

**150g/5oz dried apricots, finely chopped or sliced**

**45ml/3 tbsp pine nuts**

**1 egg**

**5ml/1 tsp *pul biber*, or 1 fresh red chilli, deseeded and finely chopped**

**a bunch of dill, chopped**

**a bunch of basil, finely shredded**

**salt and ground black pepper**

**plain (all-purpose) flour, for coating**

**sunflower oil, for shallow-frying**

**lemon wedges, to serve**

For the mint yogurt

**about 225g/8oz thick and creamy natural (plain) yogurt**

**juice of ½ lemon**

**1–2 garlic cloves, crushed**

**a bunch of mint, finely chopped**

**salt and ground black pepper**

Steam the carrot slices for about 25 minutes, or until very soft. Do not boil them as they will lose some of their flavour.

Meanwhile, make the mint yogurt. Beat the yogurt in a bowl with the lemon juice and garlic, season with salt and pepper and stir in the mint. Set aside, or chill in the refrigerator.

Mash the carrots to a paste while they are warm. Add the breadcrumbs, spring onions, apricots and pine nuts and mix well with a fork. Beat in the egg and stir in the *pul biber* or chilli, and herbs. Season with salt and pepper to taste.

Put a small heap of flour on a flat surface. Take a plum-sized portion of the carrot mixture in your fingers and mould it into an oblong roll. If the mixture is very sticky, make it easier to deal with by adding more breadcrumbs or wetting your hands.

Coat the carrot roll in the flour and put it on a plate. Repeat with the rest of the mixture, to get 12–16 rolls altogether.

Heat sunflower oil for shallow-frying in a heavy frying pan. Place the carrot rolls in the hot oil and fry over a medium heat for 8–10 minutes, turning from time to time, until golden brown on all sides.

Remove from the pan with a slotted spoon and drain on kitchen paper. Serve the rolls hot, with lemon wedges for squeezing and the mint yogurt for dipping.

## Variations

You can make similar *köfte* using cooked sweet potatoes combined with spices such as cinnamon, ground cumin or *pul biber*, or plain mashed potato with lots of fresh herbs such as parsley and dill.

# Courgette, feta and mint patties

I always make a big batch of these patties, *kabak mücver*, as they are so popular and are just as delicious cold as they are hot. They are a great addition to a meze spread or picnic and you can make miniature ones and serve them as a nibble with drinks. Don't be afraid to pack in the herbs, especially the mint. If you like a little fire on your tongue, add more *pul biber* or chilli.

## Serves four to six

**3 firm courgettes (zucchini), washed and ends trimmed**

**30–45ml/2–3 tbsp olive oil**

**1 large onion, quartered and sliced along the grain**

**4 garlic cloves, chopped**

**45ml/3 tbsp plain (all-purpose) flour**

**3–4 eggs, beaten**

**225g/8oz *beyaz peynir*, or feta cheese, crumbled**

**a big bunch each of fresh flat leaf parsley, mint and dill, chopped**

**5ml/1 tsp *pul biber*, or 1 fresh red chilli, deseeded and chopped**

**sunflower oil, for shallow-frying**

**salt and ground black pepper**

**mint leaves, to garnish**

Hold the courgettes at an angle and grate them, then put them in a sieve or strainer and sprinkle with a little salt. Leave them to weep for 5 minutes, then squeeze the grated courgettes in your hand to extract the juices.

Heat the oil in a frying pan, stir in the courgettes, onion and garlic and fry until they begin to colour. Remove from the heat.

Beat the flour and eggs in a bowl to form a smooth batter. Beat in the cooled courgette mixture. Add the *beyaz peynir* or feta, herbs and *pul biber* or chilli, and season with black pepper. Add salt if you like, but usually the feta is quite salty. Mix well.

Heat enough sunflower oil for shallow-frying in a heavy, non-stick pan. Drop four spoonfuls of the mixture into the hot oil, leaving space between each one, then fry over a medium heat for 6–8 minutes, or until firm to the touch and golden brown on both sides.

Remove from the pan with a slotted spoon and drain on kitchen paper while you fry the remainder. Serve while still warm, garnished with mint.

# Potatoes baked with tomatoes and feta

This tasty potato dish, *patates bastısı*, comes from western Anatolia. Traditionally baked in an earthenware dish, it makes a fabulous accompaniment to meat, poultry or fish. You can also serve it on its own with a squeeze of lemon or a dollop of yogurt and a green salad.

## Serves four to six

**675g/1½lb new potatoes**

**15ml/1 tbsp butter**

**45ml/3 tbsp olive oil**

**2 red onions, quartered and sliced along the grain**

**3–4 garlic cloves, chopped**

**5–10ml/1–2 tsp cumin seeds, crushed**

**5–10ml/1–2 tsp *pul biber*, or**

**1 fresh red chilli, deseeded and chopped**

**10ml/2 tsp dried oregano**

**10ml/2 tsp sugar**

**15ml/1 tbsp white wine vinegar**

**400g/14oz can of chopped tomatoes, drained of juice**

**12–16 black olives**

**115g/4oz *beyaz peynir*, or feta cheese, crumbled**

**salt and ground black pepper**

**olive oil, for drizzling**

**lemon wedges, to serve**

Preheat the oven to 200°C/400°F/Gas 6. Put the potatoes into a pan of cold water, bring to the boil and cook for 15–20 minutes, or until tender but not soft. Drain and refresh under cold running water, then peel off the skins and cut the potatoes into thick slices.

Heat the butter and 30ml/2 tbsp of the oil in a heavy pan, stir in the onions and garlic and cook until soft. Add the cumin seeds, *pul biber* or chilli, and most of the oregano – reserve a little for the top – then stir in the sugar and vinegar, then the tomatoes. Season.

Put the potatoes and olives into a baking dish – preferably an earthenware one – and spoon the tangy tomato mixture over them. Crumble the *peynir* or feta on top and sprinkle with the reserved oregano. Drizzle with the remaining oil, then bake for 25–30 minutes.

Serve hot, with lemon wedges to squeeze over.

# Artichokes with beans and almonds

One of the joys of buying seasonal vegetables in Turkey is that the people selling them know exactly what you are going to make with them so they are happy to prepare them for you. In the early summer when every stall and street seller has crates of globe artichokes on their stalks, you can have them cut, peeled and prepared right down to their meaty hearts and tender bottoms ready to take home and poach in olive oil, *zeytinyağlı enginar*. If you're not in Turkey during the artichoke season and don't want to prepare them yourself, use frozen ready-prepared artichoke bottoms.

## Serves four

**4 large globe artichokes**

**175g/6oz broad (fava) beans**

**120ml/4fl oz/½ cup olive oil**

**juice of 1 lemon, plus extra for acidulation**

**50ml/2fl oz/¼ cup water**

**10ml/2 tsp granulated sugar**

**75g/3oz blanched almonds**

**a small bunch of fresh dill, chopped**

**2 tomatoes, skinned, deseeded and diced**

**salt**

To prepare the artichokes, cut off the stalks and pull off all the leaves. Dig out the hairy chokes from the middles with a spoon, then cut away any hard bits with a sharp knife and trim into a neat cup shape. Rub the cup shapes – called bottoms – with a mixture of lemon juice and salt to prevent them from discolouring.

Put the beans in a large pan of water and bring to the boil. Lower the heat and simmer for 10–15 minutes or until tender. Drain and refresh under cold running water, then peel off the skins.

Place the artichokes in a heavy pan. Mix together the oil, lemon juice and water and pour over the artichokes. Cover the pan and poach the artichokes gently for about 20 minutes, then add the sugar, beans and almonds. Cover again and continue to poach gently for a further 10 minutes, or until the artichokes are tender.

Toss in half the dill, season with salt, and turn off the heat. Leave the artichokes to cool in the pan before lifting them out and placing them hollow-side up in a serving dish. Mix the tomatoes with the beans and almonds, spoon into the middle of the artichokes and around them, and garnish with the remaining dill. Serve at room temperature.

## Cook's tip

Buy fresh-looking almonds in their skins. Put them in a bowl and cover with boiling water. Leave to soak for a few hours until the skins loosen, then rub the skins off with your fingers. If you leave them for as long as 24 hours, the nuts soften, too.

# Green beans with tomatoes and dill

*Zeytinyağlı taze fasulye* is one of the delicious olive oil dishes that have survived from the Ottoman Empire, and which include leeks, celeriac, aubergines, green beans, artichokes or borlotti beans cooked in olive oil. When runner beans are in season it is a favourite family meal. As part of a meze spread it is served at room temperature, but it may be served hot as a side dish to accompany grilled or barbecued meat, or as a main course with yogurt. The fresh dil is essential.

## Serves four

**1–2 onions, roughly chopped**

**2 garlic cloves, roughly chopped**

**30–45ml/2–3 tbsp olive oil**

**500g/1¼lb stringless runner (green) beans, trimmed and each cut into 3–4 pieces**

**15ml/1 tbsp sugar**

**juice of 1 lemon**

**2 x 400g/14oz cans of chopped tomatoes**

**a handful of fresh dill, roughly chopped**

**salt and ground black pepper**

Put the onions, garlic and oil in a wide, heavy pan and stir over a low heat until they soften. Toss in the beans, coating them in the onions and oil, then stir in the sugar and lemon juice.

Add the tomatoes to the pan and bring to the boil, then lower the heat and add the dill. Cook gently for 35–40 minutes, or until the beans are tender and the tomato sauce is fairly thick. Season with salt and pepper to taste before serving.

# Sweet-and-sour ladies' fingers

This is a delightful way to eat okra, as they are tender and crunchy as well as being very easy to prepare. Cooked this way, they can be served as a meze dish or as a side dish, eaten hot or cold. Other dishes using okra include chicken casseroles, vegetable stews and an Anatolian soup made with small, sour-tasting okra, but this simple sweet-and-sour method is my favourite way of using them. Its name, *bamya*, is the same for both the vegetable and the dish.

## Serves four

**350g/12oz fresh, springy okra or ladies' fingers, left whole**

**juice of 2 lemons**

**45ml/3 tbsp olive oil**

**15ml/1 tbsp sugar**

**salt and ground black pepper**

Put all the okra into a wide bowl and toss them in the lemon juice. Leave them to soak in the lemon juice for 5–10 minutes (this is a traditional trick to ensure the okra retains its vibrant green colour after cooking).

Gather up the okra with your hands and place them in a colander, leaving most of the lemon juice behind. Pour this juice into a cup.

Heat the olive oil in a wide, heavy pan. Toss in the okra for 2–3 minutes, then sprinkle them with the sugar. Toss them again and pour in the reserved lemon juice.

Season the okra with salt and pepper to taste, and pour in a little water, just enough to cover the base of the pan. Keep tossing the okra over a high heat until the juices in the pan are richly coloured and almost caramelised.

Lift the okra out of the pan and arrange them on a serving dish. Drizzle the pan juices over them and serve hot or cold.

## Cook's tip

For this dish you must choose very fresh, vibrant green, firm okra and be careful not to overcook them.

# Caramelised mushrooms with allspice and herbs

Button mushrooms caramelise beautifully in their own juices while still retaining their moistness and nutty flavour. This dish, *mantar tava*, can be served as a side dish, a hot or cold meze dish with chunks of bread to mop up the tasty cooking juices, or as a snack served on toasted crusty bread.

## Serves four

**45ml/3 tbsp olive oil**

**15ml/1 tbsp butter**

**450g/1lb button (white) mushrooms, wiped clean**

**3–4 garlic cloves, finely chopped**

**10ml/2 tsp allspice berries, crushed**

**10ml/2 tsp coriander seeds**

**5ml/1 tsp dried mint**

**a bunch each of fresh sage and flat leaf parsley, chopped**

**salt and ground black pepper**

**crusty bread and lemon wedges, to serve**

Heat the oil and butter in a wide, heavy pan, then stir in the mushrooms with the garlic, crushed allspice and coriander seeds. Mix everything gently to combine.

Cover and cook for about 10 minutes, shaking the pan from time to time, until the mushrooms start to caramelise.

Remove the lid and toss in the dried mint with some of the fresh sage and parsley. Cook for a further 5 minutes, until most of the liquid has evaporated, then season.

Transfer to a serving dish and sprinkle the rest of the sage and parsley over the top. Serve hot or at room temperature, with lemon wedges for squeezing over, and crusty toasted bread.

## Cook's tip

Button white mushrooms are ideal as they don't release much liquid and caramelise well. Don't wash them before cooking, just wipe with a clean dish towel.

# Courgette and apple with a hazelnut and lemon sauce

The Turkish nut sauce, *tarator*, is delicious served with many vegetable and seafood dishes. Along the Black Sea Coast, *tarator* is often made with the local hazelnuts, which makes a lighter sauce than the walnut version in Istanbul. The courgettes and apples are roasted in this recipe, *taratorlu kabak*, but they could be cooked by any method, such as grilling or steaming. This dish can be served as a side dish or part of a meze spread.

## Serves four

**2 firm, fat courgettes (zucchini)**

**2 sweet, firm red, pink, or yellow apples**

**30–45ml/2–3 tbsp olive oil**

**15–30ml/1–2 tbsp chopped roasted hazelnuts, to garnish**

For the nut sauce

**115g/4oz hazelnuts**

**1–2 garlic cloves**

**30ml/2 tbsp olive oil**

**juice of 1 lemon**

**15ml/1 tbsp grape *pekmez*, or molasses or clear honey**

**salt and ground black pepper**

Preheat the oven to 180°C/350°F/Gas 4. Using a vegetable peeler, partially peel the courgettes in stripes. Slice them on the diagonal. Quarter and core the apples then cut each quarter into 2 or 3 segments.

Place the courgette and apple slices in an ovenproof dish and pour over the olive oil. Roast in the oven for 35–40 minutes, or until golden brown.

Meanwhile, make the nut sauce. Using a mortar and pestle, or a food processor, pound the hazelnuts with the garlic to form a thick paste. Gradually beat in the oil and lemon juice, until the mixture is quite creamy. Sweeten with the *pekmez*, molasses or clear honey, and season to taste.

Arrange the roasted courgette and apple on a serving dish and drizzle the nut sauce over them. Sprinkle the chopped roasted hazelnuts over the top and serve while still warm.

## Variation

Other vegetables served this way include whole bell peppers, sliced aubergine, pumpkin and squash, and fruit such as plums.

# Roasted courgettes and peaches

Like most Turks, I love tucking into a platter of deep-fried, grilled or roasted vegetables served with a garlic-flavoured sauce made with yogurt, nuts or tahini. The combination of summer fruit and vegetables in this baked version of *yoğurtlu kabak ve şeftali* is particularly colourful and juicy.

## Serves four

**2 courgettes (zucchini)**

**2 yellow or red bell peppers, deseeded and cut into wedges**

**100ml/3½fl oz/scant ½ cup olive oil**

**4–6 plum tomatoes, quartered lengthways**

**2 firm peaches, peeled, halved and stoned (pitted), then cut into wedges**

**30ml/2 tbsp pine nuts**

**salt**

For the yogurt sauce

**500g/1¼lb thick and creamy natural (plain) yogurt**

**2–3 garlic cloves, crushed**

**juice of ½ lemon**

**salt and ground black pepper**

Preheat the oven to 200°C/400°F/Gas 6. Using a vegetable peeler, peel the courgettes lengthways in stripes like a zebra, then cut into wedges. Place the courgettes and peppers in an earthenware baking dish. Drizzle the oil over and sprinkle with salt, then bake in the oven for 20 minutes.

Take the dish out of the oven and turn the vegetables in the oil, then mix in the tomatoes and peaches. Bake for a further 20–25 minutes, until everything is nicely browned.

Meanwhile, make the yogurt sauce. In a small bowl, beat the yogurt with the garlic and lemon juice. Season to taste and set aside until required.

Dry-roast the pine nuts in a small, heavy pan, shaking them constantly, until they turn golden brown and give off a nutty aroma. Be careful not to let them burn. Remove from the heat.

When the roasted vegetables are ready, remove the dish from the oven and sprinkle over the pine nuts. Serve immediately with the yogurt sauce and some warm bread.

## Variation

This dish is also delicious with a tahini dressing. Thin down about 30ml/ 2 tbsp sesame paste with a little water and lemon juice, then beat in some crushed garlic, seasoning and, if you like, a little roasted *pul biber*.

# Beans, peas, lentils and pilaffs

In the past, pilaffs were considered the food of nobility, and pulses the food of peasants. Today, there is not a Turk who doesn't love both. At least one meal of every day will feature a rice, grain or pulse dish. The Turkish word for pulses, *bakliyat*, derives from the Arabic word for vegetables, and beans, peas and lentils are immensely popular, used in a myriad of ways. The cooking of rice is regarded as an art, and the grain is held in high esteem, playing an important role in celebratory dishes like Veiled Pilaff.

# Lentils with carrots and sage

In Anatolia, pungent sage leaves are dried in the sun to enhance their strong herb and wood aroma, ideal for a healthy tea and for adding liberally to vegetable, meat and fish dishes. This dish is adapted from one of the Ottoman olive oil dishes; this is *zeytinyağlı havuç ve mercimek*.

## Serves four to six

**175g/6oz/scant 1 cup green lentils, rinsed and picked over**

**45–60ml/3–4 tbsp fruity olive oil**

**1 onion, cut in half lengthways, in half again crossways, and sliced along the grain**

**3–4 plump garlic cloves, roughly chopped and bruised with the flat side of a knife**

**5ml/1 tsp coriander seeds**

**a handful of dried sage leaves**

**5–10ml/1–2 tsp sugar**

**4 carrots, sliced**

**15–30ml/1–2 tbsp tomato purée (paste)**

**salt and ground black pepper**

**lemon wedges, to serve**

Bring a pan of water to the boil and add the lentils. Lower the heat, partially cover the pan and simmer gently for 10 minutes. Drain and rinse well under cold running water.

Heat the oil in a heavy pan, stir in the onion, garlic, coriander seeds, dried sage and sugar, and cook until the onion begins to colour.

Add the carrots and cook for 3 minutes, then add the lentils and pour in 250ml/9fl oz/1 cup water, making sure the lentils and carrots are covered.

Stir in the tomato purée and cover the pan, then cook gently for about 20 minutes, until most of the liquid has been absorbed. The lentils and carrots should both be tender, but still have some bite. Season with salt and pepper to taste. Serve hot or warm, with lemon wedges to squeeze over.

# Chickpea stew

Although many bean and chickpea stews are prepared with chunks of lamb or the cured spicy sausage, *sucuk*, and cured beef, *pastırma*, this recipe for *nohutlu yahnisi* is vegetarian. It can be served as a meal on its own, perhaps with a bulgur or rice pilaff, or as a side dish.

## Serves three to four

**15–30ml/1–2 tbsp ghee, or 15ml/ 1 tbsp olive oil plus a knob or pat of butter**

**2 red onions, halved and sliced**

**4 garlic cloves, chopped**

**10ml/2 tsp coriander seeds**

**5ml/1 tsp cumin seeds, crushed**

**5ml/1 tsp fennel seeds**

**5–10ml/1–2 tsp *pul biber*, or paprika**

**400g/14oz can of chopped tomatoes, drained of juice**

**10ml/2 tsp sugar**

**2 x 400g/14oz cans of chickpeas, rinsed thoroughly and drained**

**a small bunch of flat leaf parsley, leaves chopped**

**200g/7oz baby spinach leaves**

**salt and ground black pepper**

**lemon wedges, to serve**

**60–75ml/4–5 tbsp thick and creamy natural (plain) yogurt, to serve**

Heat the ghee, or oil and butter, in a heavy pan. Stir in the onions, garlic and spices, and cook until the onions begin to brown.

Stir in the tomatoes and sugar, then toss in the chickpeas to brown them lightly. Add the parsley and season with salt and pepper.

Toss in the spinach leaves, cover the pan, and let the leaves wilt in the steam. Transfer to a bowl and serve immediately. Squeeze the wedges of lemon over it and serve with a dollop of yogurt.

## Variation

You can use *sucuk*, the spicy sausage, or *pastırma*, the cured beef, in this dish. Simply slice and add to the pan with the onion and garlic, so that they flavour the cooking juices. Omit the spinach leaves.

# Chickpea patties with red onion and parsley

Healthy and vegetarian, these tasty cumin-flavoured patties, *nohutlu mücver*, can be served like burgers, slapped between two bun halves with parsley, pickles, tomato, salad leaves and a dollop of yogurt or herb mayonnaise, or they can be tucked into the pockets of toasted pitta bread. Served on their own, they are delicious with a crunchy salad.

## Serves four

**400g/14oz can of chickpeas, drained and thoroughly rinsed**

**45–60ml/3–4 tbsp olive oil**

**1 red onion, finely chopped**

**10ml/2 tsp cumin seeds, crushed**

**10ml/2 tsp ground coriander**

**5–10ml/1–2 tsp *pul biber*, or paprika**

**a small bunch of flat leaf parsley, leaves finely chopped**

**a small bunch of dill, finely chopped**

**grated rind of 1 lemon**

**plain (all-purpose) flour, for dusting**

**sea salt and ground black pepper**

To serve

**45–60ml/3–4 tbsp thick and creamy natural (plain) yogurt**

**1–2 garlic cloves, crushed**

**1 red onion, halved and sliced**

**a small bunch of flat leaf parsley, leaves roughly chopped**

**1 lemon, cut into wedges**

**toasted pitta or flat breads, optional**

In a bowl, pound the chickpeas with a potato masher, or process them to a paste in a food processor or blender.

Bind the mashed chickpeas with 15ml/1 tbsp of the olive oil and beat in the onion, cumin, coriander and *pul biber* or paprika with a wooden spoon Add the parsley, dill and lemon rind, and season the mixture with salt and pepper to taste.

Mould portions of the chickpea mixture into small balls and flatten them in the palm of your hand to form thick patties (make these as big or as small as you like).

Dust the patties in a little flour and fry them for 2 minutes on each side in the remaining olive oil in a non-stick pan. Drain them on kitchen paper.

In a small bowl, beat the yogurt with the garlic, and season to taste.

Arrange the patties on a large serving plate and serve them hot, or at room temperature, with the red onion, parsley, and lemon to squeeze over them, or a little garlic yogurt to drizzle over the top. Alternatively, you can tuck the patties into pitta pouches with the same ingredients.

# Beans with pastırma and lamb's lettuce

The flavouring of this simple dish, *bostana*, comes from the dark red fenugreek and cumin coating (called *çemen*) on the dried fillet of beef, *pastırma*. The dish is generally made with borlotti, haricot or black-eyed beans. You can serve it on its own with lemon wedges, or for a more sustaining dish, pad it out with eggs by creating pockets in the mixture and dropping them in to cook gently.

## Serves three to four

**175g/6oz/scant 1 cup dried borlotti beans, black-eyed beans (peas), haricot (navy) or butter (lima) beans, soaked overnight and rinsed**

**30ml/2 tbsp olive oil and a little butter**

**1 onion, chopped**

**2 garlic cloves, chopped**

**175g/6oz *pastırma*, finely sliced**

**400g/14oz can of chopped tomatoes, drained of juice**

**225g/8oz fresh lamb's lettuce, rinsed and drained**

**salt and ground black pepper**

**lemon wedges, to serve**

Put the beans into a pan and cover with water. Bring to the boil and simmer until tender (this will take about 30 minutes for borlotti beans, 45 minutes for black-eyed beans, 50 minutes for haricot beans and 1 hour for butter beans).

Heat the oil and butter in a heavy pan and stir in the onion and garlic, until they begin to colour. Toss in the beans, followed by the *pastırma*, and sauté for 3–4 minutes to release the flavour. Add the tomatoes and cook for 2–3 minutes, then toss in the lamb's lettuce until it just begins to wilt.

Season and serve with wedges of lemon to squeeze over the top.

# Borlotti beans with tomato and garlic

Meaty and pinkish in dappled pods, borlotti beans are a huge favourite amongst Turks and sit very comfortably in this dish. Cooked in lots of olive oil, this is one of the esteemed *zeytinyağlı* dishes, which you will encounter all over the western region of Turkey. This is called *zeytinyağlı barbunya.*

## Serves four

**175g/6oz/scant 1 cup dried borlotti beans, soaked in cold water overnight**

**45–60ml/3–4 tbsp olive oil**

**2 red onions, quartered and sliced along the grain**

**4 garlic cloves, chopped**

**400g/14oz can of chopped tomatoes**

**10ml/2 tsp sugar**

**a bunch each of fresh flat leaf parsley and dill, coarsely chopped**

**4 ripe plum tomatoes**

**salt and ground black pepper**

**lemon wedges, to serve**

Drain the beans, transfer them to a pan and fill the pan with plenty of cold water. Bring to the boil and boil for 1 minute, then lower the heat and partially cover the pan. Simmer the beans for about 30 minutes, or until they are tender but not soft or mushy. Drain, rinse well under cold running water and remove any loose skins.

Heat the oil in a heavy pan and stir in the onions and garlic. When they begin to soften, add the canned tomatoes, sugar and half the herbs. Toss in the beans, pour in 300ml/½ pint/1¼ cups water and bring to the boil. Lower the heat, partially cover the pan, then simmer for about 20 minutes, until most of the liquid has gone.

Meanwhile, bring a small pan of water to the boil, drop in the plum tomatoes for a few seconds, then plunge them into a bowl of cold water. Peel off the skins and coarsely chop the tomatoes.

Add the tomatoes to the beans with the rest of the herbs. Season and cook for a further 5–10 minutes. Serve hot or at room temperature, with lemon wedges for squeezing.

# Black-eyed bean stew with spicy sausage

Black-eyed beans are common in the stews and salads of the Aegean region. If you can't get hold of them for *sucuk ve fasulye yahnisi* you can substitute haricot, borlotti or chickpeas. Accompany with a salad of hot green peppers and parsley, or pickled vegetables.

## Serves four to six

- **175g/6oz/scant 1 cup dried black-eyed beans (peas), soaked in cold water overnight**
- **30ml/2 tbsp ghee or 15ml/1 tbsp each of olive oil and butter**
- **1 large onion, cut in half lengthways and sliced along the grain**
- **2–3 garlic cloves, roughly chopped and bruised with the flat side of a knife**
- **5ml/1 tsp cumin seeds**
- **5–10ml/1–2 tsp coriander seeds**
- **5ml/1 tsp fennel seeds**
- **5–10ml/1–2 tsp sugar or clear honey**
- **1 spicy cured sausage, about 25cm/10in long, sliced**
- **150ml/¼ pint/⅔ cup white wine**
- **400g/14oz can of chopped tomatoes**
- **a bunch of fresh flat leaf parsley, roughly chopped**
- **salt and ground black pepper**

Drain the beans, transfer them to a pan and fill the pan with plenty of cold water. Bring to the boil and boil for 1 minute, then lower the heat and partially cover the pan. Simmer the beans for about 25 minutes, or until they are just cooked but still with a bite. Drain, rinse well under cold running water and remove any loose skins.

Preheat the oven to 180°C/350°F/Gas 4. Melt the ghee or olive oil and butter in a heavy pan or flameproof earthenware pot. Stir in the onion, garlic and spices and fry until the onion begins to colour.

Stir in the sugar or honey, toss in the sliced spicy sausage and cook until it begins to brown. Add the beans, followed by the wine. Bubble up the wine, then lower the heat and add the tomatoes. Stir in half the parsley and season with salt and pepper.

Cover and bake for about 40 minutes. Before serving, taste for seasoning and sprinkle with the remaining parsley.

## Variation

This dish uses the cumin-spiked horseshoe-shaped sausage, *sucuk*, but any Turkish, Greek or Italian spicy sausage will work; it can also be made with *pastırma*, the spiced cured fillet of beef.

# Broad bean purée

I know so many people who love this dish for its smooth, silky texture but I would have to say it is an acquired taste. Traditionally *fava* is made when the beans are in season, and it is much sought after at that time. Serve with strips of toasted flat bread as part of a meze spread.

## Serves four

**225g/8oz/1¼ cups dried broad (fava) beans, soaked overnight**

**175g/6oz fresh broad (fava) beans, shelled**

**550ml/18fl oz/2¼ cups water**

**1 onion, chopped**

**1 potato, peeled and chopped**

**150ml/¼ pint/⅔ cup olive oil**

**5ml/1 tsp salt**

**10ml/2 tsp sugar**

For the garnish

**1 tomato**

**a few dill fronds**

Put the dried and fresh beans into a pan with the water and bring to the boil. Add the onion and potato and reduce the heat.

Pour in the olive oil and sprinkle the salt and sugar over the top. Cover and simmer for 1 hour, stirring occasionally and topping up the water if necessary, until it has a pouring consistency.

Press through a sieve or strainer, or process it in a food processor or blender, to make a purée. Pour the purée into a wet mould or bowl. Leave to cool and set.

To make the garnish, plunge the tomato into a bowl of boiling water for 30 seconds, then refresh in cold water. Peel away the skin. Remove and discard the seeds and finely chop the flesh.

Invert the mould or bowl on to a serving plate and garnish the dome with chopped tomato and dill feathers. Serve at room temperature.

# Bulgur wheat with yogurt

A simple bowl of cooked bulgur with yogurt is incredibly nourishing and satisfying, often served for breakfast or as a hot snack. For some, *kürt bulgur pilavı* might be the only meal of the day, often eaten from a communal pot. In the east of Anatolia, it is both a Turkish and Kurdish dish traditionally made with the strong-tasting fat from the sheep's tail, or with ghee.

## Serves four to six

**45ml/3 tbsp ghee or butter**

**2 onions, chopped**

**350g/12oz/2 cups bulgur wheat, thoroughly rinsed and drained**

**600ml/1 pint/2½ cups water or lamb stock**

**500g/1¼lb thick and creamy natural (plain) yogurt**

**salt and ground black pepper**

Melt 30ml/2 tbsp of ghee or butter in a heavy pan and stir in the onions. Cook the onions to soften. Add the bulgur wheat, tossing it thoroughly.

Pour in the water or stock, season with salt and pepper to taste and stir to combine thoroughly. Bring to the boil for 1–2 minutes, then reduce the heat and simmer until all the liquid has been completely absorbed.

Turn off the heat, cover the pan with a clean dish towel, and press the lid on top. Leave to steam for a further 10–15 minutes, then fluff it up with a fork and form it into a mound on a serving dish. Make a well in the centre and spoon the yogurt into it.

Melt the remaining ghee or butter in a small pan. Drizzle it over the yogurt and serve the bulgur wheat immediately.

## Variation

A similar dish, *kuskus*, can be made with couscous. Soak the couscous first, then rub with oil to separate the grains, and heat them in the oven with 45ml/3 tbsp ghee. Serve this simple couscous dish straight from the oven with a dollop of creamy natural yogurt.

# Anatolian bulgur with nuts and dates

There are several hearty Anatolian dishes made with bulgur that include vegetables, dried fruit and nuts. This one, *arap pilav*, is often attributed to the Bedouin, nomadic herdsmen in the deserts of Arabia and North Africa who depended heavily on dates. It is delicious served with roasted meat or chicken. You can add dried figs, prunes or apricots, if you like.

## Serves four to six

**350g/12oz/2 cups coarse bulgur wheat, rinsed under running water and drained**

**30ml/2 tbsp ghee or butter**

**2 medium carrots, cut into matchsticks**

**75g/3oz blanched almonds**

**30–45ml/2–3 tbsp pine nuts**

**30–45ml/2–3 tbsp shelled pistachio nuts, chopped**

**175g/6oz soft dried dates, roughly chopped**

**salt**

To serve

**a handful of fresh coriander (cilantro), chopped**

**about 30ml/2 tbsp ghee or butter, melted (optional)**

**thick and creamy natural (plain) yogurt**

Put the bulgur wheat into a bowl, add salt, pour over enough boiling water to cover it by 2.5cm/1in, and give it a quick stir. Cover the bowl and leave the bulgur wheat to steam for about 25 minutes, until it has soaked up the water and doubled in volume.

Meanwhile, melt the ghee in a wide, heavy pan, add the carrots and fry for about 10 minutes, until tender and golden. Toss in the nuts and cook for a further minute, or until they give off a nutty aroma and begin to colour.

Add the dates and, if they look dry, splash in 15–30ml/1–2 tbsp water. Transfer the bulgur wheat to the pan, check the seasoning for salt, and toss until everything is mixed well together. Turn off the heat, cover the pan with a dish towel and lid, and leave to steam for 5–10 minutes.

To serve, stir the coriander through the bulgur, and pour over the melted ghee or butter, if you like. Hand round yogurt in a small bowl.

## Cook's tip

In Bedouin camps in eastern Turkey, this dish is normally served piled in a mound with yogurt spooned into a hollow, and eaten communally.

# Tomato bulgur with spicy lamb

*Kuzulu bulgur pilavı* is a very tasty dish from the area around Kayseri in central Anatolia, which is well known for its meat dishes. Traditionally, sheep's tail fat is used, but you can substitute with ghee. The dish is typically served with yogurt or *cacik*, the cucumber, mint and yogurt salad.

## Serves four

**30ml/2 tbsp ghee, or butter**

**2 onions, chopped**

**10ml/2 tsp sugar**

**350g/12oz/2 cups bulgur wheat, rinsed and drained**

**10ml/2 tsp tomato purée (paste)**

**600ml/1 pint/2½ cups lamb or chicken stock, or water**

**10ml/2 tsp *pul biber*, or paprika**

**5–10ml/1–2 tsp ground cumin**

**5ml/1 tsp ground coriander**

**250g/9oz shoulder of lamb, cut into bitesize pieces**

**salt and ground black pepper**

**a small bunch of flat leaf parsley, roughly chopped, to garnish**

**sliced lemon or yogurt, to serve**

Melt the ghee or butter in a heavy pan. Stir in the onions with the sugar and fry gently for 3–4 minutes, or until golden brown.

Toss in the bulgur wheat, coating it in the onion and ghee, and stir in the tomato purée.

Pour in the stock or water, season with salt and pepper, and bring it to the boil. Reduce the heat and simmer until all the water has been absorbed. Turn off the heat, cover the pan with a clean dish towel, place the lid on firmly, and leave to steam for 10–15 minutes.

Put the spices and lamb pieces in a plastic bag and shake to coat. Heat a wide, heavy, non-stick frying pan. Toss the meat quickly on its own in the pan, frying it in its own juices, until it is lightly browned.

Add the bulgur wheat to the pan and toss with the meat over heat for 2–3 minutes, or until the flavours are thoroughly mixed.

Transfer the bulgur wheat and lamb to a serving dish, garnish with the parsley and serve hot with lemon slices or yogurt.

# Anchovy and rice dome

The people of the Black Sea coast sing about anchovies, write poetry about them, and prepare many savoury dishes with them as well as one or two sweet. Some versions of this dish toss fried anchovies through the rice, or bake them in layers, but *hamsili pilav* tops them all for ingenuity and opulent design – a perfect anchovy dome, like a Sultan's turban, encasing succulent grains.

## Serves four to six

**600g/1lb 6oz fresh anchovies, gutted, with heads and backbones removed**

**30ml/2 tbsp olive oil**

**15ml/1 tbsp butter**

**1 onion, finely chopped**

**30ml/2 tbsp pine nuts**

**15ml/1 tbsp dried mint**

**5ml/1 tsp ground allspice**

**450g/1lb/2¼ cups long grain rice, thoroughly rinsed and drained**

**a small bunch of fresh dill, finely chopped, plus a few fronds to garnish**

**salt and ground black pepper**

**lemon wedges, to serve**

Rinse the anchovies and pat dry. Open them out like butterflies and sprinkle with salt. Lightly grease a dome-shaped ovenproof dish or bowl and line it with anchovies, skin side down. Reserve some for the top.

Heat the oil and butter in a heavy pan, stir in the onion and cook until soft. Add the pine nuts and cook until golden, then stir in the mint, allspice and rice. Season and pour in enough water to cover the rice by 2cm/¾in.

Bring to the boil, lower the heat, partially cover and simmer for 10–12 minutes, until the water has been absorbed. While the rice is cooking, preheat the oven to 180°C/350°F/Gas 4.

Turn off the heat under the pan and sprinkle the dill over the rice. Cover the pan with a dish towel, put the lid tightly on top and leave the rice to steam for 10 minutes. Fluff up the rice with a fork to mix in the dill, then tip it into the anchovy mould. Lay the remaining anchovies, skin side up this time, over the rice.

Splash a little water over the top of the fish and place the dish in the oven for 25 minutes.

To serve, invert a serving plate over the dish and carefully turn out the anchovy mould encasing the rice. Garnish with dill, and serve immediately with lemon wedges to squeeze over.

# Pumpkin stuffed with jewelled rice

Cappadocia – an extraordinary landscape of troglodyte cave dwellings, fairy chimneys and churches carved out of the rock – is also one of the key regions for apricot production and the harvesting of pumpkins, which make ideal cooking vessels. This sumptuous fruit and nut pilaff, *bal kabağı dolması*, would normally be reserved for special occasions, such as a wedding feast.

## Serves four to six

**1 medium-sized pumpkin, weighing about 1.2kg/2½lb**

**225g/8oz/generous 1 cup long grain rice, well rinsed**

**30–45ml/2–3 tbsp olive oil**

**15ml/1 tbsp butter**

**a fingerful of saffron threads**

**5ml/1 tsp coriander seeds**

**2–3 strips of orange peel, pith removed and finely sliced**

**45–60ml/3–4 tbsp shelled pistachio nuts**

**30–45ml/2–3 tbsp dried cranberries, soaked in boiling water for 5 minutes and drained**

**175g/6oz dried apricots, sliced or chopped**

**a bunch of fresh basil, leaves loosely torn**

**a bunch each of fresh coriander (cilantro), mint and flat leaf parsley, coarsely chopped**

**salt and ground black pepper**

**lemon wedges and thick and creamy natural (plain) yogurt, to serve**

Preheat the oven to 200°C/400°F/Gas 6. Wash the pumpkin and cut off the stalk end to use as a lid. Scoop all the seeds out of the middle with a spoon, and pull out the stringy bits. Replace the lid, put the pumpkin on a baking tray and bake for 1 hour.

Meanwhile, put the rice in a pan and pour in just enough water to cover. Add a pinch of salt and bring to the boil, then lower the heat and partially cover the pan. Simmer for 10–12 minutes, until all the water has been absorbed and the grains of rice are cooked but still have a bite.

Heat the oil and butter in a wide, heavy pan. Stir in the saffron, coriander seeds, orange peel, pistachios, cranberries and apricots, then toss in the rice, making sure everything is thoroughly combined. Season to taste.

Turn off the heat, cover the pan with a clean, dry dish towel and press the lid tightly on top of the pan. Set to one side and leave the pilaff to steam for 10 minutes, then toss in the herbs.

Take the pumpkin out of the oven. Lift off the lid and spoon the pilaff into the cavity. Replace the lid and pop it back in the oven for 20 minutes.

To serve, remove the lid and slice a round off the top of the pumpkin. Place the ring on a plate and spoon some pilaff into the middle. Prepare the rest in the same way. Serve with lemon wedges and a bowl of yogurt.

# Aubergine pilaff with cinnamon and mint

Often served cold, this is a delicious combination of aubergines and rice, and the cinnamon and mint lift it to another level. The dish varies from region to region, some with bulgur rather than rice; in Istanbul this version bears the grand name *Sultan Reşat pilav*.

## Serves four to six

**2 large aubergines (eggplants)**

**30–45ml/2–3 tbsp olive oil**

**30–45ml/2–3 tbsp pine nuts**

**1 large onion, finely chopped**

**5ml/1 tsp coriander seeds**

**30ml/2 tbsp currants, soaked in warm water for 5–10 minutes and drained**

**10–15ml/2–3 tsp sugar**

**15–30ml/1–2 tbsp ground cinnamon**

**15–30ml/1–2 tbsp dried mint**

**a small bunch of fresh dill, finely chopped**

**3 tomatoes, skinned, deseeded and finely chopped**

**350g/12oz/2 cups long or short grain rice, well rinsed and drained**

**sunflower oil, for deep-frying**

**juice of ½ lemon**

**salt and ground black pepper**

**fresh mint sprigs and lemon wedges, to serve**

Using a vegetable peeler or a small, sharp knife, peel the aubergines lengthways in stripes like a zebra. Quarter them lengthways, then slice into bitesize chunks and place in a bowl of salted water. Cover with a plate to keep them submerged, and leave to soak for at least 30 minutes.

Meanwhile, heat the oil in a heavy pan, stir in the pine nuts and cook until they turn golden. Add the onion and soften it, then stir in the coriander seeds and currants. Add the sugar, cinnamon, mint and dill, and stir in the tomatoes.

Toss in the rice, coating it well in the tomato and spices, then pour in 900ml/ 1½ pints/3¾ cups water, season with salt and pepper and bring to the boil. Lower the heat and partially cover the pan, then simmer for 10–12 minutes, until almost all of the water has been absorbed. Turn off the heat, cover the pan with a dish towel and press the lid tightly on top. Leave the rice to steam for about 15 minutes.

Heat enough sunflower oil for deep-frying in a suitable pan. Drain the aubergines and squeeze them dry, then toss them in batches in the oil, for a few minutes at a time. When they are golden brown, lift them out with a slotted spoon and drain on kitchen paper.

Transfer the rice to a serving bowl and toss the aubergine chunks through it with the lemon juice. Garnish with fresh mint sprigs and serve warm or cold, with lemon wedges for squeezing.

# Rice with green peas, mint and dill

This plain buttery pilaff, *bezeliyeli pilav*, is a popular one to serve with fried or grilled chicken and fish dishes. Dotted with fresh green peas, it is delicious served hot or at room temperature and makes an attractive addition to a buffet spread or barbecue.

## Serves four

**15ml/1 tbsp olive oil**

**25g/1oz/2 tbsp butter**

**1 onion, finely chopped**

**350g/12oz/2 cups long grain rice, thoroughly rinsed and drained**

**750ml/1¼ pints/3 cups chicken stock or water**

**200g/7oz fresh or frozen peas**

**a small bunch of dill, finely chopped**

**a small bunch of mint, leaves finely chopped**

**salt and ground black pepper**

Heat the oil and butter in a heavy pan and stir in the onion. Cook until softened. Add the rice, coating it in the butter and onion, and pour in the stock or water.

Season and bring the stock to the boil. Reduce the heat and simmer for 10 minutes, or until almost all the liquid has been absorbed.

Toss the peas into the rice with half the fresh herbs. Cover the pan with a clean dish towel and a lid and leave the rice to steam with the peas for a further 10 minutes.

Transfer the cooked rice mixture to a serving dish, garnish with the remaining fresh herbs, and serve the pilaff hot or at room temperature.

## Variation

To make a more substantial dish, you can add diced carrot and diced artichoke bottoms with the peas.

# Sultan's chickpea pilaff

There is a story that Mahmut Pasha, the Grand Vizier of Mehmet the Conqueror, used to invite his ministers to lunch every Friday, when he would serve a special mound of rice and chickpea pilaff at the end of the meal. As each minister dipped into the rice with his spoon, solid gold balls the same size as the chickpeas would be revealed, bringing good fortune to those who managed to get one on their spoon. A classic buttery pilaff, fit for a sultan, this dish *nohutlu pilav* is a perfect accompaniment to almost any meat or fish dish.

## Serves four

**50g/2oz dried chickpeas, soaked in cold water overnight**

**30ml/2 tbsp butter**

**15ml/1 tbsp olive or sunflower oil**

**1 onion, chopped**

**225g/8oz/generous 1 cup long grain rice, well rinsed and drained**

**600ml/1 pint/2½ cups water or chicken stock**

**salt and ground black pepper**

Drain the chickpeas, put them in a pan and fill the pan with plenty of cold water. Bring to the boil and boil for 1 minute, then lower the heat and partially cover the pan. Simmer the chickpeas for about 45 minutes, or until tender.

Drain the chickpeas in a colander, rinse well under cold running water and remove any loose skins by rubbing them in a dry, clean dish towel.

Gently melt the butter with the oil in a heavy pan, stir in the onion and cook until it softens. Add the rice and chickpeas to the pan and cover with the water or stock. Season with salt and pepper and bring to the boil. Lower the heat, partially cover the pan and simmer for about 10 minutes, until almost all of the water has been absorbed.

Turn off the heat, cover the pan with a clean, dry dish towel and put the lid tightly on top. Leave the rice to steam for 10 minutes, then fluff up with a fork before serving.

# Sour cherry pilaff

This popular summer pilaff *vişneli pilav* is made with fresh, small, sour cherries rather than the more common plump, sweet ones. With its refreshing bursts of flavour, it makes a good accompaniment to most vegetable, meat and fish dishes. If you are unable to obtain fresh sour cherries, you can use dried ones or dried cranberries instead – or barberries if you can find them.

## Serves three to four

**30ml/2 tbsp butter**

**225g/8oz fresh or dried sour cherries, such as morello, pitted if fresh**

**5–10ml/1–2 tsp sugar**

**5ml/1 tsp caraway seeds**

**225g/8oz/generous 1 cup long grain rice, well rinsed and drained**

**salt and ground black pepper**

Melt the butter in a heavy pan. Set a handful of the cherries aside, and toss the rest in the butter with the sugar and caraway seeds. Cook for a few minutes, then add the rice and 600ml/1 pint/2½ cups water. Season with salt and pepper to taste.

Bring the mixture to the boil, lower the heat and partially cover the pan. Simmer for 10–12 minutes, until most of the water has been absorbed. Turn off the heat, cover with a dish towel, and put the lid tightly on top. Leave for 20 minutes.

Fluff up the rice with a fork, transfer to a serving dish and garnish with the reserved cherries.

## Cook's tip

Due to their acidity, sour cherries are often consumed cooked or poached with sugar in sorbets, jam, bread pudding, cakes, and in a pretty compôte that is traditionally spooned over rice or yogurt.

# Chicken liver pilaff with currants, pine nuts and almonds

This is such a traditional Istanbul dish. Flavoured with cinnamon and rich morsels of chicken liver, *iç pilavı* is in a league of its own. Sophisticated and tasty, it is delicious by itself with lemon or natural yogurt but is also served as an accompaniment to meat dishes.

## Serves four to six

**30ml/2 tbsp currants**

**45ml/3 tbsp ghee, butter or olive oil**

**1 onion, chopped**

**30–45ml/2–3 tbsp pine nuts**

**45ml/3 tbsp blanched almonds**

**5–10ml/1–2 tsp ground allspice**

**5ml/1 tsp ground cinnamon**

**350g/12oz/2 cups long grain rice, thoroughly rinsed and drained**

**about 750ml/1¼ pints/3 cups chicken stock**

**250g/9oz chicken livers, cut into bitesize pieces**

**a bunch of flat leaf parsley, leaves finely chopped**

**a small bunch of dill, finely chopped, plus a few fronds for garnish**

**15ml/1 tbsp pine nuts**

**salt and ground black pepper**

**lemon wedges, to serve**

Soak the currants in warm water for 15 minutes and then drain. Melt 30ml/2 tbsp of the ghee in a heavy pan and stir in the onion. Cook until softened.

Add the pine nuts and almonds. When they begin to turn golden, stir in the currants, spices and rice and mix well.

Pour in the stock, season with salt and pepper, and bring to the boil. Reduce the heat and simmer until the liquid has been absorbed. Turn off the heat, cover the pan with a clean dish towel, and place the lid on tightly. Leave to steam for 10–15 minutes.

Meanwhile, melt the remaining ghee in a heavy pan and sauté the chicken livers until nicely browned. Fluff up the rice with a fork and toss in the chicken livers and herbs.

Dry-roast the pine nuts in a small frying pan until golden. Transfer the pilaff to a serving dish and garnish with the extra dill fronds. Sprinkle over the pine nuts and serve with lemon wedges for squeezing.

## Cook's tip

At Kurban Bayramı, the liver of the slaughtered lamb is used instead of chicken livers.

# Rice with spiced lamb

When you travel in central and eastern Anatolia you come across substantial rice anc bulgur dishes named after the regions they hail from, such as Uzbekistan, Turkmenistan, and Azerbaijan. The roots of this particular dish, *kaşgar pilav*, are in Mongolia. Cooked in a large pan it is eaten communally with yogurt as a meal on its own.

## Serves four

**about 450g/1lb lamb, cubed**

**30ml/2 tbsp ghee, or olive oil and butter**

**2 onions, chopped**

**4 garlic cloves, chopped**

**2 medium carrots, peeled and coarsely grated**

**350g/12oz/2 cups long grain rice, rinsed and thoroughly drained**

**5ml/1 tsp ground cinnamon**

**10ml/2 tsp ground allspice**

**1 litre/1¾ pints/4 cups lamb or chicken stock**

**salt and ground black pepper**

**a few sprigs of flat leaf parsley, to garnish**

**thick and creamy natural (plain) yogurt, to serve**

Heat a wide, heavy, non-stick frying pan. Toss the meat quickly on its own in the pan, frying it in its own juices, until it is lightly browned. Remove the lamb and keep to one side.

Heat the ghee, or olive oil and butter, in the pan and stir in the onions and garlic. Cook until they begin to colour. Toss in the cubed lamb and cook for 1–2 minutes, then stir in the carrots.

Toss in the rice with the spices and pour in the stock. Stir the rice and season with salt and pepper. Bring to the boil and boil for 1–2 minutes, then reduce the heat and simmer for 10–12 minutes, or until all the liquid has been absorbed.

Turn off the heat, cover the pan with a clean dish towel and place the lid on top. Leave to steam for 10–15 minutes.

Transfer to a serving dish, garnish with the parsley sprigs and serve with dollops of creamy natural yogurt.

## Cook's tip

Use leftover cooked lamb if you have available.

# Veiled pilaff

This splendid-looking rice dish is traditionally prepared for weddings in parts of Anatolia. Literally translated as 'veiled' or 'curtained' rice, *perdeli pilav* is prepared by baking the grains within a *yufka* dome. Medieval recipes for this dish included partridges which symbolised peace; the pistachio nuts and almonds represented children; and the rice was a symbol of abundance. In the modern version chicken has replaced the partridges and, although some village versions still encase the rice in sheets of *yufka*, the more elaborate creations utilise puff pastry to create the desired shape of an Ottoman headdress decorated with nuts to represent jewels.

## Serves six to eight

**45ml/3 tbsp olive oil**

**30ml/2 tbsp butter**

**175g/6oz blanched almonds**

**115g/4oz blanched pistachio nuts**

**350g/12oz/2 cups medium grain rice, rinsed thoroughly**

**10ml/2 tsp sugar**

**900ml/1½ pints/3¾ cups chicken stock**

**225g/8oz puff pastry, thawed if frozen**

**flour, for dusting**

**500g/1¼lb cooked chicken meat, shredded or cut into small pieces**

**1 egg yolk**

**10ml/2 tsp nigella seeds**

**salt and ground black pepper**

To garnish

**30ml/2 tbsp blanched pistachio nuts**

**15ml/1 tbsp butter**

Preheat the oven to 180°C/350°F/Gas 4 and lightly grease a round baking tin or pan.

Heat 15ml/1 tbsp of the olive oil and butter in a large, heavy pan and stir in the blanched almonds and pistachio nuts for 3 minutes, until they begin to colour. Add the rice and the sugar, making sure the rice grains are completely coated in the butter. Pour in the stock and bring to the boil. Season to taste with salt and pepper, reduce the heat, and simmer for 10–12 minutes, or until the stock has been absorbed.

On a floured surface roll out the puff pastry thinly into a circle (reserve a small, apricot-sized portion for the top). Press the pastry into the baking tin with the edges overlapping the sides.

Form the rice into a dome in the middle and arrange the cooked chicken shreds over the top and around the edges. Pull up the sides of the pastry over the rice and chicken, overlapping the edges to seal in the rice.

Roll out the reserved portion of pastry into a square. Trim off six thin strips (the width of matchsticks) and set aside for decorating. Brush the top of the dome with a little egg yolk and place the pastry square over the top to cover the sealed edges – or you can roll the square of pastry into a ball to represent a jewel at the top of the dome.

Beat the remainder of the egg yolk with the remaining olive oil and brush it all over the pastry dome. Decorate the dome with the pastry strips, placing them on the pastry to create segments over the dome so that it looks like a turban. Brush the strips with the egg and olive oil mixture. Sprinkle a few nigella seeds over the dome and place it in the oven.

Bake for about 25–30 minutes, or until the pastry is golden brown all over. Carefully remove the domed pastry from the tin and place it on a serving dish. For the garnish, melt the butter in a frying pan and toss in the pistachio nuts, until they begin to brown. Pour the nuts and the butter over the pastry dome and serve immediately.

# Fish and shellfish

Buying fish straight off the boats or from the markets is an education. There's such a wonderful variety, often still swimming around in buckets or kept fresh on beds of ice. The fishermen and market sellers are often knowledgeable and willing to help you select and prepare the fish for your chosen dish, such as a good-sized mackerel to stuff with nuts and spices, the right size of anchovy to poach in vine leaves, or perfect baby squid to stuff and poach in saffron oil.

# Anchovies poached in vine leaves

This is an ingenious way of cooking small anchovies and sprats that you can just pick up with your fingers and pop into your mouth. Popular with street vendors and fish restaurants, especially in early summer, *hamsi sarması* are sweet and juicy in their vine leaf wraps, which add texture and a slight malty flavour. They are best served with a squeeze of lemon or sprinkling of sumac.

## Serves four to six

**about 24 fresh anchovies, gutted and cleaned, with the backbone removed**

**about 24 fresh or preserved vine leaves, plus extra for lining the pan**

**60ml/4 tbsp olive oil**

**juice of 1 lemon**

**1–2 garlic cloves, crushed (optional)**

**5–10ml/1–2 tsp sumac**

**salt and ground black pepper**

**lemon wedges, to serve**

Place the anchovies on a flat surface and wrap them individually in vine leaves with their heads poking out.

Line a shallow pan with a few of the extra vine leaves and place the wrapped anchovies on top, packing them together quite tightly.

Mix the olive oil and lemon juice together, beat in the garlic, if using, and salt and pepper. Pour the mixture over the anchovies.

Place a plate directly on top of the wrapped anchovies to keep them in place while cooking. Cover the pan and poach the anchovies gently for 10 minutes.

Arrange the anchovies on a serving dish with the lemon wedges for squeezing over. Sprinkle a little sumac over the top of the fish and eat them whole while still hot, or at room temperature.

# Jewelled mackerel salad in a dome

Shaped like a Sultan's turban, *uskumru salatası* is another Ottoman classic. Artistically prepared with fresh mackerel, tomatoes, pine nuts and currants, it is often served at celebratory feasts or as part of an elaborate meze spread.

## Serves two to four

**15ml/1 tbsp currants**

**3 tomatoes**

**sunflower oil, for shallow-frying**

**2 fresh mackerel, gutted and thoroughly cleaned**

**45ml/3 tbsp pine nuts**

**30ml/2 tbsp olive oil**

**1 crisp cos or romaine lettuce, cut into thin strips**

**a handful of fresh rocket (arugula) leaves**

**a bunch of fresh dill fronds, stalks removed**

**1 red onion, sliced into thin rings**

For the dressing

**60–75ml/4–5 tbsp olive oil**

**juice of 1 lemon**

**15ml/1 tbsp apple or white wine vinegar**

**5ml/1 tsp yellow mustard**

**5–10ml/1–2 tsp clear honey**

**salt and ground black pepper**

Soak the currants in warm water for 15 minutes then drain them.

Plunge the tomatoes into a large bowl of boiling water for 30 seconds, then refresh immediately in cold water. Peel away the tomato skins with your fingers, then remove the seeds and cut the flesh into thin strips (reserve one slice for the top of the dome).

Heat enough sunflower oil in a heavy pan for shallow-frying, and fry the mackerel for 5–6 minutes on each side. Drain on kitchen paper and leave to cool. Alternatively, you can grill or broil the mackerel. Peel the skin off the mackerel and cut the flesh into long fingers.

In a small, heavy pan, fry the pine nuts in the olive oil, until they begin to colour. Toss in the currants to plump them up, then pour them on to kitchen paper to drain. Leave to cool.

Arrange the lettuce and rocket leaves in a dome in the centre of a round serving dish. Arrange the mackerel fingers around the sides of the dome, laying them gently on top of the leaves, and interspersing them with strips of tomato. Place the reserved slice of tomato on the very top of the dome.

Decorate the dome with the dill fronds, placing a little sprig on the top, and arrange the red onion rings around the base. Sprinkle the pine nuts and currants over the dome and around the base. The whole effect should be like an elaborately jewelled crown.

To make the dressing, mix together all the ingredients in a bowl and season to taste. Pour over the salad and serve immediately, with fresh, crusty bread.

# Mackerel pilâki

*Pilâki* dishes are distinctive in their use of root vegetables – usually carrots, potatoes and celeriac – cooked in tomato, garlic and olive oil. The most common *pilâki* are prepared with borlotti beans, fish or shellfish. It can be served hot or cold, or baked in the oven like this classic *uskumru pilâki*.

## Serves four to six

**2 good-sized fresh mackerel, gutted and rinsed**

**120ml/4fl oz/½ cup olive oil**

**2 onions, chopped**

**3–4 garlic cloves, chopped**

**1 mild fresh green chilli, deseeded and chopped**

**2–3 carrots, diced**

**2–3 potatoes, diced**

**1 medium celeriac, weighing about 450g/1lb, peeled, trimmed and diced**

**2 large tomatoes, skinned and chopped, or 400g/14oz can of chopped tomatoes, drained of juice**

**5ml/1 tsp sugar**

**2–3 bay leaves**

**juice of 2 lemons**

**a small bunch of fresh flat leaf parsley**

**salt and ground black pepper**

Preheat the oven to 170°C/325°F/Gas 3. Using a large, sharp knife, cut into the fish crossways, 2cm/¾in apart, keeping it intact at the backbone.

Heat the oil in a large, heavy pan. Stir in the onions, garlic and chilli and cook until soft. Add the carrots, potatoes and celeriac to the pan and cook for 1–2 minutes, then stir in the tomatoes, sugar and bay leaves.

Pour in 600ml/1 pint/2½ cups water and bring the mixture to the boil. Lower the heat, cover the pan and simmer for 5–10 minutes, until the vegetables are tender but not mushy. Season with salt and pepper to taste.

Spoon half the vegetables over the bottom of an ovenproof dish, then place the fish on top and spoon the remaining vegetables over them. Sprinkle with the lemon juice and lay a few sprigs of parsley on top.

Cover with baking parchment that has been soaked in water and squeezed out, then place in the oven for 20 minutes, or until the fish is cooked.

Remove the paper and parsley sprigs and serve the fish immediately, garnished with some roughly chopped parsley. If you like you can leave the *pilâki* to cool in the dish and serve at room temperature.

## Variation

Mussel *pilâki* is sought-after in Istanbul and Izmir, and an old Ottoman favourite, oyster *pilâki*, is appearing again on the culinary scene.

# Stuffed mackerel

During the inventive years in the Ottoman Palace kitchens, where many stuffed dishes were created, this inspired one emerged. A genuine classic, *uskumru dolması* is more often a restaurant dish than a home-cooked one as it is quite fiddly to make. First you have to skilfully massage the mackerel to empty it of flesh and bones while keeping the skin intact, so that it can be stuffed to resemble the whole fish once more before it is fried, baked or grilled to serve. The result is impressive and tasty.

## Serves four

**1 large, fresh mackerel, scaled and thoroughly washed, but not gutted**

**30–45ml/2–3 tbsp olive oil**

**4–5 shallots, finely chopped**

**30ml/2 tbsp pine nuts**

**30ml/2 tbsp blanched almonds, finely slivered**

**45ml/3 tbsp walnuts, finely chopped**

**15–30ml/1–2 tbsp currants, soaked in warm water for 5–10 minutes and drained**

**6–8 dried apricots, finely chopped**

**5–10ml/1–2 tsp ground cinnamon**

**5ml/1 tsp ground allspice**

**5ml/1 tsp *pul biber*, or 2.5ml/½ tsp chilli powder**

**2.5ml/½ tsp ground cloves**

**5ml/1 tsp sugar**

**a small bunch each of fresh flat leaf parsley and dill, finely chopped, retaining a few sprigs for garnish**

**juice of 1 lemon**

**plain (all-purpose) flour, for dusting**

**sunflower oil, for shallow-frying**

**salt and ground black pepper**

**lemon wedges, to serve**

Take a sharp knife and cut an opening just below the gills of the mackerel, making sure the head and backbone remain intact. Push your finger into the opening and remove the guts, then rinse the fish inside and out. Using a rolling pin or mallet, gently bash the fish on both sides, making sure you smash the backbone. Now, with your hands, gently massage the skin to loosen it away from the flesh – don't pummel it too hard or the skin will tear.

Working from the tail end towards the head, squeeze the loosened flesh out of the opening below the gills – use a similar motion to squeezing a half-empty tube of toothpaste. Remove any bones from the loosened flesh, then rinse out the mackerel sack and set aside.

Heat the oil in a frying pan, stir in the shallots and cook until soft. Add the nuts and stir until they just begin to colour. Add the currants, apricots, spices and sugar and mix thoroughly. Mix in the fish flesh and cook through for 2–3 minutes, then toss in the herbs and lemon juice and season to taste with salt and pepper.

Lift up the empty mackerel skin and carefully push the filling through the opening, shaking the sack a little to jiggle the filling down towards the tail. As the skin begins to fill, gently squeeze the mixture downwards to make it compact, until it looks like a plump, fresh mackerel once more.

To cook the mackerel, toss it in flour and fry it in sunflower oil, or brush with a little oil and grill or broil until the skin begins to turn brown and buckle.

To serve, cut the fish crossways into thick slices and arrange on a dish in the shape of the fish. Garnish with dill and parsley and serve with lemon wedges for squeezing over.

# Baked sardines with tomatoes

With the hillsides covered in herbs, aromatic fish dishes like this *fırında sardalya* are a common feature of the Aegean and Mediterranean coasts. Purple basil, which has a mild aniseed taste, is used frequently, although the green-leafed sweet basil and lemon basil work just as well as they impart their own aroma and flavour. Serve with crusty bread.

## Serves four

**8 large sardines, scaled, gutted and thoroughly washed**

**6–8 fresh thyme sprigs**

**juice of ½ lemon**

**2 x 400g/14oz cans of chopped tomatoes, drained of juice**

**60–75ml/4–5 tbsp olive oil**

**4 garlic cloves, smashed flat**

**5ml/1 tsp sugar**

**a bunch of fresh purple basil**

**salt and ground black pepper**

**lemon wedges, to serve**

Preheat the oven to 180°C/350°F/Gas 4.

Lay the sardines side by side in an ovenproof dish, place sprigs of thyme between and over the fish, and squeeze the lemon juice over them.

In a bowl, mix the tomatoes, olive oil, garlic and sugar. Season the mixture and stir in the basil leaves, then spoon the mixture over the sardines.

Bake, uncovered, for 25 minutes. Serve hot with lemon wedges for squeezing over.

# Stuffed sardines

When you buy your fish at the market you will be told exactly which sardines to use for this dish, *ızgara sardalya dolması*, as you need nice plump ones to hold the stuffing. This is a great dish for cooking outdoors on the barbecue but you can also cook under a conventional grill. If you can't find sardines you can adapt the recipe to red mullet, small mackerel or trout.

## Serves four

**15ml/1 tbsp currants**

**4 good-sized sardines, gutted**

**30ml/2 tbsp olive oil**

**6 spring onions (scallions), finely sliced**

**2–3 garlic cloves, crushed**

**5ml/1 tsp cumin seeds, crushed**

**5ml/1 tsp sumac**

**15ml/1 tbsp pine nuts**

**a small bunch of flat leaf parsley, leaves finely chopped**

**salt and ground black pepper**

**lemon wedges, to serve**

For basting

**45ml/3 tbsp olive oil**

**juice of 1 lemon**

**5–10ml/1–2 tsp sumac**

Prepare the barbecue, if using. Soak four wooden skewers in cold water for 30 minutes. Soak the currants in warm water for 15 minutes, then drain them.

Slit the sardines from head to tail and remove each backbone by gently massaging the area around it to loosen it. Using your fingers, carefully prise out the bone, snapping it off at each end, while keeping the fish intact. Rinse the fish and pat it dry.

Heat the oil in a heavy pan, stir in the spring onions and cook until soft. Add the garlic, cumin and sumac. Stir in the pine nuts and currants, and fry until they begin to turn golden. Toss in the parsley, and season to taste with salt and pepper. Leave to cool.

Heat the grill, if using. Place each sardine on a flat surface and spread the filling inside each one. Seal by threading the skewers through the soft belly flaps. Mix together the olive oil, lemon juice and sumac, and brush some of it over the sardines.

Place the fish on the rack over the hot coals and cook them for 2–3 minutes each side over a medium heat, basting them with the remainder of the olive oil mixture. Serve immediately, with lemon wedges for squeezing.

# Chargrilled sardines in vine leaves

My favourite way to enjoy fresh fish plucked straight from sea is to chargrill it in the open air – nothing quite beats the smoky aroma and taste of *ızgara sardalya*. The tangy, charred vine leaves and tomatoes make perfect partners for the oily flesh of the fish, which only requires a little lemon to refresh it.

## Serves three to four

**12 sardines, scaled, gutted and thoroughly washed**

**30ml/2 tbsp olive oil, plus extra for brushing**

**juice of ½ lemon**

**12 fresh or preserved vine leaves (see Cook's tip)**

**4–6 vine tomatoes, halved or quartered**

**salt and ground black pepper**

**lemon wedges, to serve**

For the dressing

**60ml/4 tbsp olive oil**

**juice of 1 lemon**

**15ml/1 tbsp balsamic or white wine vinegar**

**5–10ml/1–2 tsp clear honey**

**5ml/1 tsp *pul biber*, or 1 fresh red chilli, finely chopped**

**a few fresh dill fronds and flat leaf parsley sprigs, finely chopped**

**salt and ground black pepper, to taste**

Prepare the barbecue half an hour before you want to cook and eat.

Put all the dressing ingredients in a medium-sized bowl, and mix well to combine thoroughly.

Pat the sardines dry with kitchen paper and lay them in a flat dish. Mix 30ml/2 tbsp of the olive oil with the lemon juice and brush the mixture over all the sardines.

Spread the vine leaves out on a flat surface and place a sardine on each leaf. Sprinkle each one with a little salt and wrap loosely in the leaf like a cigar, with the tail and head poking out.

Brush each vine leaf with a little olive oil and place seam-side down to keep it from unravelling. Thread the tomatoes on skewers and sprinkle them with a little salt.

Place the sardines and tomatoes on the prepared barbecue and cook for 2–3 minutes on each side, until the vine leaves are charred and the tomatoes are soft.

Transfer the vine leaves and tomatoes to a large serving dish and drizzle with the dressing. Serve immediately, with lemon wedges.

## Cook's tip

Fresh vine leaves are sold in Turkish markets, and you can get them in Middle Eastern and Mediterranean stores when they are in season in the autumn. Plunged into boiling water for a minute, the bright green leaves soften and turn a deep olive colour, indicating they are ready for use. If you can't get fresh, you can use the ones preserved in brine that are available in packets. They require soaking to remove the salt. In a bowl, pour boiling water over and leave to soak for about an hour. Drain and rinse under cold running water, then pat dry.

# Swordfish, lemon and red pepper kebabs

Any firm-fleshed fish, such as tuna, trout, salmon, monkfish or sea bass, can be used for kebabs, but the classic *kiliç şiş*, made with meaty chunks of swordfish, is a favourite in restaurants. Usually served as a main course with a rocket and herb salad, they are light and tasty – ideal for a summer lunch or a light supper.

## Serves four

**500g/1¼lb boneless swordfish loin or steaks, cut into bitesize chunks**

**1 lemon, halved lengthways and sliced**

**1 large tomato, halved, deseeded and cut into bitesize pieces**

**2 hot green peppers (see Cook's tip) or 1 green bell pepper, deseeded and cut into bitesize pieces**

**a handful of bay leaves**

**lemon wedges, to serve**

For the marinade

**1 onion, grated**

**1–2 garlic cloves, crushed**

**juice of ½ lemon**

**30–45ml/2–3 tbsp olive oil**

**10ml/2 tsp tomato purée (paste)**

**salt and ground black pepper**

Mix together the marinade ingredients in a large, shallow bowl. Toss in the chunks of swordfish and set aside for about 30 minutes to marinate and absorb the flavours.

Thread the fish chunks on to skewers, alternating with the lemon slices, tomato and peppers and the occasional bay leaf. If there is any marinade left, brush it over the kebabs.

Put a cast-iron griddle pan over a medium heat and leave until very hot. Place the skewers on the pan and cook for 2–3 minutes on each side until the kebab ingredients are quite charred. Serve the kebabs hot, with lemon wedges for squeezing.

## Cook's tip

In Turkish, hot green peppers are called *çarliston biber*. They are light green, and shaped like Turkish slippers. Most *çarliston biber* are sweet, and mainly used raw in meze and salads, but some have a hint of heat and are good for cooked dishes like the kebabs here. Look out for them in Turkish and Middle Eastern stores.

# Seared tuna with sage, parsley and dill

In general, Turks cook their fish and meat to a point that some Western cultures would consider overcooked. As both are often marinated with spices and herbs, this affects the texture more than taste, but tuna steaks are undoubtedly best when they are simply seared to ensure the flesh is pink inside, as in this version of *ızgara orkinos*.

## Serves four

**60ml/4 tbsp olive oil, plus extra for greasing**

**juice of 1 lemon**

**a small bunch of fresh sage, leaves finely chopped or shredded**

**a small bunch of flat leaf parsley, leaves finely chopped**

**a small bunch of fresh dill, finely chopped, plus fronds to garnish**

**4 thick tuna steaks**

**salt and ground black pepper**

In a small bowl, mix together the olive oil and lemon juice with the herbs and season it with salt and pepper. Set this dressing aside.

Smear a couple of drops of olive oil over the surface of a heavy frying pan or griddle. Place it over the heat until hot. Sear the tuna steaks for 1 minute on both sides and sprinkle them with a little salt.

Quickly transfer the steaks to a serving dish and spoon the dressing over them. Garnish with the dill fronds and serve immediately.

## Cook's tip

Raw tuna features in a popular meze dish called *lekerda*. Cured in a mixture of lemon juice and dill, the meltingly succulent tuna fillets are a frequent sight on the meze tables of Istanbul and Izmir.

# Sea perch baked on a tile with poppy seeds

Along the Black Sea coast and in parts of central Anatolia, the curved earthenware tiles, used for the roofs of houses, also serve as practical cooking vessels. The shape of the tile lends itself ideally to containing whole fish, the favourite being blue fish, but whole trout, sea bass or salmon can be also be cooked in this way. For this recipe, *kiremitte haşhaş lüfer*, the fish is wrapped in cabbage leaves. If you don't have a suitable tile you can bake the fish in an ovenproof dish.

## Serves two

**1 good-sized blue fish or sea perch, or sea bass, trout or salmon, about 500g/1¼lb, gutted and cleaned**

**5–6 red or green cabbage leaves**

**50g/2oz butter, melted**

**30ml/2 tbsp poppy seeds**

**lemon wedges, to serve**

For the marinade

**2 large onions, grated**

**sea salt**

**30ml/2 tbsp olive oil**

**juice of 1 lemon**

**10ml/2 tsp pink peppercorns, crushed**

**2–3 bay leaves, crushed with your fingers**

To make the marinade, put the grated onion on a plate and sprinkle with salt. Leave to weep for 5 minutes. Transfer the mixture to a piece of muslin or cheesecloth, and squeeze tightly to extract the juice. Mix the juice with the olive oil and lemon juice and stir in the peppercorns and bay leaves.

Place the fish in a dish and spoon the marinade all over it, inside and out. Cover and refrigerate for 2 hours.

Preheat the oven to 200°C/400°F/Gas 6. Soften the cabbage leaves by plunging them into a pan of boiling water for 1 minute.

If using a tile, heat it in the oven for 10 minutes, then remove with oven gloves. Brush a little oil over the surface of the tile, or an ovenproof dish. Line with several cabbage leaves, then lay the fish on top, and place the remaining cabbage leaves over the top to totally enclose the fish.

Return to the oven and bake for about 20 minutes. Remove the top cabbage leaves and pour the melted butter over the fish. Sprinkle with poppy seeds and return it to the oven for a further 10 minutes. Serve immediately with lemon to squeeze over.

Left **Sea bass with rakı** Right **Deep-fried red mullet with rocket**

# Sea bass with rakı

Aniseed-flavoured *rakı* is Turkey's national spirit and the preferred drink to accompany meze and fish dishes. On occasion it is used for cooking seafood, particularly fried prawns and octopus, or whole fish such as red mullet and sea bass. For this dish, *rakı soslu levrek*, the fish is first grilled and then doused in *rakı* and set alight; a trick that restaurant waiters carry out with great panache.

## Serves four

**2 good-sized sea bass, gutted and cleaned**

**30–45ml/2–3 tbsp olive oil**

**about 150ml/¼ pint/⅔ cup *rakı***

**2 large white radishes, grated**

**juice of 1 lemon, and lemon wedges to serve**

**salt and ground black pepper**

**flat leaf parsley, to garnish**

First preheat the grill or broiler. Line the grill pan with a piece of foil and place the fish on it. Brush the fish on both sides with the olive oil and season with salt and pepper. Place the fish under the preheated grill and cook for 6–8 minutes on each side, allowing the skin to buckle and brown.

Remove the fish from the grill and pour the *rakı* over them. Set the *rakı* alight and flambé the fish until the flames die down. (If you prefer, you could fry the fish and flambé it in the pan.)

In a bowl, toss the grated radish with the lemon juice and a sprinkling of salt. Divide the fish among serving plates and garnish with chopped parsley. Serve immediately with the grated radish and lemon to squeeze.

# Deep-fried red mullet with rocket

The sweet flesh of red mullet is a huge favourite in Istanbul and Izmir. Grilled or deep-fried with garlic, sprinkled with sumac, and served with rocket leaves and a glass of *rakı*, *barbunya tavası* spells perfection to many Turks who enjoy their fish or meat fairly plain after meze dishes.

## Serves two to four

**a bunch of fresh flat leaf parsley, leaves chopped**

**15–30ml/1–2 tbsp sumac**

**4–5 garlic cloves, crushed**

**4 red mullet, gutted and cleaned**

**salt**

**plain (all-purpose) flour, for coating**

**sunflower oil, for deep-frying**

**a bunch of fresh rocket (arugula) leaves**

**lemon wedges, to serve**

Mix the chopped parsley with half the sumac and half the crushed garlic, and stuff it into the gutted cavity of each fish. Mix the remainder of the garlic with some salt and rub it all over the outside of the fish.

Roll each fish in flour, until it is completely coated.

Heat enough oil in a large, heavy pan for deep-frying. Pop in the fish and fry for about 5 minutes until golden brown. Lift the fish out of the oil and drain on kitchen paper.

Arrange the rocket leaves on a serving dish. Place the fish on the rocket, sprinkle with the remaining sumac, and serve with the lemon wedges to squeeze over them.

# Sea bass parcels with cinnamon and mastic

With a delightful hint of tree resin and a mild chewy twang from the mastic, this dish – *kağitta levrek* – is a pleasant surprise. To cook with mastic, you first need to pulverise it with salt in a pestle and mortar, and then seal it with the fish in foil or parchment paper to capture the flavour.

## Serves four

**4 tomatoes**

**30ml/2 tbsp olive oil**

**30ml/2 tbsp butter**

**2–3 red onions, cut in half lengthways and sliced along the grain**

**2 light green peppers, or 1 green bell pepper, deseeded and sliced**

**5ml/1 tsp sugar**

**2 bay leaves, crushed**

**4 cloves, crushed**

**4 sea bass fillets**

**4 pieces of mastic, pulverised with a little salt**

**1 cinnamon stick, broken into 4 pieces**

**salt and ground black pepper**

Preheat the oven to 180°C/350°F/Gas 4. Plunge the tomatoes into boiling water for 30 seconds, then refresh in cold water. Peel away the skins, remove the seeds and chop the flesh.

In a heavy pan, heat the oil with the butter until it has melted. Stir in the onions and peppers, and cook until soft. Add the tomatoes, sugar, bay leaves and cloves, and cook gently for about 5 minutes. Season with salt and pepper, and leave to cool.

Cut four pieces of foil large enough to enclose a fish fillet each, and spread them out on a flat surface. Spoon a little of the onion and tomato mixture on to each piece of foil, spreading it flat, and place a fish fillet on top. Sprinkle the pulverised mastic over the fillets.

Spoon the remaining onion and tomato mixture over and around the fillets, and place a piece of cinnamon stick on top of each one.

Wrap up the parcels into little packets, by pulling up the sides and pinching the edges tightly, leaving a little room for steam to escape. Brush some water over the parcels and place them on a baking tray. Put them in the oven for about 15–20 minutes.

Place the parcels on individual plates, or on a serving dish, and open them up to let the aroma whet the appetite.

# Cinnamon fishcakes with currants, pine nuts and herbs

I often prepare these fishcakes, *balık köftesi*, as a hot meze dish but they are also delicious served on their own for lunch or supper. Flavoured with cinnamon and the ubiquitous triad of herbs – parsley, mint and dill – variations are popular throughout the Aegean and Mediterranean regions.

## Serves four

**450g/1lb skinless fresh white fish fillets, such as haddock or sea bass**

**2 slices of day-old bread, sprinkled with water and left for a few minutes, then squeezed dry**

**1 red onion, finely chopped**

**30ml/2 tbsp currants, soaked in warm water for 5–10 minutes and drained**

**30ml/2 tbsp pine nuts**

**a small bunch each of fresh flat leaf parsley, mint and dill, finely chopped, plus extra to garnish**

**1 egg**

**5–10ml/1–2 tsp tomato purée (paste) or ketchup**

**15ml/1 tbsp ground cinnamon**

**45–60ml/3–4 tbsp plain (all-purpose) flour, for coating**

**45–60ml/3–4 tbsp sunflower oil, for shallow-frying**

**salt and ground black pepper**

**lemon or lime wedges, to serve**

In a bowl, break up the fish with a fork. Add the bread, onion, currants and pine nuts, toss in the chopped fresh herbs, and mix.

In another small bowl, beat the egg with the tomato purée and 10ml/2 tsp of the cinnamon. Pour the mixture over the fish and season with salt and pepper to taste, then mix with your hands and mould into small balls.

Mix the flour on a plate with the remaining cinnamon. Press each ball into a flat cake and coat in the flour.

Heat the oil in a wide, shallow pan and fry the fishcakes in batches for 8–10 minutes, until golden brown. Lift out and drain on kitchen paper. Serve hot with a garnish of fresh herbs, and lemon or lime wedges for squeezing.

# Sea bass baked in salt

This ancient method of cooking in salt to intensify the freshness of the fish and to bleach the colour of the flesh does emphasise the taste of the sea. However, depending on the size of your fish, it does require a lot of salt. The fish is completely concealed in a mask of salt and then baked in the oven until it resembles a hard shell. If you are eating this in a restaurant, the waiters will proudly bring this baked shell to your table and crack it open with a mallet in front of you for effect. When the shell is lifted off, the skin comes off too, revealing the beautiful white flesh of the cooked fish. For supreme enjoyment, little else is needed – sauces would disguise the freshness. Serve *turzlanmış balık* on its own with lemon wedges, freshly ground black pepper and a tomato or rocket salad.

## Serves two to four

**1.2kg/2½lb very fresh sea bass, gutted, with head and tail left on**

**about 1kg/2¼lb coarse sea salt**

**ground black pepper and lemon wedges, to serve**

Preheat the oven to 190°C/375°F/Gas 5. Rinse the fish well, inside and out.

Find an ovenproof dish to fit the fish and cover the base with a thick layer of salt, pressing it down with the heel of your hand. Place the fish on top and spoon salt over it until it is completely covered, then press down gently to compact the salt.

Put the dish in the preheated oven and bake for 1 hour, until the salt has formed a hard crust.

Place the dish on the table and make a show of cracking open the salt crust with a heavy object, such as a meat cleaver or a pestle.

Carefully peel off the top layer of salt using a knife, removing the skin of the fish with it.

Serve chunks of the delicate white flesh immediately, with nothing more than a little black pepper and a squeeze of lemon.

## Cook's tip

In Turkey, blue fish (also known as sea perch) is popular for this dish, but if you are unable to get it sea bass is a good alternative. You could also use any other firm-fleshed white fish, such as turbot or sole.

# Baked bonito with bay leaves

This is often a home-cooked dish in the coastal regions. A simple oven dish delicately perfumed with herbs and lemon. In this recipe, *fırında palamut*, fresh bay leaves are used but you can use dried ones or purple basil, lime leaves, rosemary, sage or thyme.

## Serves four

**4 tomatoes**

**2 fresh bonito, gutted, cleaned, and cut crossways into thick slices with the bone intact**

**2 red onions, halved lengthways and sliced**

**3 hot green peppers, or 2 green chillies, deseeded and cut in half lengthways**

**a bunch of flat leaf parsley, leaves chopped**

**6–8 fresh bay leaves**

**60–75ml/4–5 tbsp olive oil**

**30ml/2 tbsp butter**

**salt and ground black pepper**

**lemon wedges, to serve**

Preheat the oven to 180°C/350°F/Gas 4. Plunge the tomatoes into boiling water for 30 seconds, then refresh in cold water. Peel away the skins, then cut the tomatoes in half and slice them.

Arrange the fish in a shallow ovenproof earthenware dish and sprinkle them with a little salt and pepper. Arrange the onions, tomatoes and peppers over and around the fish, and sprinkle the parsley over the top. Tuck the bay leaves around the fish and pour over the olive oil.

Cover the dish with foil and place it in the oven for 30 minutes. Remove the foil and dot the fish with little pieces of butter. Place the dish back in the oven and leave for a further 10–15 minutes for the fish to brown slightly.

Serve hot with wedges of lemon to squeeze over the fish.

## Variation

This dish is also delicious with other fresh fish such as trout, salmon, sea bass or mackerel.

# Blue fish stew

This fish stew, *lüfer yahnisi*, epitomises basic home-cooked food in the coastal regions using simple, traditional ingredients: currants to sweeten, cinnamon to spice, and vinegar to sharpen. Serve the stew with plenty of crusty bread or a plain pilaff.

## Serves three to four

**30ml/2 tbsp currants**

**30ml/2 tbsp olive oil**

**15ml/1 tbsp butter**

**2 onions, halved lengthways and sliced with the grain**

**2 green bell peppers, deseeded and sliced**

**2–3 garlic cloves, chopped**

**10ml/2 tsp ground cinnamon**

**4 blue fish (sea perch) fillets, or sea bass or trout**

**15ml/1 tbsp apple or white wine vinegar**

**400g/14oz can of chopped tomatoes**

**120ml/4fl oz/½ cup water**

**salt and ground black pepper**

**a bunch of flat leaf parsley, leaves chopped, to garnish**

**pilaff, to serve (optional)**

Soak the currants in a bowl of warm water for 15 minutes and then drain.

Heat the olive oil and butter in a large, heavy pan, or a flameproof earthenware pot. Add the onions, peppers, garlic and currants, stir to mix thoroughly and cook until the onions begin to colour.

Stir in the cinnamon and add the fish fillets, making sure they are coated with the onions and peppers.

Add the vinegar, tomatoes and water, and bring the liquid to the boil.

Reduce the heat and simmer gently for 15–20 minutes, or until the fish is completely cooked. Season to taste with salt and pepper.

Serve the fish stew immediately, garnished with the flat leaf parsley, and accompanied by a plain pilaff or chunks of warm, crusty bread to mop up the sauce.

# Herb-stuffed squid with saffron

With their tradition of stuffing cavities, it is no surprise that the Turks have stuffed the sacs of tender baby squid to perfection. Impressive-looking and tasty, *kalamar dolması* can be served as a hot meze dish or as a main dish. In this recipe the sacs are stuffed Anatolian-style with bulgur wheat and herbs and baked in saffron oil, but you could use the Ottoman rice filling flavoured with allspice and cinnamon that is used in many of the stuffed vegetables.

## Serves four to six

**12 baby squid, thoroughly cleaned and prepared with the body sacs left whole (see Cook's Tip, page 288)**

**50g/2oz fine bulgur wheat, rinsed and drained**

**45ml/3 tbsp olive oil**

**juice of 1 lemon**

**120ml/4fl oz/½ cup white wine**

**a generous pinch of saffron threads**

**30ml/2 tbsp tomato purée (paste)**

**a large bunch of flat leaf parsley, leaves finely chopped**

**a large bunch of mint, leaves finely chopped**

**a large bunch of dill fronds, finely chopped**

**2–3 garlic cloves, finely chopped**

**salt and ground black pepper**

Prepare the squid. Preheat the oven to 180°C/350°F/Gas 4.

Put the bulgur wheat in a bowl and pour over just enough boiling water to cover it and no more. Place a clean dish towel over the bowl and leave for about 20 minutes to absorb the liquid. Once the water has been absorbed, the quantity of bulgur wheat will double in size.

In a small bowl whisk together 30ml/2 tbsp of the olive oil with the lemon juice, white wine and saffron. Put the mixture aside to allow the saffron to release its colour.

Using your fingers, rub the tomato purée into the bulgur wheat with the remaining olive oil, or combine everything well with a fork. Toss in the fresh herbs and garlic, and mix well to combine. Season to taste.

Using your fingers, or a teaspoon, stuff the herby bulgur wheat into the empty body sacs and plug the hole with the tentacles.

Place the stuffed squid into a shallow earthenware or ovenproof dish and pour over the saffron-coloured olive oil and lemon juice mixture. Place the dish in the preheated oven and bake for about 25 minutes. Serve immediately.

## Cook's tip

The common Turkish saffron is an imposter for the real thing as it is extracted from a variety of wild flowers rather than the crocus. It does lend a vibrant yellow-orange colour to dishes, but it doesn't have any taste and doesn't dissolve into the dish like the real thing, so you feel you are eating dried petals. Although real saffron is produced in small amounts in Turkey, most of it comes from Iran.

# Squid with olives and red wine

Although many Muslims do not drink alcohol, there are some surprisingly good wines available in Turkey and along the Mediterranean and Aegean coasts, and some restaurants incorporate wine in dishes. With olives and red wine, *sarhoş kalamar* is a delicious way to enjoy squid.

## Serves four

**30–45ml/2–3 tbsp olive oil**

**2 red onions, halved lengthways and sliced along the grain**

**3–4 garlic cloves, chopped**

**about 750g/1lb 10oz fresh squid, prepared (see Cook's tip) and cut into thick rings**

**45–60ml/3–4 tbsp black olives, pitted**

**5–10ml/1–2 tsp ground cinnamon**

**5–10ml/1–2 tsp sugar**

**300ml/½ pint/1¼ cups red wine**

**2 bay leaves**

**a small bunch each of fresh flat leaf parsley and dill, finely chopped**

**salt and ground black pepper**

**lemon wedges, to serve**

Heat the oil in a heavy pan and cook the onions and garlic until golden. Add the squid heads and rings and toss them in the pan for 2–3 minutes, until they begin to colour. Toss in the olives, cinnamon and sugar, pour in the wine and add the bay leaves.

Bubble up the liquid, then lower the heat and cover the pan. Cook gently for 35–40 minutes, until most of the liquid has reduced and the squid is tender.

Season the squid with salt and pepper to taste and toss in the herbs. Serve immediately, with lemon wedges to squeeze over.

## Cook's tip

Fresh squid should smell slightly sweet. Rinse it and peel off the thin film of skin, then sever the head and trim the tentacles with a sharp knife. With your finger, pull out the backbone and reach down into the body pouch to remove the ink sac and any mushy bits. Rinse the empty pouch thoroughly inside and out and pat dry. Use the pouch and trimmed head for cooking; discard the rest.

# Baked prawns with tomatoes, pepper and garlic

Lunch, supper, or a hot meze dish, *karides güveç* works for all. Traditionally cooked in a large earthenware pot (*güveç*), or in individual ones, it is delicious served with a salad.

## Serves four

**30–45ml/2–3 tbsp olive oil**

**1 onion, halved lengthways and finely sliced along the grain**

**1 green bell pepper, deseeded and finely sliced**

**2–3 garlic cloves, chopped**

**5–10ml/1–2 tsp coriander seeds**

**5–10ml/1–2 tsp *pul biber*, or 1 fresh red chilli, deseeded and chopped**

**5–10ml/1–2 tsp sugar**

**a splash of white wine vinegar**

**2 x 400g/14oz cans of chopped tomatoes**

**a small bunch of fresh flat leaf parsley, chopped**

**500g/1¼lb fresh raw prawns (shrimp), shelled, thoroughly cleaned and drained**

**about 120g/4oz *kaşar peyniri*, Parmesan or a strong, dry Cheddar, grated**

**salt and ground black pepper**

Heat the oil in a heavy pan, stir in the sliced onion, green pepper, garlic, coriander seeds and *pul biber* or chilli, and cook until they just begin to colour.

Stir in the sugar, vinegar, tomatoes and parsley, then cook gently for about 25 minutes, until you have a chunky sauce. While the sauce is cooking, preheat the oven to 200°C/400°F/Gas 6.

Season the sauce with salt and pepper to taste, and toss in the prawns, making sure that everything is thoroughly combined.

Spoon the mixture into individual earthenware pots and sprinkle the top with the grated cheese. Bake in the oven for 25 minutes, or until the cheese is nicely browned on top.

# Mussels stuffed with aromatic pilaff

Classic Ottoman food, and a popular meze dish in the fish restaurants and street food of Istanbul and Izmir, *midye dolması* are simply a delight. I love the sight of street vendors steaming them in big cauldrons on the Golden Horn and Bosphorus, wherever the boats and ferries come in.

## Serves four

**16 large fresh mussels**

**45–60ml/3–4 tbsp olive oil**

**2–3 shallots, finely chopped**

**30ml/2 tbsp pine nuts**

**30ml/2 tbsp currants, soaked in warm water for 5–10 minutes and drained**

**10ml/2 tsp ground cinnamon**

**5ml/1 tsp ground allspice**

**5–10ml/1–2 tsp sugar**

**5–10ml/1–2 tsp tomato purée (paste)**

**115g/4oz/generous ½ cup short grain or pudding rice, well rinsed and drained**

**a small bunch each of fresh flat leaf parsley, mint and dill, finely chopped**

**salt and ground black pepper**

**lemon wedges and fresh flat leaf parsley sprigs, to serve**

Clean the mussels as described in the Cook's tip. Keep them in a bowl of cold water while you prepare the stuffing.

Heat the oil in a heavy pan, stir in the shallots and cook until they soften. Add the pine nuts and currants, stir for 1–2 minutes until the pine nuts turn golden and the currants plump up, then stir in the cinnamon, allspice, sugar and tomato purée. Now add the rice, and stir until it is well coated.

Pour in enough water to just cover the rice. Season to taste with salt and pepper and bring to the boil. Lower the heat, partially cover the pan and simmer for 10–12 minutes, until all the water has been absorbed. Transfer the rice to a plate, leave to cool, then toss in the fresh herbs.

Using a sharp knife, prise open each mussel shell wide enough to fill with rice. Stuff a spoonful of rice into each shell, then close the shells and pack the mussels tightly into a steamer filled with water. Cover with a sheet of dampened baking parchment, put a plate on top and weigh it down with a stone – a clean one from the garden will do – to prevent the mussels from opening during steaming.

Place the lid on the steamer and bring the water to the boil. Lower the heat and steam the mussels gently for 15–20 minutes, then leave to cool a little in the pan.

Serve warm or at room temperature on a bed of parsley, with lemon wedges for squeezing over.

## Cook's tip

Place the mussels in a bowl of cold water and scrub the shells with a stiff brush. Pull out the tough beards and cut off the barnacles with a knife. Discard any mussels that are open, or that do not close when tapped on the work surface.

# Meat and poultry

The Turks are renowned carnivores, with a preference for lamb and mutton, and the enticing smell of spicy grilling is never far away. However there is more to Turkish meat dishes than the ubiquitous kebabs in their many guises. Lamb, beef and chicken are cooked every day, but goat, rabbit, quail and duck also appear in some traditional dishes. Notable meat favourites featured here include a variety of delicious Palace specialities, and the stews featuring nuts or fruits lend a medieval air to the predominantly grilled-meat table.

# Lamb kebabs in flat bread wraps

This popular Anatolian kebab, *çöp şiş*, is traditionally made with lamb scraps – *çöp* means rubbish – that are flavoured with onion, cumin and garlic and chargrilled on swords or skewers. The small pieces of cooked meat are then wrapped in freshly griddled flat bread with red onion, flat leaf parsley and a squeeze of lemon – like a modern wrap.

## Serves four to six

**2 onions**

**7.5ml/1½ tsp salt**

**2 garlic cloves, crushed**

**10ml/2 tsp cumin seeds, crushed**

**900g/2lb boneless shoulder of lamb, trimmed of fat and cut into bitesize pieces**

For the flat breads

**225g/8oz/2 cups strong white bread flour, plus extra for dusting**

**50g/2oz/½ cup wholemeal flour**

**5ml/1 tsp salt**

To serve

**1 large onion, halved lengthways, halved again crossways, and sliced along the grain**

**a large bunch of fresh flat leaf parsley, roughly chopped**

**2–3 lemons, cut into wedges**

Grate the onions on to a plate, sprinkle with the salt and leave them to weep for about 15 minutes. Place a strainer over a large bowl, add in the onions and press down with the back of a wooden spoon in order to extract the onion juice. Discard the onions left in the sieve, then mix the garlic and cumin seeds into the onion juice and toss in the lamb. Cover and leave the lamb to marinate for 3–4 hours.

Meanwhile, prepare the dough for the flat breads. Sift the flours and salt together into a large bowl. Make a well in the middle and gradually add 200ml/7fl oz/scant 1 cup lukewarm water, drawing in the flour from the sides. Using your hands, knead the dough until firm and springy – if it is at all sticky, add more flour.

Divide the dough into 24 pieces and knead each one into a ball. Place on a floured surface and cover with a damp cloth. Leave to rest for 45 minutes while you get the barbecue ready.

Just before cooking, roll each ball of dough into a wide, thin circle. Dust each circle with flour so they don't stick together, and keep them covered until required with a damp dish towel to prevent them drying out.

Thread the meat on to flat kebab swords or metal skewers. Cook the kebabs on the barbecue for 2–3 minutes on each side.

At the same time, cook the flat breads on a hot griddle or other flat pan, flipping them over as they begin to go brown and buckle. Pile up on a plate.

Slide the meat on to the flat breads. Sprinkle onion and parsley over each pile and squeeze lemon juice over the top. Wrap the breads into parcels and eat with your hands.

# Lamb shish kebab

This is the ultimate kebab – chargrilled meat served on flat bread with yogurt and tomatoes. Designed to use up day-old *pide*, for which you can substitute pitta bread or a plain Indian naan, *şiş kebab* is succulent and tasty, and should be devoured as a dish on its own.

## Serves four

For the kebabs

**500g/1¼lb minced (ground) lean lamb**

**2 onions, finely chopped**

**1 fresh green chilli, deseeded and finely chopped**

**4 garlic cloves, crushed**

**5ml/1 tsp *pul biber*, or paprika**

**5ml/1 tsp ground sumac**

**a bunch of flat leaf parsley, finely chopped, plus extra to garnish**

For the sauce

**30ml/2 tbsp olive oil**

**15ml/1 tbsp butter**

**1 onion, finely chopped**

**2 garlic cloves, finely chopped**

**1 fresh green chilli, deseeded and finely chopped**

**5–10ml/1–2 tsp sugar**

**400g/14oz can of chopped tomatoes**

**salt and ground black pepper**

For serving

**12 plum tomatoes**

**30ml/2 tbsp butter**

**1 large pide, or 4 pitta or small naan, cut into bitesize pieces**

**5ml/1 tsp ground sumac**

**5ml/1 tsp dried oregano**

**225g/8oz thick and creamy natural (plain) yogurt**

**salt and ground black pepper**

Make the kebabs. Put the lamb into a bowl with all the other ingredients and knead well to a smooth paste. Cover and chill for about 15 minutes.

Meanwhile, make the sauce. Heat the oil and butter in a pan, add the onion, garlic and chilli, and cook until they begin to colour. Add the sugar and tomatoes and cook, uncovered, for 30 minutes. Season and remove from the heat.

Get the barbecue ready for cooking and shape the lamb mince around skewers. Cook them on the barbecue for 6–8 minutes, turning once.

Meanwhile, thread the whole plum tomatoes on to skewers, place them on the barbecue and cook until they are charred.

While the kebabs and tomatoes are cooking, melt the butter in a heavy pan, add the *pide* or bread pieces and cook until golden. Sprinkle with some of the sumac and oregano, then arrange on a serving dish, spreading the pieces out. Spoon a little tomato sauce over the pide – not too much or it will go soggy – and spoon on some yogurt.

When the kebabs are cooked on both sides, slip the meat off the skewers. Arrange the meat on the *pide* with the cooked tomatoes, sprinkle with salt and the rest of the sumac and oregano, then garnish with the chopped fresh parsley.

Serve hot, topped with dollops of the remaining sauce and yogurt.

# Lamb kebab in puff pastry

Kebabs in pastry are neither Anatolian nor Ottoman, but a more recent addition to the culinary culture of Turkey. Over the last hundred years, new methods of cooking have had an impact on traditional techniques, and the effect of this can be seen in this dish, *talaş kebab*, which reflects a French influence. You can make your own buttery puff pastry for this kebab, or use the ready-prepared packs, which is easier.

## Serves six to eight

**450g/1lb lean shoulder of lamb**

**30ml/2 tbsp butter**

**2 onions, quartered then sliced**

**7.5ml/1½ tsp tomato purée (paste)**

**10ml/2 tsp sugar**

**5ml/1 tsp dried mint**

**500g/1¼lb puff pastry, thawed if frozen**

**a little flour, for dusting**

**1 egg yolk, beaten**

**salt and ground black pepper**

Cut the shoulder of lamb into thin strips using a sharp knife.

Melt the butter in a heavy pan, add the onions and cook until they have softened. Add the strips of lamb and cook for 3–4 minutes, or until most of the liquid has evaporated.

Stir in the tomato purée and sugar, and pour in about 250ml/8fl oz/1 cup of water. Reduce the heat, cover the pan and cook gently for about 40 minutes, or until the meat is tender.

Meanwhile, preheat the oven to 180°C/350°F/Gas 4 and lightly grease a baking tray.

Drain the meat over a pan to catch the cooking liquid. Reserve the cooking liquid and place the meat in a dish. Sprinkle the meat with a little salt and the dried mint. Leave to cool.

On a lightly floured board, roll out the puff pastry into a rectangle. Cut out squares, about 10 x 10cm/4 x 4in square. Place a little of the cooked lamb in the centre of each square and fold over the edges to form a neat packet.

Place the packets, seam-side down, in the baking tray. Brush the egg yolk over to glaze. Put the pastries in the oven and bake them for about 35 minutes, or until puffed up and golden brown.

Heat up the reserved cooking liquid, season it and serve as a sauce with the puff parcels.

# Lamb stew with roasted chestnuts

In western Anatolia, *kestaneli kuzu* is a popular stew to cook at home in the late autumn, and there is also a classic early summer version that is made with apricots. Easy to prepare, it benefits from being made in advance. You can roast your own chestnuts at home, or you can buy them ready-roasted in cans and vacuum-sealed packs in health food shops, some supermarkets and delicatessens. Serve with a plain pilaff and salad.

## Serves four to six

**1kg/2¼lb shoulder of lamb**

**45ml/3 tbsp olive oil**

**30ml/2 tbsp butter**

**450g/1lb shallots, peeled and left whole**

**4–6 garlic cloves, smashed**

**2 cinnamon sticks**

**10ml/2 tsp allspice berries, crushed**

**15ml/1 tbsp clear honey**

**450g/1lb roasted chestnuts, peeled**

**salt and ground black pepper**

Trim the lamb of fat and cut the meat into chestnut-sized pieces.

Heat the oil and butter in a large, heavy, flameproof earthenware pot or casserole. Stir in the shallots and fry until they turn golden brown. Transfer the shallots to a plate and set aside.

Add the garlic, cinnamon sticks and allspice berries to the oil. Toss in the lamb pieces to brown a little. Stir in the honey and pour in just enough water to cover the meat.

Bring the water to the boil and reduce the heat. Cover the pot or casserole and cook gently for 45 minutes.

Remove the lid and return the shallots to the pot. Add the chestnuts and cook gently for a further 10 minutes. Season to taste with salt and pepper, and serve.

# Aubergine musakka

There are several versions of *musakka* in Turkey, as the word simply denotes a dish comprising minced meat and vegetables, such as courgettes, cabbage and potatoes. The aubergine version, *patlıcan musakkası*, is a classic, and was probably devised in the Ottoman Palace kitchens, as it includes a milk-based sauce, which was sometimes used to lend an air of sophistication to dishes. For this recipe, which is similar to the Greek version, you can fry, grill or roast the aubergine slices.

## Serves four to six

**4 good-sized aubergines (eggplants), sliced crossways**

**30ml/2 tbsp currants**

**sunflower oil or olive oil, for shallow-frying, plus 30ml/2 tbsp olive oil**

**2 onions, chopped**

**4 garlic cloves, chopped**

**10ml/2 tsp sugar**

**500g/1¼lb minced (ground) lamb**

**25ml/1½ tbsp ground cinnamon**

**10ml/2 tsp dried thyme or oregano**

**5–10ml/1–2 tsp tomato purée (paste)**

**salt and ground black pepper**

For the sauce

**2 egg yolks**

**450ml/¾ pint/2 cups milk**

**25ml/1½ tbsp butter**

**45ml/3 tbsp plain (all-purpose) flour**

**2.5ml/½ tsp freshly grated nutmeg**

Place the aubergine slices on a tray or shallow bowl and sprinkle them with salt. Leave them to weep for 10-15 minutes. Soak the currants in warm water for 15 minutes then drain. Rinse and drain the aubergines and squeeze dry.

Heat a layer of oil in a frying pan and fry the aubergine slices in batches until lightly golden (you will need to top up the oil during cooking, as the aubergines absorb it). Drain them on kitchen paper.

Heat the 30ml/2 tbsp of olive oil in a heavy pan. Stir in the onions and garlic with the sugar and cook until golden. Add the currants to plump them up and stir in the minced lamb. Cook for 2–3 minutes, then add the cinnamon, thyme or oregano, and tomato purée. Stir to combine and cook for a further 2 minutes, then season to taste with salt and pepper.

Layer the aubergines and minced meat in an ovenproof dish, starting and finishing with a layer of aubergines (this can be prepared ahead of time). Preheat the oven to 200°C/400°F/Gas 6.

To make the sauce, put the egg yolks in a bowl. Stir in 15–30ml/1–2 tbsp of the milk and set aside. Melt the butter in a pan over a medium heat. Take the pan off the heat and stir in the flour to make a paste. Return the pan to the heat and pour in the milk, whisking constantly, until the sauce begins to thicken. Beat in the nutmeg, and season.

Stir 15–30ml/1–2 tbsp of the hot sauce into the egg yolks and then pour them into the pan. Keep stirring until the sauce is smooth and thick. Pour the sauce over the top layer of aubergines and place the dish in the preheated oven.

Bake for 25–30 minutes, or until the top of the *musakka* is beautifully browned. Serve immediately.

# Lamb cutlets with tomato sauce

Quick and easy to prepare, lamb or veal cutlets are popular griddled for lunch or supper. Generally the butchers bash them flat with a meat cleaver so they only take minutes to cook, seared in their own fat. To serve *sahanda pirzola*, sprinkle with dried oregano, squeeze lemon juice over, and spoon the tomato sauce around them.

## Serves four

**30ml/2 tbsp olive oil**

**10ml/2 tsp butter**

**12 lamb cutlets, trimmed and flattened with a cleaver (or ask the butcher to do this)**

**1 onion, finely chopped**

**1 fresh green chilli, deseeded and finely chopped**

**2 garlic cloves, finely chopped**

**5ml/1 tsp sugar**

**5–10ml/1–2 tsp white wine vinegar**

**2–3 large tomatoes, skinned and chopped, or 400g/14oz can of tomatoes**

**1 green bell pepper, deseeded and finely chopped**

**a sprinkling of dried oregano**

**salt and ground black pepper**

Heat the oil and butter in a large pan and brown the cutlets on both sides.

Remove the cutlets from the pan and put to one side, then add the onion, chilli and garlic, and fry gently until the onion begins to brown.

Stir in the sugar and vinegar, then add the tomatoes and green pepper. Lower the heat, cover and simmer for about 30 minutes, until the mixture is thick and saucy. Season with salt and pepper to taste.

Return the cutlets to the pan, covering them completely in the sauce. Cook for about 15 minutes, until the meat is tender.

Spoon the sauce on to a serving dish and arrange the cutlets on top. Sprinkle with oregano, and serve immediately.

# Ladies' thighs

Nowadays, you wouldn't get away with some of the names that came out of the Ottoman kitchens, such as 'young girls' breasts', 'sweetheart's lips' and these meat and rice *köfte*, 'ladies' thighs'. Plump, juicy and packed with flavour, *kadinbudu köfte* are often served as a hot meze dish or on their own with a chickpea pilaff.

## Serves four

**15ml/1 tbsp olive oil**

**1 onion, finely chopped**

**500g/1¼lb minced (ground) lean lamb or beef**

**115g/4oz/generous ½ cup long grain rice, cooked**

**a bunch of flat leaf parsley, leaves finely chopped**

**5ml/1 tsp ground cumin**

**5ml/1 tsp dried thyme**

**plain (all-purpose) flour, for coating**

**sunflower oil, for deep-frying**

**2 eggs, beaten**

**salt and ground black pepper**

**lemon wedges, to serve**

Heat the olive oil in a heavy pan and stir in the onion. Cook until it begins to colour. Add half the minced meat and fry over a high heat until all the liquid has evaporated. Add the cooked rice to the pan and stir well to mix. Transfer the meat and rice mixture to a bowl.

Add the remainder of the raw minced meat with the parsley, cumin and thyme. Season with salt and pepper. Using a wooden spoon, combine the mixture until it is thoroughly mixed.

Take small, apricot-sized portions of the mixture in the palm of your hand and mould them into oval shapes. Flatten the ovals slightly with the heel of your hand, then dip them in the flour to coat completely.

Heat enough oil for deep-frying in a pan. Dip the flour-coated 'thighs' into the beaten egg and drop them into the oil. Cook in batches for about 2 minutes each side, until crisp and golden. Drain on kitchen paper and serve hot with lemon wedges for squeezing over.

# Meat-stuffed vine leaves

Most people are familiar with the rolled vine leaves stuffed with aromatic rice served as a meze dish but in Turkey these are called *yalanıc yaprak dolması*, meaning 'false stuffed vine leaves', because they do not contain meat - this version, *etli yaprak dolması*, is regarded as the real thing.

## Serves four to six

**25–30 fresh or preserved vine leaves**

**350g/12oz minced (ground) lean lamb or beef**

**2 onions, finely chopped**

**115g/4oz/generous ½ cup long grain rice, thoroughly rinsed and drained**

**a bunch each of fresh dill, flat leaf parsley and mint, finely chopped**

**45–60ml/3–4 tbsp olive oil**

**juice of 1 lemon**

**150ml/¼ pint/⅔ cup water**

**salt and ground black pepper**

To serve

**60–90ml/4–6 tbsp thick and creamy natural (plain) yogurt**

**lemon wedges**

If using fresh vine leaves, bring a pan of water to the boil and plunge the leaves into it for 1–2 minutes. Drain and refresh under cold running water, then drain thoroughly. Trim off the stems, and keep covered in the refrigerator for 2–3 days. If using preserved leaves, place in a bowl and cover with boiling water. Soak for 15–20 minutes, using a fork to separate the leaves. Drain and soak in cold water for 2–3 minutes, then drain again.

Put the lamb mince in a bowl and stir in the onions, rice and herbs. Season, bind with 15ml/1 tbsp of the oil, and mix together thoroughly.

Lay one of the vine leaves on a flat surface and spoon some filling at the top of the leaf. Pull this over the filling, fold in the sides, then roll into a tight log. Repeat with the remaining leaves and filling.

Arrange the vine leaves, seam side down, in a deep, wide pan. Pack them together in circles, making more than one layer if necessary. In a bowl, mix the remaining oil with the lemon juice and water, and pour over the vine leaves. The liquid should come at least halfway up the top layer, so you may need to add extra liquid.

Put the pan over a medium heat. Once the liquid begins to bubble, place a plate over the leaves to stop them from unravelling, followed by a lid or foil. Lower the heat and leave the vine leaves to steam gently for 45 minutes, until the rice and meat are cooked. Serve hot, with yogurt and lemon wedges to squeeze over.

# Meatballs with pine nuts and cinnamon

Meatballs come in various shapes and sizes, made with lamb, beef or chicken, grilled or fried and some are even stuffed in true Turkish fashion! They all fall under the generic name *köfte* and are as popular as kebabs. Serve these *klasik köfte* with *cacık*, cucumber yogurt.

## Serves four to six

**250g/9oz minced (ground) lean lamb**

**1 onion, finely chopped**

**2 garlic cloves, crushed**

**10–15ml/2–3 tsp ground cinnamon**

**30ml/2 tbsp pine nuts**

**30ml/2 tbsp currants, soaked in warm water for 5–10 minutes and drained**

**5ml/1 tsp *pul biber*, or paprika**

**2 slices of day-old white or brown bread, ground into crumbs**

**1 egg, lightly beaten**

**15ml/1 tbsp tomato ketchup**

**a bunch each of fresh flat leaf parsley and dill, finely chopped**

**60ml/4 tbsp plain (all-purpose) flour, for coating**

**sunflower oil, for shallow-frying**

**salt and ground black pepper**

**lemon wedges, to serve**

In a large bowl, pound the minced lamb with the chopped onion, garlic and cinnamon. Knead the mixture with your hands and knock out the air, then add the pine nuts with the currants, *pul biber* or paprika, breadcrumbs, egg and ketchup. Season with salt and pepper to taste.

Knead the herbs into the meat mixture, making sure all the ingredients are well combined.

Take apricot-size portions of the meat mixture in your hands and roll into balls. Flatten each ball with the heel of your hand so that it resembles a thick disc, then coat lightly in the flour, shaking off any excess.

Heat a thin layer of sunflower oil in a large, heavy pan. Add the meatballs and cook for 8–10 minutes, until browned on all sides. Remove the meatballs with a slotted spoon and drain on kitchen paper.

Serve hot, garnished with herbs and with lemon wedges for squeezing.

## Variation

For a tasty version to eat on the go, omit the currants and pine nuts, and add 5ml/1 tsp ground cumin and 1 chopped fresh hot chilli. Shape into small balls and cook as above, then tuck the meatballs into toasted pitta pockets with slices of red onion, chopped flat leaf parsley, and a dollop of yogurt. Or make with beef mince and onions, *kuru köfte*, for picnics.

# Mother-in-law's meatballs

These meatballs, *içli köfte*, are from the southern region of Turkey where they were traditionally prepared by the mother-in-law of a new bride. Great care is taken over the making of the balls, which are hollowed out to form shells for a spicy, nutty filling and then pushed together again to seal and form a round or oval-shaped *köfte*. The ritual of filling and sealing and presenting the meatballs to the new daughter-in-law is to signify that her lips must now be sealed with discretion.

## Serves four to six

**225g/8oz bulgur wheat**

**225g/8oz finely minced (ground) beef or lamb**

**10ml/2 tsp *pul biber*, or paprika**

**plain (all-purpose) flour, for dusting**

**sunflower oil, for deep-frying**

**salt**

**flat leaf parsley, to garnish**

For the filling

**15–30ml/1–2 tbsp ghee, or olive oil with a knob or pat of butter**

**1 onion, finely chopped**

**4 garlic cloves, finely chopped**

**50g/2oz walnuts, chopped**

**50g/2oz blanched pistachio nuts, finely chopped**

**5ml/1 tsp ground cumin**

**5ml/1 tsp ground coriander**

**5ml/1 tsp dried thyme**

**115g/4oz finely minced (ground) beef or lamb**

**a small bunch of flat leaf parsley, finely chopped**

**salt and ground black pepper**

To make the filling, melt the ghee, or olive oil and butter, in a heavy pan and stir in the onion and garlic until they begin to colour. Add the nuts, spices and thyme, and fry for 1–2 minutes. Toss in the minced meat and cook for 4–5 minutes, then stir in the parsley, and season with salt and pepper. Leave the mixture to cool.

Meanwhile, put the bulgur wheat into a bowl and pour in enough boiling water to just cover it. Cover the bowl and leave the bulgur wheat to absorb the water for about 25 minutes.

Squeeze the bulgur wheat to make sure there is no excess water, then add the minced meat, *pul biber* or paprika, and salt to taste. Using your hands, knead the ingredients together thoroughly so that the mixture has a pasty consistency.

Take a small portion of the mixture in the palm of your hand and mould it into a ball. Using your thumb, hollow out an opening in the middle of the ball. Put the ball on to a flat surface. Repeat with the remainder of the mixture.

Using a teaspoon, spoon a little filling into each hollow and pinch the edges of the ball together to seal. Gently squeeze the *köfte* to form a ball or a cone shape. Toss them in a little flour to coat lightly.

Heat enough sunflower oil for deep-frying in a pan. Fry the *köfte* in batches for 3–4 minutes, or until golden brown. Drain on kitchen paper and serve hot, garnished with parsley leaves.

# Stir-fried liver with red onion

Over the years I've managed to change the minds of many who have claimed not to like liver. This is such a simple and delicious way to prepare it and retain a tender texture. Translated as 'Albanian Liver', *Arnavut ciğeri* is one of the dishes that was adopted by the Palace kitchens as the Ottoman Empire consumed vast expanses of Eastern Europe. It is often served as a cold meze dish but I prefer it hot with a squeeze of lemon, which lifts and refreshes it.

## Serves four

**500g/1¼lb fresh lamb's liver**

**30ml/2 tbsp plain (all-purpose) flour**

**5–10ml/1–2 tsp *pul biber*, or paprika**

**45–60ml/3–4 tbsp olive oil**

**2 garlic cloves, finely chopped**

**5–10ml/1–2 tsp cumin seeds**

**salt**

To serve

**1 large red onion, cut in half lengthways, in half again crossways, and sliced along the grain**

**a handful of fresh flat leaf parsley**

**lemon wedges**

Using a sharp knife, remove any skin and ducts from the liver, then cut it into thin strips or bitesize cubes. Mix the flour and *pul biber* or paprika, and toss the liver in it.

Heat the olive oil in a heavy pan. Add the garlic and cumin seeds, season with salt and cook until the cumin gives off a nutty aroma.

Toss in the strips of liver and stir-fry quickly for 2–3 minutes so that it cooks on all sides and browns slightly. Remove with a slotted spoon and drain on kitchen paper.

Spread the sliced red onion on a serving dish, spoon the hot liver in the middle and garnish with parsley leaves. Serve hot or cold, with the lemon wedges for squeezing over.

# Spicy liver sausage

This spicy sausage, *bumbar dolmasi*, is so popular in south-east Anatolia that there is even a *bumbar* festival in Siirt, when it is served with a dried apricot compôte, *hoşaf*. It also plays a role in the marriages of the region, as the new bride is required to present her mother-in-law with annual gifts of home-cooked *bumbar*. The most traditional sausage casing is a sheep's intestine that has been thoroughly cleaned, rubbed in salt, soaked in vinegar, then rinsed and patted dry.

## Serves four

**225g/8oz lamb's liver, minced (ground) (you could ask the butcher to do this)**

**90g/3½oz long grain rice, rinsed and drained**

**5–10ml/1–2 tsp *pul biber*, or paprika**

**5ml/1 tsp ground cinnamon**

**5ml/1 tsp ground cumin**

**2.5ml/½ tsp ground allspice**

**2.5ml/½ tsp ground black pepper**

**5ml/1 tsp salt**

**2 sausage skins or casings (available in most butchers)**

**flat leaf parsley, to garnish**

For the compôte

**175g/6oz ready-to-eat dried apricots**

**175g/6oz/¾ cup caster (superfine) sugar**

**juice of 1 lemon**

In a large bowl, mix the liver with the rice and spices. Add the salt and bind with a little water, about 15ml/1 tbsp. Mix well.

Tie one end of each sausage skin in a knot, or with a piece of string. Fill them with the liver mixture (this is much easier if you have a funnel to insert into the other end of the sausage skin), and tie the ends.

Place the sausages in a pan and cover with salted water. Bring the water to the boil and skim off any scum. Reduce the heat, cover the pan, and simmer for 15 minutes.

Prick the sausages in several places with the sharp point of a knife and simmer for a further 15–20 minutes, or until tender.

Meanwhile, prepare the compôte. Put the apricots and sugar into a heavy pan and pour in enough water to cover. Heat gently and bring to the boil, stirring constantly. Reduce the heat, stir in the lemon juice, and leave to cook gently for 10 minutes. Leave to cool.

Drain the sausages and return them to the pan of compôte. Cover with a clean dish towel and the lid, and leave for 15 minutes.

Place the sausages on a serving dish, garnish with parsley and serve with the apricot compôte.

# Chicken casserole with okra and lemon

This classic Turkish dish, *güveçte piliçli bamya*, is found in various forms throughout Turkey and the Middle East. It is most often served on its own with chunks of bread to mop up the sauce, or with a plain pilaff. In south-east Anatolia, a generous dose of hot red pepper is added for a fiery kick. A similar dish is made with chicken and artichoke bottoms.

## Serves four

**30ml/2 tbsp olive oil**

**30ml/2 tbsp butter**

**1 small free-range chicken, trimmed of excess fat and cut into quarters**

**2 onions, cut in half lengthways and finely sliced**

**2–3 garlic cloves, finely chopped**

**5–10ml/1–2 tsp *pul biber*, or 1 fresh red chilli, deseeded and finely chopped**

**10ml/2 tsp coriander seeds**

**10ml/2 tsp dried oregano**

**5–10ml/1–2 tsp sugar**

**15ml/1 tbsp tomato purée (paste)**

**400g/14oz can of chopped tomatoes**

**450g/1lb fresh okra/ladies' fingers (see Cook's tip)**

**juice of 1 lemon**

**salt and ground black pepper**

**thick and creamy natural (plain) yogurt, to serve**

Heat the oil with the butter in a wide, heavy pan or flameproof casserole. Add the chicken pieces and brown them on all sides. Remove from the pan with tongs and set aside.

Add the sliced onions, chopped garlic, *pul biber* or chilli, coriander seeds and oregano to the pan. Stir in the sugar and cook the mixture over a medium heat until the onions just begin to turn golden brown, then stir in the tomato purée and tomatoes and add 150ml/¼ pint/⅔ cup of water. Mix to combine thoroughly.

Bring the liquid to the boil, then reduce the heat and simmer gently for 2–3 minutes, to thicken the sauce. Slip in the chicken pieces and baste them all over with the sauce. Cover the pan and cook gently on top of the stove, or put the casserole in the oven at 180°C/350°F/Gas 4, and leave to cook for about 30 minutes.

Place the prepared okra over the chicken and pour the lemon juice on top. Cover the pan again and cook gently for a further 20 minutes, until the okra are tender but not soggy.

Transfer the chicken pieces to a serving dish. Ensure that the okra is completely coated with the tomato sauce, season to taste with salt and pepper, and spoon over and around the chicken.

Serve immediately, with a bowl of yogurt for spooning over.

## Cook's tip

To retain colour and reduce sliminess when okra are cooked, prepare them as follows. Cut off the stalks, then place the okra in a bowl and sprinkle with 15ml/1 tbsp salt and 30–45ml/2–3 tbsp white wine vinegar or cider vinegar. Toss well and leave to sit for 1–2 hours. Rinse thoroughly and pat dry.

# Chicken with green plums and grape syrup

Tart green plums are popular as a snack dipped in salt or cooked in stews. Cooking fruit with meat and poultry was a great Persian tradition that filtered through to the cuisine of the Seljuk Turks in Konya where the mystic poet, Mevlana Jalal-al Din Rumi, kept records of recipes and the healing properties of the food of this period. Grapes, quinces, apples, figs, apricots and plums have all been cooked in medieval stews like this one, *erikli tavuk*.

## Serves four

**30ml/2 tbsp olive oil with a knob or pat of butter**

**3–4 garlic cloves, smashed**

**8 chicken thighs, skinned if preferred**

**30ml/2 tbsp blanched almonds**

**8–10 green plums, or other tart plums, stoned and halved**

**15ml/1 tbsp grape *pekmez* (molasses) or honey**

**salt and ground black pepper**

**flat leaf parsley, chopped roughly, to garnish**

**lemon wedges, to serve**

Heat the oil and butter in a heavy pan and stir in the garlic. Add the chicken thighs and cook for 2–3 minutes to brown them, then stir in the almonds.

When the almonds turn golden, toss in the plums, cover the pan and cook gently for 10–15 minutes.

Stir in the *pekmez* or honey, to give a hint of sweetness, and season the dish with salt and pepper.

Serve the chicken dish hot or at room temperature, garnished with parsley and with wedges of lemon to squeeze over.

# Chicken stew with walnuts and pomegranate juice

With medieval origins in the Persian classic version, *fesinjan*, variations of this dish, *acem yahnisi*, pop up all over Turkey. Although traditionally prepared with pheasant, modern adaptations are more often made with chicken or duck. It is generally served with a plain pilaff and leafy salad.

## Serves four

**3 pomegranates**
**juice of 1 lemon**
**30ml/2 tbsp ghee or butter**
**2 onions, finely chopped**
**1 medium-size chicken, jointed**
**5–10ml/1–2 tsp ground cinnamon**
**5ml/1 tsp sugar**
**225g/8oz walnuts, chopped**
**salt and ground black pepper**
**a few shredded mint leaves, to garnish**

Halve the pomegranates. Extract the seeds from one of the halves and set them aside for a garnish. Squeeze the remaining pomegranate halves over a bowl to extract the juice. Add the lemon juice and mix well.

Melt the butter or ghee in a heavy ovenproof pan or flameproof casserole dish. Stir in the onions and fry until they begin to colour. Add the chicken joints to the pan and brown them lightly. Pour over the pomegranate and lemon juices and stir in the cinnamon and sugar. Season with salt and pepper. Bring the liquid to a gentle boil, then turn down the heat. Cover the pan and simmer for about 35 minutes – top up the liquid with a little water if the mixture becomes dry.

Meanwhile, heat the oven to 200°C/400°F/Gas 6. Transfer the chicken and all the juices to an ovenproof dish if necessary, and sprinkle the walnuts over the chicken. Place in the oven and roast for about 10 minutes, or until the walnuts become golden.

Transfer the chicken pieces to a serving dish if you like, spooning all the walnuts and cooking juices over and around the chicken. Sprinkle the reserved pomegranate seeds over the top and garnish with the shredded mint before serving.

# Circassian chicken

I have fond memories of this dish in meze restaurants along the Bosphorus. It is a classic Ottoman dish with an unusual story. At the height of the Ottoman Empire, young Circassian women were captured to serve as concubines to the sultans, who appreciated their renowned beauty and fair features, so the traditional version of this dish is pale in colour like the complexion and hair of the women. The version from eastern Anatolia, a region that was never reached by the Ottomans, contains coriander – a herb that was rarely used in Ottoman cooking. To my mind *Çerkez tavuğu* is a delightful addition to a meze or buffet spread, but the history of it could be considered controversial.

## Serves six

**1 chicken, trimmed of excess fat**

**3 slices of day-old white bread, crusts removed**

**150ml/¼ pint/⅔ cup milk**

**175g/6oz walnuts**

**4–6 garlic cloves**

**salt and ground black pepper**

For the stock

**1 onion, quartered**

**1 carrot, chopped**

**2 celery sticks, chopped**

**4–6 cloves**

**4–6 allspice berries**

**4–6 black peppercorns**

**2 bay leaves**

**5ml/1 tsp coriander seeds**

**a small bunch of fresh flat leaf parsley, stalks bruised and tied together**

For the garnish

**30ml/2 tbsp butter**

**5ml/1 tsp *pul biber*, or paprika**

**a few fresh coriander (cilantro) leaves**

Put the chicken into a deep pan with all of the ingredients for the stock. Pour in enough water to just cover the chicken, and bring to the boil. Lower the heat, cover the pan and simmer the chicken for about 1 hour. Remove the chicken from the pan and leave until cool enough to handle. Meanwhile, boil the stock with the lid off for 15 minutes until reduced, then strain and season with salt and pepper.

When the chicken has cooled a little, pull off the skin and discard it. Tear the chicken flesh into thin strips, and put them into a large bowl.

In a small bowl, soak the bread in the milk for a few minutes until the milk is totally absorbed. Using a mortar and pestle, pound the walnuts with the garlic to form a paste, or blend them in a food processor. Beat the soaked bread into the walnut paste, then add to the chicken. Beat in spoonfuls of the warm stock to bind the chicken and walnut mixture until it is light and creamy. Spoon the mixture into a serving dish, forming a rounded mound.

To garnish the chicken in the Istanbul fashion, gently melt the butter over a low heat, stir in the *pul biber* or paprika, then drizzle the mixture in a cross shape over the top of the mound. Serve at room temperature, garnished with the fresh coriander leaves.

## Variations

The Çerkez of eastern Anatolia often make this dish with coriander (cilantro) leaves tossed through, which adds freshness. A similar dish, *Çerkez fasulye*, is made with green beans.

# Lemon chicken thighs wrapped in aubergine

This elegant Ottoman dish, *patlıcanlı tavuk kebabı*, is usually made with chicken thighs or veal fillet. Wrapping the meat in strips of fried aubergine may take a little time and effort to prepare, but the result is both impressive and tasty. Serve as a main course with a tomato and cucumber salad, or a salad of parsley, pepper and onion, and a buttery rice pilaff.

## Serves four

**juice of 2–3 lemons**

**2 garlic cloves, crushed**

**4–6 allspice berries, crushed**

**8 chicken thighs, skinned and boned**

**3–4 aubergines (eggplants)**

**sunflower oil, for deep-frying**

**30ml/2 tbsp flaked (sliced) almonds, toasted**

**lemon wedges, to serve**

In a shallow bowl, mix together the lemon juice, garlic and allspice berries. Toss the chicken in the mixture, rolling the pieces over in the juice to coat them thoroughly, then cover and leave to marinate in a cold place or the refrigerator for about 2 hours.

Using a vegetable peeler or a small, sharp knife, peel the aubergines lengthways in stripes like a zebra.

Slice the aubergines thinly lengthways using a large, sharp knife – you need 16 strips in total – then soak the slices in a bowl of salted cold water for about 30 minutes.

Preheat the oven to 180°C/350°F/Gas 4. Drain the aubergines and squeeze out the excess water.

Heat enough oil for deep-frying in a suitable deep-sided pan, and deep-fry the aubergines in batches for 2–3 minutes until golden brown. Remove with a slotted spoon and drain on kitchen paper.

On a board or plate, lay two strips of aubergine over one another in a cross shape, then place a chicken thigh in the middle. Tuck the thigh into a bundle and wrap the aubergine around it.

Place the aubergine parcel, seam-side down, in a lightly greased ovenproof dish and repeat the process with the remaining aubergine strips and chicken.

Pour any remaining marinade over the parcels and sprinkle with the toasted almonds. Cover with foil and bake for 40 minutes. Serve hot, with lemon wedges for squeezing over.

# Roast wild duck with honey, thyme and almonds

Wild ducks are a common sight in the lakes and marshes of Anatolia and some end up in the village pot. Reared ducks, on the other hand, are sold alongside hens in rural and city markets. This village recipe, called *ördek fırında*, can be made with wild or reared duck. A tomato and cucumber salad makes a perfect accompaniment.

## Serves two or more

**1 wild duck, well hung, gutted and cleaned, with trimmed giblets**

**15ml/1 tbsp butter**

**a bunch of fresh thyme sprigs**

**4 slices day-old bread, crumbled**

**45ml/3 tbsp olive oil, plus an extra 15ml/1 tbsp for roasting**

**2 garlic cloves, crushed**

**10ml/2 tsp dried oregano**

**45ml/3 tbsp blanched almonds**

**45ml/3 tbsp wild clear honey**

Soak a wooden skewer in water for 30 minutes. Preheat the oven to 230°C/450°F/Gas 8. Place the duck in an ovenproof dish, reserving the giblets, and smear the breasts in butter. Place a few sprigs of thyme into the body cavity and scatter the remainder of the leaves over the top of the duck.

Put the crumbled bread into a dish and pour the oil over it, rubbing the oil into the bread. Toss in the garlic and oregano, and pack the mixture into the cavity on top of the thyme sprigs. Skewer the legs with the wooden skewer to prevent the filling from oozing out.

Sprinkle the giblets and almonds around the duck and drizzle the honey and the reserved oil over the top. Place the duck in the oven and roast for about 25 minutes until the skin is browned.

Serve straight from the oven, with the stuffing.

# Chargrilled marinated quails

Small birds, such as quails, poussins or grouse, are often chargrilled in the countryside. The aroma can lure you from afar as there is nothing quite so appetising as the smell of grilling meat. The sharp, tangy marinade tenderises the meat, as well as enhancing its flavour. Served straight off the charcoal grill, these quails are usually tucked into half a loaf of bread with some chopped raw onions, parsley and yogurt. Here the *ızgara bılıdrcın* are served with warm flat bread.

## Serves four

**4 quails, cleaned and boned**

**4 pomegranates**

**juice of 1 lemon**

**30ml/2 tbsp olive oil**

**5–10ml/1–2 tsp *pul biber*, or 5ml/1 tsp chilli powder**

**30–45ml/2–3 tbsp thick and creamy natural (plain) yogurt**

**salt**

**a bunch of fresh flat leaf parsley**

Soak eight wooden skewers in hot water for about 15 minutes. Thread one skewer through the wings of each bird and a second skewer through the legs to keep them together. Place the birds in a wide, shallow dish.

Halve the pomegranates. Extract the seeds from one of the halves and set aside for a garnish. Squeeze the remaining pomegranate halves over a bowl to extract the juice. Add the lemon juice and mix well.

Beat the pomegranate and lemon juices with the oil and *pul biber* or chilli powder, pour over the quails and rub it into the skin. Cover with foil and leave to marinate in a cold place or the refrigerator for 2–3 hours, turning the birds over from time to time.

Get the barbecue or grill ready for cooking. Lift the birds out of the marinade and pour what is left of it into a bowl. Beat the yogurt into the leftover marinade and add a little salt.

Brush some of the yogurt mixture over the birds and place them on the prepared barbecue. Cook for 4–5 minutes on each side, brushing with the yogurt as they cook, to form a crust.

Chop some of the parsley and lay the rest on a serving dish. Place the quails on top and garnish with pomegranate seeds and chopped parsley.

# Spicy rabbit stew with shallots and figs

There are records from the Seljuk and Ottoman periods of many recipes for rabbit, quails, pigeon, wild duck and deer. At that time hunting was regarded as a recreation, but the modern culinary culture doesn't include much game. In central Anatolia, however, you come across villagers who still enjoy hunting wild rabbit, duck and quails. This stew, *tavşan yahnisi*, is delicious served with sautéed potatoes or a bulgur pilaff.

## Serves two to three

**1 good-sized rabbit, gutted, cleaned, and jointed into 4 or 6 portions**

**30ml/2 tbsp ghee, or olive oil with a knob or pat of butter**

**12 shallots, peeled and left whole**

**10 garlic cloves, peeled, left whole and lightly smashed**

**5–10ml/1–2 tsp *pul biber*, or paprika**

**10ml/2 tsp coriander seeds**

**8–10 allspice berries, crushed**

**6 cloves, crushed**

**1 cinnamon stick**

**6–8 dried figs, halved**

**30ml/2 tbsp sultanas (golden raisins)**

**15ml/1 tbsp grape *pekmez* (molasses), or clear honey**

**150ml/¼ pint/⅔ cup water**

**salt and ground black pepper**

**a bunch of fresh parsley, roughly chopped, to garnish**

For the marinade

**200ml/7fl oz/scant 1 cup red wine**

**30ml/2 tbsp olive oil**

**30ml/2 tbsp red wine vinegar**

**2–3 bay leaves, crumpled**

Mix the marinade ingredients together. Place the rabbit joints in a shallow dish and pour the marinade over them. Cover and leave in the refrigerator for 6–8 hours, turning the joints in the marinade from time to time.

Transfer the rabbit joints to a plate and reserve the marinade. Melt the ghee, or olive oil and butter, in a wide, heavy pan or flameproof earthenware dish, and brown the joints all over.

Return the cooked rabbit joints to the plate, and add the shallots, garlic and spices to the pan. Cook gently for 2–3 minutes, or until the shallots turn golden brown. Add the figs and sultanas and stir in the *pekmez* or clear honey.

Return the rabbit joints to the pan, pour in the reserved marinade and the water, and bring the liquid to the boil. Reduce the heat, cover and cook for about 1 hour, or until the rabbit is tender.

Transfer the joints to a serving dish. Bubble up the syrupy, spicy sauce and season it with salt and pepper. Spoon the sauce and shallots over and around the rabbit, garnish with some chopped parsley and serve.

# Sweet snacks and jams

With pudding and pastry shops around every corner, Turkish sweet dishes lure you in. They play an important role in religious festivals, celebrations, hospitality, goodwill and general contentment. "Eat sweet, talk sweet" say the Turks as they stop to enjoy a plate of syrupy baklava, chewy ice cream, or the delectable burnt chicken breast pudding – typically eaten at any time of day along with a glass of tea or a small cup of strong Turkish coffee.

# Rose petal sorbet

The ancient Egyptians, Romans, Persians and seafaring Arabs all used sweet-scented roses for culinary purposes, producing perfumed water, pure oil and wine. The Ottoman chefs carried on the tradition by splashing rose water into their syrupy pastries and milk puddings, and infusing the pretty petals in syrup to make fragrant jams and sorbets. Served in frosted glasses, decorated with fresh or crystallised rose petals, this sorbet, *gül dondurması*, looks quite special.

## Serves four

**fresh petals of 2 gloriously scented red or pink roses, free from pesticides**

**600ml/1 pint/2½ cups water**

**225g/8oz/1 cup caster (superfine) sugar**

**juice of 1 lemon**

**15ml/1 tbsp rose water**

Wash the rose petals and cut off the white bases. Place in a pan with the water and bring to the boil. Turn off the heat, cover the pan and leave to steep for 10 minutes.

Strain off the infused water, reserving the petals. Pour the water into the pan, add the sugar and bring to the boil, stirring, until the sugar has dissolved. Boil for 1–2 minutes, then lower the heat and simmer for 5–10 minutes, until the syrup thickens a little. Stir in the lemon juice, rose water and reserved petals, then turn off the heat and leave to cool in the pan.

Once cool, pour into a freezer container and freeze until beginning to set. Take the sorbet out of the freezer at 2–3 hour intervals and whisk to disperse the ice crystals. Alternatively, freeze in an electric sorbetière.

Before serving, take the sorbet out of the freezer for 5–10 minutes, so that it softens enough to scoop.

## Cook's tip

Clear, fragrant rose water is much prized in Turkish households. It is splashed on the face and hands to freshen up before or after a meal, and it is used to scent many sweet dishes.

# Mastic ice cream

There are many delicious flavours of ice cream, *dondurma*, in Turkey, but there is one unusual one which is well worth trying. A feature of Istanbul street life and ice-cream parlours, it is served from vats using a large wooden paddle. The resin-tasting tree gum, mastic (*mastika*) provides the chewy consistency, while the silky, ground orchid root (*salep*) contributes to its pearly white colour and thick texture. Both *mastika* and *salep* are available online and in some Turkish and Middle Eastern stores.

## Serves four

**900ml/1½ pints/3¾ cups full-fat (whole) milk**

**300ml/½ pint/1¼ cups double (heavy) cream**

**225g/8oz/1 cup sugar**

**45ml/3 tbsp ground *salep***

**1–2 pieces of mastic (see Cook's tip), crushed with a little sugar**

Put the milk, cream and sugar into a heavy pan and bring to the boil, stirring all the time, until the sugar has dissolved. Lower the heat and simmer for 10 minutes.

Put the *salep* into a bowl. Moisten it with a little cold milk, add a spoonful of the hot, sweetened milk, then transfer it to the pan, stirring all the time.

Beat the mixture gently and stir in the *mastika*, then continue simmering for 10–15 minutes. Pour the liquid into a freezer container, cover with a dry dish towel and leave to cool.

Remove the dish towel, cover the container with foil and place it in the freezer. Leave to set, beating it at intervals to disperse the ice crystals. Alternatively, churn the cooled liquid in an ice-cream maker.

Before serving, allow the ice cream to sit out of the freezer for 5–10 minutes so that it becomes soft enough to scoop.

## Cook's tip

*Mastika*, also called *sakız*, is the aromatic gum from the Pistacia lentiscus tree that grows wild in the Mediterranean region. When sold in the markets, *mastika* is in clear crystal form, often containing a few ants that managed to get caught in the sticky gum. The aroma will indicate the strength of the resinous taste, which the crystals impart to the dish along with the chewy texture. To use the crystals, they must first be pulverised with a little sugar, using a mortar and pestle.

# Poached apricots with buffalo cream

Perfect for just popping into your mouth with your fingers, these apricots, filled with the clotted cream (*kaymak*) of water buffalo milk, are delicious. You come across trays of *kaymaklı kayısı* on display at the Sweet Festival (Şeker Bayramı) to mark the end of Ramazan. You can flavour the syrup with orange blossom or rose water, and use ordinary clotted cream or crème fraiche to fill the succulent apricots.

## Serves six to eight

**250g/9oz dried apricots, soaked in cold water for at least 6 hours or overnight**

**250g/9oz/1¼ cups sugar**

**juice of 1 lemon**

**30ml/2 tbsp orange blossom or rose water**

**225g/8oz *kaymak*, clotted cream or crème fraiche**

Strain the soaked dried apricots over a large bowl and pour the soaking water into a measuring jug up to the 250ml/8fl oz/1 cup mark. Pour the measured liquid into a heavy pan, add the sugar and bring to the boil, stirring all the time.

Stir in the lemon juice and scented water, simmer for 5 minutes, and slip in the apricots. Bring the syrup back to the boil then reduce the heat and simmer for 30–40 minutes, until the apricots are golden orange and gleaming. Leave to cool.

Lift an apricot out of the syrup. Gently pull it open with your fingers – there is a slit where the stone has been removed – and fill the apricot with a spoonful of *kaymak*. Place the filled apricot, cream-side up, in a shallow serving dish and repeat the process with the remaining apricots and cream.

Place the dish in the refrigerator to chill until ready to eat. Just before serving, spoon a little of the syrup around the apricots – if you do this too early the cream weeps into the syrup.

# Pumpkin poached in clove syrup

I love the colour, flavour and texture of this dish, *bal kabağı tatısı*, and often prepare pumpkins this way in the autumn. They also store well in a jar so you can keep them in a cool place for several months. Generally, the poached pumpkin is served on its own with clotted buffalo cream (*kaymak*) and sometimes sprinkled with chopped walnuts.

## Serves four to six

**450g/1lb/2¼ cups sugar**

**250ml/9fl oz/1 cup water**

**juice of 1 lemon**

**6–8 cloves**

**1kg/2¼lb pumpkin flesh, peeled, deseeded and cut into cubes or rectangular blocks**

***kaymak* or clotted cream, to serve, optional**

Put the sugar into a deep, wide, heavy pan and pour in the water. Bring to the boil, stirring all the time, until the sugar has dissolved, then boil gently for 2–3 minutes.

Lower the heat and stir in the lemon juice and cloves, then add the pumpkin pieces and bring back to the boil. Lower the heat and put the lid on the pan. Poach the pumpkin gently in the syrup, turning the pieces over from time to time, until they are tender and a rich, gleaming orange colour. This may take 1½–2 hours, depending on the size of the pumpkin pieces.

Leave the pumpkin to cool in the pan, then lift the pieces out of the syrup and place them in a serving dish. Drizzle a little of the syrup over them and serve at room temperature, or chilled with a dollop of *kaymak*.

# Fresh figs baked with honey

Baking fruit with honey is an ancient cooking method. Apricots, peaches and figs are all delicious cooked this way and served with strained yogurt (*süzme*) or clotted cream (*kaymak*) – some people serve bread with it to mop up the yogurt and honey. Spices and herbs, such as aniseed, cinnamon, rosemary and lavender, are often used for flavouring, and the aroma of your chosen honey can make a difference to the dish, *fırında incir*.

## Serves four

**12 ripe figs**

**30ml/2 tbsp vanilla sugar (see Cook's tip)**

**3–4 cinnamon sticks**

**45–60ml/3–4 tbsp clear honey**

**225g/8oz chilled thick and creamy natural (plain) yogurt, *kaymak* or clotted cream**

Preheat the oven to 200°C/400°F/Gas 6. Wash the figs and pat them dry. Using a sharp knife, cut a deep cross from the top of each fig to the bottom, keeping the skin at the bottom intact. Fan each fig out, so it looks like a flower, then place them upright in a baking dish, preferably an earthenware one.

Sprinkle the vanilla sugar over each fig flower, tuck in the cinnamon sticks and drizzle with honey.

Bake in the oven for 15–20 minutes, until the sugar is slightly caramelised but the honey and figs are still moist.

Spoon a dollop of yogurt or cream into the middle of each fig, or serve them in bowls and let everyone help themselves to the yogurt or cream.

## Cook's tip

To make the vanilla sugar, split a vanilla pod (bean) lengthways in half, scrape out the seeds and mix thoroughly with the sugar, or you can whizz the whole pod with the sugar in an electric blender. Vanilla sugar keeps well in an airtight container.

# Sour cherry summer pudding

Known as *vişne tiridi* or *vişneli ekmek tatlısı*, this is a popular summer dessert of bread soaked in cherry compôte. Vibrant purple in colour, the pudding is usually served with clotted cream (*kaymak*) and can be made in one large dish or individual ones. It is a great way of using up day-old bread and slightly over-ripe cherries.

## Serves four to six

**½ loaf day-old Turkish white bread, or a small French baguette**

**250g/9oz fresh sour cherries**

**250g/9oz/1¼ cups sugar**

**about 550ml/18fl oz/2¼ cups water**

***kaymak* or clotted cream, to serve**

Remove the crusts of the loaf or baguette and cut the bread into thin slices, approximately 2cm/¾in thick. Arrange the bread slices in a double layer in a shallow dish suitable for serving from.

Wash and pit the cherries and place them in a deep, heavy pan with the sugar and the water. Bring to the boil, stirring from time to time. Reduce the heat and simmer for 5–6 minutes, until the cherry skins begin to crack.

Pour the hot liquid and cherries over the bread, making sure it is evenly distributed, so that every piece of bread is soaked in the juice.

Leave the pudding to cool and then place it in the refrigerator and leave for about 6 hours.

Lift individual portions of the bread pudding out of the dish and place them on small plates. Serve immediately, with *kaymak* or clotted cream.

## Cook's tip

If you do want to use fresh bread, just toast the slices lightly before arranging them in the dish.

# Classic almond milk pudding

This Ottoman milk pudding, *keşkül*, is thought to have got its name from the oval bowl called keşkul that beggars would carry from house to house seeking food. Perhaps for that reason it is revered, and always served in individual bowls. Traditionally, it is decorated with grated pistachios.

## Serves four

**115g/4oz blanched almonds**

**600ml/1 pint/2½ cups milk**

**25g/1oz rice flour**

**115g/4oz/generous ½ cup sugar**

**15–30ml/1–2 tbsp finely grated pistachio nuts**

Using a mortar and pestle, food processor or nut mill, pound or grind the almonds to a paste. Blend the paste with a little of the milk until smooth, and set aside. In a small bowl, slake the rice flour with a little more milk to form a paste with the consistency of thick cream. Set the bowl aside.

Pour the rest of the milk into a heavy pan. Add the sugar and bring the milk to the boil, stirring constantly. Stir 30ml/2 tbsp of the hot milk into the slaked rice flour and then add this paste to the pan. Make sure you keep stirring to prevent the rice flour from cooking in clumps. Cook until the mixture coats the back of the wooden spoon.

Stir in the almond paste and reduce the heat. Simmer the mixture gently for about 25 minutes, stirring from time to time, until the mixture is thick. Pour into individual bowls or glasses and leave to cool.

Sprinkle the grated pistachio nuts over each bowl of *keşkul* – this is often done in a thin line across the middle – and chill in the refrigerator.

## Variation

Another classic milk pudding is *mulhallebi*, which is made in a similar way but without the nuts, and which is flavoured with *mastick* and dusted with icing (confectioner's) sugar. It can also be set in a mould and cut into blocks, then served with rose water.

# Noah's pudding

According to legend, Noah came up with this unusual pudding, *aşure*, on the Ark by combining whatever stores were left – grains, pulses and dried fruit – when the Flood subsided. It is also the traditional dessert to serve on the tenth day of Muharrem, the first month of the Muslim calendar, to mark the martyrdom of the Prophet's grandson. It requires a fair amount of advance preparation and is always made in large quantities to be shared with friends.

## Serves ten to twelve

**50g/2oz each of dried haricot (navy) beans, dried broad (fava) beans, and dried chickpeas, all soaked separately for at least 6 hours, and drained**

**115g/4oz pot barley, husks removed, soaked for 24 hours**

**50g/2oz short grain rice, washed and drained**

**115g/4oz dried apricots**

**50g/2oz sultanas (golden raisins)**

**50g/2oz raisins**

**50g/2oz currants**

**225g/8oz/1 cup sugar**

**30ml/2 tbsp cornflour (cornstarch), or rice flour**

**150ml/¼ pint/⅔ cup rose water**

To decorate

**15ml/1 tbsp pine nuts**

**seeds of ½ pomegranate**

**4–5 dried figs, sliced**

**4–5 ready-to-eat dried apricots, sliced**

**15ml/1 tbsp sultanas, soaked in warm water for 10 minutes**

Cook the dried beans and chickpeas in separate pans of fresh water until just tender. The haricot beans will require about 50 minutes; the broad beans and chickpeas about 1 hour.

Transfer the barley and its soaking water to a large, deep pan and bring to the boil. Reduce the heat and simmer for about 45 minutes, or until the barley is tender, topping up the water during the cooking time if necessary. Add the cooked beans and chickpeas, and the short grain rice, and bring the liquid to the boil again. Reduce the heat and simmer for about 15 minutes.

Meanwhile, place all the dried fruit in a bowl and cover with boiling water. Leave to soak for 10 minutes, then drain. Add the fruit to the pan with the beans, and stir in the sugar. Continue to simmer, stirring from time to time, until the mixture thickens.

Mix the cornflour or rice flour with a little water to form a creamy paste. Mix in 30ml/2 tbsp of the hot liquid from the pan, then add all the paste to the pan, stirring constantly. Add the rose water and continue to simmer the mixture for another 15 minutes, stirring from time to time, until it is very thick.

Transfer the mixture to a large serving bowl. Shake the bowl to make sure the surface is flat, and leave the pudding to cool. Arrange the pine nuts, pomegranate seeds, sliced dried figs and apricots, and the drained sultanas, over the top. Serve chilled or at room temperature.

## Cook's tip

Another traditional grain pudding that is thickened with cornflour is the rose-scented, saffron-coloured *zerde* prepared for wedding feasts. Its name derives from the Persian word 'zerd', meaning 'yellow'.

# Helva with pine nuts

*Helva*, derived from the Arabic word for 'sweet', signifies good fortune and is made for events such as moving house, starting a new job, the birth of a child and the arrival of guests. There are many different types of *helva*, some soft, others hard, and usually combined with seeds or nuts, but this recipe is for the semolina *helva* that is traditionally offered to guests at a bereavement.

## Serves six to eight

**225g/8oz butter**

**450g/1lb/2¾ cups semolina**

**45ml/3 tbsp pine nuts**

**900ml/1½ pints/3¾ cups milk**

**225g/8oz/1 cup sugar**

**5–10ml/1–2 tsp ground cinnamon**

Melt the butter in a heavy pan, stir in the semolina and pine nuts, and cook over a medium heat, stirring all the time, until lightly browned.

Lower the heat and pour the milk into the pan. Mix well, cover the pan with a dish towel and press the lid down tightly to form a seal. Pull the flaps of the dish towel up and over the lid and simmer gently for 10–12 minutes, until the milk has been absorbed.

Add the sugar and stir until it has dissolved completely. Cover the pan with the dish towel and lid again, remove from the heat and leave it to stand for 1 hour.

To serve, mix well with a wooden spoon and spoon into bowls, then dust with cinnamon.

# Dried fruit compôte with rose water

Served as a winter dessert, or at ceremonial feasts, *hoşaf* is a classic dish held in high esteem. When the Ottomans dined in the Topkapi Palace, *hoşaf* was often spooned over plain rice as a final touch to a splendid meal. The syrup can be flavoured with rose or orange blossom water.

## Serves six to eight

**225g/8oz ready-to-eat dried apricots**

**175g/6oz ready-to-eat prunes**

**115g/4oz sultanas (golden raisins)**

**115g/4oz blanched almonds**

**30ml/2 tbsp pine nuts**

**45–60ml/3–4 tbsp sugar**

**30–45ml/2–3 tbsp rose water**

**15ml/1 tbsp orange flower water**

Put the dried fruit and nuts into a large bowl and cover them with water. Add the sugar according to taste, the rose water and orange flower water, and gently stir until the sugar has completely dissolved.

Cover the bowl and place it in the refrigerator. Leave the fruit and nuts to soak for 48 hours, during which time the liquid will turn syrupy and golden. Serve chilled, on its own, or with cream or ice cream, or with rice pudding.

## Cook's tip

You can make this dessert as sweet as you like using sugar or scented, runny honey.

Left **Festive helva with pine nuts** Right **Dried fruit compôte with rose water**

# Chilled baked rice pudding

From the Ottoman Palace kitchens to your table at home, *sütlaç* is the best-ever baked rice pudding. Some traditional 'pudding shops' burn the top of the pudding to give the skin a charred look and taste, contrasting with the delectable creaminess beneath. The concept of the 'pudding shop' is unique to Turkey and is devoted to the Palace milk puddings, such as *sütlaç*, *keşkül* (almond milk pudding) and *tavuk göğsü* (chicken breast pudding, see overleaf).

## Serves four to six

**100g/3¾oz/½ cup short grain pudding rice, rinsed thoroughly under running water and drained**

**2 litres/3½ pints/8 cups full-fat (whole) milk**

**90g/3½oz/½ cup sugar**

**5–10ml/1–2 tsp vanilla extract, or the seeds scraped from a juicy vanilla pod (bean)**

**30ml/2 tbsp rice flour**

Place the pudding rice in a deep, heavy pan, pour in enough water to just cover the rice and bring to the boil. Lower the heat and simmer the mixture for 5–6 minutes, until the water has been absorbed.

Pour in the milk and bring to the boil, stirring, then lower the heat and simmer until the liquid begins to thicken.

Add the sugar, stirring all the time until the sugar has dissolved, then stir in the vanilla and simmer for a further 15–20 minutes.

Meanwhile, preheat the oven to 200°C/400°F/Gas 6.

In a bowl, moisten the rice flour with a little water to make a smooth paste. Stir in a spoonful of the hot liquid. Tip the rice flour mixture into the pan of rice, stirring all the time to prevent lumps forming.

Once the liquid has thickened a little, transfer the mixture to a large ovenproof dish and bake in the oven for about 25 minutes, until the pudding is lightly browned on top.

Remove the pudding from the oven and leave to cool, allowing a skin to form on top, then chill well in the refrigerator, preferably overnight.

# Burnt chicken breast pudding

For the 'eat sweet, talk sweet' Turks, there is one pudding above all others that they will insist you try. A classic Ottoman dish that may even have had its origins in the lavish feasting of the Romans when Anatolia was part of its eastern empire, this dessert emerged from the Topkapi kitchens as *tavuk göğsü*, a milk pudding containing threads of cooked chicken breast for texture. In many pudding shops you will find the pudding has been burnt in a pan and then rolled into logs. The burnt version – *tavuk göğsü kazandibi* – is one of my favourite Turkish puddings.

## Serves six

**1 skinless, boneless chicken breast**

**75ml/5 tbsp rice flour**

**900ml/1½ pints/3¾ cups milk**

**300ml/½ pint/1¼ cups double (heavy) cream**

**a pinch of salt**

**175g/6oz/¾ cup sugar**

**ground cinnamon, for dusting**

Place the chicken breast fillet in a pan with enough water to just cover it. Bring the water to the boil, lower the heat and simmer for 6–7 minutes, until the breast is tender. Drain the chicken and tear the meat into very fine threads.

In a small bowl, moisten the rice flour with a little of the milk and mix to form a smooth paste that has the consistency of double cream.

Pour the rest of the milk and the cream into a heavy pan, add the salt and sugar and bring the mixture to the boil, stirring all the time, until the sugar has dissolved completely. Add a few spoonfuls of the hot milk mixture to the moistened rice flour, then transfer it all to the pan and stir vigorously with a wooden spoon. Lower the heat and stir constantly until it begins to thicken. If you do not stir constantly, the mixture will stick on the bottom of the pan and burn. Gently beat in the shredded, cooked chicken and continue to simmer for about 5 minutes, until the mixture is very thick.

Lightly grease a non-stick frying pan and place it over the heat. When the pan is hot, transfer the pudding mixture to it and keep it over the heat for 5 minutes to brown, or burn, the bottom – check by lifting up an edge to peep beneath. Move the pan around to make sure the bottom is evenly burned, then turn off the heat and leave the pudding to cool in the pan.

Using a sharp-pointed knife, cut the pudding into rectangles. Lift each rectangle out of the pan with a palette knife or metal spatula and place on a flat surface. Roll each rectangle over so that it resembles a log, and place seam-side down in a serving dish.

Serve chilled or at room temperature as a sweet snack or dessert, dusted with a little cinnamon.

# Cheese-filled pastry in lemon syrup

This delectable sweet pastry, *künefe*, from the south of Turkey, is another favourite of mine. It is made with thin strands of pastry that look like shredded wheat or pale vermicelli, called *kadayıf*, which is difficult to make at home as the batter requires tossing through a strainer on to a hot metal sheet over an open fire. However, you can buy the pastry online and in Middle Eastern and Turkish food stores. Sometimes this sweet dish is simply called *kadayıf*.

## Serves six

**225g/8oz ready-prepared *kadayıf* pastry, thawed if frozen**

**115g/4oz clarified butter, or ghee, melted**

**350g/12oz *dil peyniri*, or mozzarella, sliced**

**15–30ml/1–2 tbsp pistachio nuts, coarsely chopped**

For the syrup

**225g/8oz/1 cup sugar**

**120ml/4fl oz/½ cup water**

**juice of 1 lemon**

Preheat the oven to 180°C/350°F/Gas 4. To make the syrup, put the sugar and water into a pan and bring it to the boil, stirring with a wooden spoon until the sugar has dissolved. Add the lemon juice, reduce the heat, and simmer for 15 minutes, until it coats the back of the wooden spoon. Turn off the heat and leave the syrup to cool.

Put the shredded pastry into a bowl and separate the strands. Pour the clarified butter or melted ghee over them and, using your fingers, rub it all over the strands so that they are completely coated. Spread half the pastry in the base of a baking tin or pan (the Turks use a round 27cm/10½in tin), and press it down with your fingers.

Lay the slices of cheese over and cover with the remainder of the pastry, pressing down firmly and tucking it down the sides of the tin.

Bake in the oven for about 45 minutes, or until it is golden brown. Remove from the oven and cool slightly for 10 minutes. Loosen the edges of the pastry with a sharp knife and pour the cold syrup over it. Sprinkle the pistachios over the top. Cut into squares or segments, depending on the shape of your tin, and serve while still warm.

## Cook's tips

✻ The same pastry is used to make *kiz memesi kadayıf* – 'young girls' breasts' – a great favourite of the Ottoman Palace kitchens. Traditionally, the pastry chefs made these filled shredded pastries in special, individual, non-stick pans cooked on the stove, but the homemade version is baked in the oven.

✻ The cheese most commonly used for the filling is the elastic *dil peyniri*, which peels off in threads, but mozzarella is similar.

# Yogurt cake in orange syrup

Not every cake has had its moment in history but this one, *yoğurt tatlısı*, was served on Fridays at the court of Mehmet the Conqueror in the fifteenth century. There are many versions – some include coconut, sultanas or ground walnuts, others are soaked in syrup – and all are enjoyed with a dollop of *kaymak* or clotted cream.

## Serves six

**a little butter or oil, for greasing**

**4 eggs**

**115g/4oz/generous ½ cup sugar**

**115g/4oz/1 cup self-raising (self-rising) flour**

**400g/14oz thick and creamy natural (plain) yogurt**

**grated rind and juice of 1 lemon**

***kaynak*, or clotted cream, to serve (optional)**

For the syrup

**225g/8oz/1 cup sugar**

**120ml/4fl oz/½ cup water**

**juice and finely shredded rind of 1 orange**

Preheat the oven to 180°C/350°F/Gas 4. Prepare a baking tin, pan or dish (the Turks use a round tepsi approximately 23cm/9in in diameter) by greasing it lightly with oil or butter.

In a bowl, beat the eggs with the sugar until light and fluffy. Beat in the flour, then the yogurt, lemon rind and lemon juice.

Transfer the mixture to the prepared tin or dish and bake it in the oven for about 45 minutes. The cake should rise and turn golden brown on top.

Meanwhile, prepare the syrup. Heat the sugar and water in a heavy pan, stirring constantly, until the sugar has dissolved. Stir in the orange juice and rind and bring the liquid to the boil. Reduce the heat and simmer for 10–15 minutes. Leave the syrup to cool.

When the cake is ready, turn it out on to a serving dish and pour the cold syrup over it. Serve warm or at room temperature on its on, or with *kaymak* if you like.

## Cook's tip

The Turkish rule with all their syrupy pastries and sponges is that if the pudding is hot, then the syrup should be cold, even chilled, and vice versa.

# Ladies' navels

This classic fried pastry, bathed in syrup, *kadin göbeği*, is one of the inventions from the Topkapi Palace kitchens. The chefs of the time shaped moulded pastries into deliberate shapes and gave them names like Ladies' Navels, and Young Girls' Breasts – descriptions they wouldn't get away with now. It can be served with *kaymak* or clotted cream.

## Serves four to six

**50g/2oz butter**

**2.5ml/½ tsp salt**

**250ml/9fl oz/1 cup water**

**175g/6oz/1½ cups plain (all-purpose) flour**

**50g/2oz semolina**

**2 eggs**

**sunflower oil, for deep-frying**

For the syrup

**450g/1lb/2¼ cups sugar**

**300ml/½ pint/1¼ cups water**

**juice of 1 lemon**

Make the sugar syrup. Put the sugar and water into a large, heavy pan and bring to the boil, stirring all the time. When the sugar has dissolved completely, stir in the lemon juice and lower the heat, then simmer for about 10 minutes, until the syrup has thickened a little. Remove from the heat and leave to cool.

Put the butter, salt and the 250ml/8fl oz/1 cup of water in another heavy pan and bring to the boil. Remove from the heat and add the flour and semolina, beating all the time, until the mixture becomes smooth and leaves the side of the pan. Leave to cool.

Beat the eggs into the cooled mixture so that it gleams. Add a tablespoon of the cooled syrup and beat well.

Pour enough oil for deep-frying into a suitable deep-sided pan. Heat until warm, then remove from the heat.

Wet your hands and take an apricot-size piece of dough in your fingers. Roll it into a ball, flatten it in the palm of your hand, then use your finger to make an indentation in the middle.

Drop the balls of dough into the pan of warmed oil. Repeat with the rest of the mixture to make about 12 navels. Place the pan back over the heat. As the oil heats up, the pastries will swell, retaining the dip in the middle. Swirl the oil, until the navels turn golden all over.

Remove the navels from the oil with a slotted spoon, then toss them in the cooled syrup. Leave to soak for a few minutes, arrange in a serving dish and spoon some of the syrup over.

# Baklava

For many Turks *baklava* is the grandest pastry of them all. An Ottoman legacy, it is prepared by specialist chefs, with great attention to detail – paper-thin dough made with clarified butter and the finest flour; finely chopped nuts with walnuts regarded as king; a light syrup to cling to each pastry sheet so it melts in your mouth. Traditionally assembled with eight layers of pastry and seven of chopped nuts, there are many versions with different nuts and syrups, but this recipe is for the classic *baklava*, often enjoyed as a mid-morning sweet snack with a cup of Turkish coffee.

## Serves twelve

**175g/6oz clarified or plain butter**

**100ml/3½fl oz/scant ½ cup sunflower oil**

**450g/1lb filo pastry (or at least 12 sheets), thawed if frozen**

**450g/1lb walnuts, or a mixture of walnuts, pistachios and almonds, finely chopped**

**5ml/1 tsp ground cinnamon**

For the syrup

**450g/1lb/2¼ cups sugar**

**250ml/9fl oz/1 cup water**

**juice of 1 lemon, or 30ml/2 tbsp rose water**

Preheat the oven to 160°C/325°F/Gas 3. Melt the butter and oil in a small pan, then brush a little over the bottom and sides of a 30cm/12in cake tin or pan, or one that fits your sheets of filo.

Place a sheet of filo in the bottom and brush it with melted butter and oil. Continue layering until you have used about seven filo sheets, brushing each one with butter and oil. Ease the sheets into the corners and trim the edges if they flop over the rim of the tin.

Spread the nuts over the last buttered sheet and sprinkle with the cinnamon, then continue as before with the remaining filo sheets. Brush the top one as well, then, using a sharp knife, cut diagonal parallel lines right through all the layers to the bottom to form small diamond shapes.

Bake the *baklava* in the oven for about 1 hour, until the top is golden – if it is still looking pale, increase the temperature for a few minutes at the end.

While the *baklava* is in the oven, make the syrup. Put the sugar into a medium, heavy pan, pour in the water and bring the mixture to the boil, stirring constantly. When the sugar has dissolved, lower the heat and stir in the lemon juice, then simmer for 15 minutes, until the syrup thickens. Leave to cool in the pan.

Remove from the oven and pour the cooled syrup over the hot pastry. Return to the oven for 2–3 minutes, then take it out and leave to cool. Once the baklava is cool, carefully lift the individual diamond-shaped pieces out of the tin and arrange them in a serving dish.

# Rose petal jam

Thick with delicate, scented rose petals, *gül reçeli* is one of the most traditional of the Turkish jams. Spooned over yogurt, rice pudding or clotted cream, or over thin sheets of pastry or chunks of warm, crusty bread, the taste is exquisite. Any sweet-scented rose petals can be used, but the pink or lilac cottage-garden rose is particularly good. Some Middle Eastern stores sell bags of dried, scented rose petals specially for jam making.

## Makes enough for 1–2 × 450g/1lb jars

**450g/1lb fresh or dried scented rose petals**

**about 350ml/12fl oz/1½ cups water**

**450g/1lb/2¼ cups sugar**

**juice of 1 lemon**

If necessary, trim and clean the petals but, if you need to rinse them, make sure they are thoroughly drained. Pour the measured water into a large, heavy pan. Add the rose petals and bring to the boil.

Strain the petals into a bowl and return the rose-scented water to the pan. Set the strained petals aside.

Add the sugar to the rose-scented water and bring it to the boil, stirring constantly. Reduce the heat and simmer for 10 minutes, or until the liquid thickens and coats the back of a wooden spoon.

Stir in the lemon juice and the strained rose petals, and simmer for a further 10 minutes.

Leave the mixture to cool and thicken in the pan – it should be thick but still runny, requiring a spoon for serving, not a knife.

Spoon the cooled jam into sterilised jars and keep in a cool, dry place for up to 6 months.

# Sour cherry jam

Stunning in colour and taste, *vişne reçeli* is one of Turkey's most popular summer jams. When the cherries are in season, the plump, sweet ones, *kiraz*, are picked to eat, whereas the sour variety, *vişne*, is coveted for this jam and to make a fruit syrup, which is deep purple in colour and is used as the basis of the cool, refreshing drink, *vişne suyu*. As with most Turkish jams, this recipe is for a runny conserve, which is spooned on to bread or drizzled over yogurt.

## Makes about 2kg/4½lb

**1kg/2¼lb fresh sour cherries**
**1kg/2¼lb/5 cups sugar**
**juice of 1 lemon**

Pick over the cherries and remove the stalks. (You can remove the stones, too, if you like, but this is a laborious task and few Turkish cooks bother – though be careful when you eat the jam not to crack your teeth.)

Rinse and drain the cherries and put them into a large, heavy pan. Spoon the sugar over them, making sure they are all covered, and leave the cherries to weep overnight.

Place the pan over the heat and bring the liquid (there will be a substantial amount of cherry juice in the pan) to the boil, stirring from time to time.

Add the lemon juice, reduce the heat, and simmer for about 25 minutes, or until the liquid thickens, bearing in mind that this is a fairly liquid jam.

Leave the jam to cool in the pan and then spoon it into sterilised jars. It can be kept in a cool, dry place, ready to enjoy with bread, or to spoon over milk and rice puddings. The jam will keep well for up to 6 months.

# Dried fig and pine nut jam with aniseed

When the fresh figs are green and unripe a very special jam is prepared with them – they are kept whole and float like globes of precious jade in a pale, transparent syrup. The taste of each bite of green fig is more reminiscent of honeycomb than the fruit itself. Less well known, but equally good, is this delectable homemade winter jam prepared with soft, ready-to-eat dried figs and pine nuts. *Kuru incir reçeli* is delicious spooned on to hot fresh bread or served with strained yogurt (*süzme*) as a sweet snack.

## Makes enough for 3–4 × 450g/1lb jars

**450g/1lb/2¼ cups sugar**

**600ml/1 pint/2½ cups water**

**juice of 1 lemon**

**5ml/1 tsp ground aniseed**

**about 700g/1lb 9oz ready-to-eat dried figs, coarsely chopped**

**45–60ml/3–4 tbsp pine nuts**

Put the sugar and water into a heavy pan and bring to the boil, stirring all the time, until the sugar has dissolved. Lower the heat and simmer for 5–10 minutes, until the syrup begins to thicken.

Stir the lemon juice, aniseed and chopped figs into the sugar syrup.

Bring to the boil once more, then lower the heat again and simmer for 15–20 minutes, until the figs are tender. Add the pine nuts and simmer for a further 5 minutes.

Leave the jam to cool in the pan before spooning into sterilised jars and sealing. Stored in a cool, dry place, the jam will keep for several months.

# Plum tomato and almond jam

Homemade jams come in many guises, in combinations of fruit, vegetables and nuts that you might not find in the shops. Always in the syrupy style of a conserve, these jams are designed to be spooned rather than spread. This summer jam, *domates reçeli*, is best made with small plum tomatoes as ideally you want to keep them whole.

## Makes enough for 2–3 × 450g/1lb jars

**1kg/2¼lb firm fresh plum tomatoes**

**500g/1¼lb/2½ cups sugar**

**115g/4oz whole blanched almonds**

**8–10 whole cloves**

Skin the plum tomatoes. Submerge them for a few seconds in a bowl of boiling water, then plunge them straight away into a bowl of cold water. Remove them from the water one at a time and peel off the skins with your fingers or a small knife.

Place the skinned tomatoes in a heavy pan and cover with the sugar. Leave them to sit for a few hours, or overnight, to draw out some of the juices, then stir in 150ml/¼ pint/⅔ cup of water. The tomatoes should be quite juicy – if not, stir in some more water; you may need up to 300ml/½ pint/1¼ cups. Place the pan over a low heat and stir gently with a wooden spoon until the sugar has completely dissolved.

Bring the syrup to the boil and boil for a few minutes, skimming off any froth, then lower the heat and stir in the almonds and cloves. Simmer gently for about 25 minutes, stirring from time to time to prevent the mixture from sticking to the bottom of the pan and burning, which would spoil the flavour.

Turn off the heat and leave the jam to cool in the pan before spooning into sterilised jars and sealing. Stored in a cool, dry place, the jam will keep for several months.

# Nutritional notes

The nutritional analysis given for each recipe is calculated per portion (i.e. serving or item), unless otherwise stated. If the recipe gives a range, such as Serves 4–6, then the nutritional analysis will be for the smaller portion, i.e. 6 servings. The analysis does not include optional ingredients, such as salt added to taste.

p97 | **Humus** Energy 190kcal/798kJ; Protein 8.4g; Carb 19.3g, of which sugars 1.4g; Fat 9.4g, of which saturates 1.3g; Chol 0mg; Calcium 70mg; Fibre 4.1g; Sodium 19mg.

p98 | **Smoked aubergine and yogurt purée** Energy 103kcal/431kJ; Protein 4.4g; Carb 7.7g, of which sugars 6.4g; Fat 6.5g, of which saturates 1.2g; Chol 1mg; Calcium 118mg; Fibre 2.3g; Sodium 49mg.

p101 | **Tahini and lemon dip** Energy 160kcal/664kJ; Protein 4.3g; Carb 6.4g, of which sugars 6.2g; Fat 13.3g, of which saturates 1.9g; Chol 0mg; Calcium 155mg; Fibre 1.8g; Sodium 6mg.

p101 | **Carrot and caraway purée with yogurt** Energy 157kcal/651kJ; Protein 4.2g; Carb 15.3g, of which sugars 13.6g; Fat 9.2g, of which saturates 1.6g; Chol 1mg; Calcium 140mg; Fibre 3.3g; Sodium 78mg.

p102 | **Hot humus with pine nuts and melted butter** Energy 433kcal/1803kJ; Protein 15g; Carb 29.5g, of which sugars 3g; Fat 29.2g, of which saturates 7.7g; Chol 21mg; Calcium 160mg; Fibre 6.8g; Sodium 91mg.

p105 | **Fiery cheese and parsley dip** Energy 170kcal/705kJ; Protein 10.7g; Carb 2.4g, of which sugars 1.5g; Fat 13.2g, of which saturates 8.6g; Chol 44mg; Calcium 262mg; Fibre 0.6g; Sodium 908mg.

p106 | **Smoked cod's roe dip** Energy 118kcal/495kJ; Protein 9.6g; Carb 5.1g, of which sugars 1.2g; Fat 6.8g, of which saturates 1.1g; Chol 125mg; Calcium 48mg; Fibre 0.5g; Sodium 94mg.

p109 | **Tangy charred pepper and smoked aubergine** Energy 102kcal/425kJ; Protein 1.8g; Carb 10.5g, of which sugars 9.8g; Fat 6.2g, of which saturates 1g; Chol 0mg; Calcium 19mg; Fibre 3.1g; Sodium 6mg.

p110 | **Spicy walnut and red pepper dip** Energy 339kcal/1399kJ; Protein 4.8g; Carb 5.1g, of which sugars 2.8g; Fat 33.4g, of which saturates 3.5g; Chol 0mg; Calcium 34mg; Fibre 1.2g; Sodium 32mg.

p113 | **Stuffed vine leaves** Energy 411kcal/1702kJ; Protein 5g; Carb 39g, of which sugars 7.5g; Fat 26.1g, of which saturates 3.4g; Chol 0mg; Calcium 58mg; Fibre 2.2g; Sodium 7mg.

p114 | **Tomato, pepper and chilli salsa** Energy 101kcal/420kJ; Protein 2.3g; Carb 9.3g, of which sugars 8g; Fat 6.3g, of which saturates 0.9g; Chol 0mg; Calcium 66mg; Fibre 2.7g; Sodium 15mg.

p117 | **Fresh bulgur salad with mint and lemon** Energy 149kcal/620kJ; Protein 3g; Carb 21.6g, of which sugars 5.4g; Fat 6.1g, of which saturates 0.8g; Chol 0mg; Calcium 54mg; Fibre 1.7g; Sodium 19mg.

p118 | **Fried vegetables with garlic yogurt** Energy 225kcal/933kJ; Protein 6.5g; Carb 13.3g, of which sugars 11.6g; Fat 17.1g, of which saturates 4.2g; Chol 0mg; Calcium 104mg; Fibre 4g; Sodium 43mg.

p121 | **Warm aubergine salad with pepper and tomatoes** Energy 102kcal/424kJ; Protein 3.2g; Carb 8.2g, of which sugars 7.5g; Fat 6.5g, of which saturates 1g; Chol 0mg; Calcium 59mg; Fibre 4g; Sodium 14mg.

p122 | **Spinach with currants, pine nuts and yogurt** Energy 145kcal/603kJ; Protein 5.8g; Carb 10.2g, of which sugars 9.8g; Fat 9.3g, of which saturates 1.3g; Chol 1mg; Calcium 252mg; Fibre 2.2g; Sodium 165mg.

p125 | **Haricot bean salad with eggs and anchovies** Energy 402kcal/1674kJ; Protein 28g; Carb 10.4g, of which sugars 4.2g; Fat 28g, of which saturates 4.4g; Chol 149mg; Calcium 221mg; Fibre 10g; Sodium 696mg.

p126 | **Orange and onion salad with olives** Energy 150kcal/629kJ; Protein 3g; Carb 18.9g, of which sugars 16.4g; Fat 7.6g, of which saturates 1.1g; Chol 0mg; Calcium 102mg; Fibre 3.8g; Sodium 292mg.

p129 | **Salad with feta, chillies and parsley** Energy 253kcal/1049kJ; Protein 11.1g; Carb 13.4g, of which sugars 11g; Fat 17.6g, of which saturates 8.6g; Chol 39mg; Calcium 260mg; Fibre 3.2g; Sodium 824mg.

p130 | **Melon and feta salad with pastirma** Energy 172kcal/716kJ; Protein 10.2g; Carb 5.4g, of which sugars 5.3g; Fat 12.4g, of which saturates 5.8g; Chol 34mg; Calcium 145mg; Fibre 0.7g; Sodium 520mg.

p133 | **Lamb's lettuce salad** Energy 78kcal/328kJ; Protein 6.8g; Carb 10.3g, of which sugars 10.3g; Fat 1.5g, of which saturates 0.7g; Chol 2mg; Calcium 253mg; Fibre 0.5g; Sodium 106mg.

p133 | **Cucumber and mint salad** Energy 83kcal/348kJ; Protein 7.4g; Carb 11.2g, of which sugars 10.1g; Fat 1.4g, of which saturates 0.6g; Chol 2mg; Calcium 273mg; Fibre 0.4g; Sodium 107mg.

p134 | **Celery and coconut salad with lime and yogurt dressing** Energy 126kcal/521kJ; Protein 2.1g; Carb 2.9g, of which sugars 2.9g; Fat 11.9g, of which saturates 10.1g; Chol 0mg; Calcium 63mg; Fibre 3.6g; Sodium 69mg.

p137 | **Grated beetroot and yogurt salad** Energy 95kcal/403kJ; Protein 7.8g; Carb 14.4g, of which sugars 13g; Fat 1.4g, of which saturates 0.6g; Chol 2mg; Calcium 249mg; Fibre 1.3g; Sodium 137mg.

p141 | **Sour pomegranate broth** Energy 62kcal/260kJ; Protein 2g; Carb 3.9g, of which sugars 2.3g; Fat 4.4g, of which saturates 0.4g; Chol 0mg; Calcium 14mg; Fibre 0.6g; Sodium 205mg.

p142 | **Fish broth with celeriac** Energy 169kcal/712kJ; Protein 24.9g; Carb 14.9g, of which sugars 7.1g; Fat 1.5g, of which saturates 0.2g; Chol 120mg; Calcium 117mg; Fibre 3.3g; Sodium 195mg.

p145 | **Meadow soup with rice and mint** Energy 187kcal/781kJ; Protein 7.6g; Carb 30.3g, of which sugars 11.1g; Fat 4.4g, of which saturates 2.5g; Chol 9mg; Calcium 215mg; Fibre 1g; Sodium 108mg.

p146 | **Leek soup with feta, dill and paprika** Energy 203kcal/844kJ; Protein 10g; Carb 10.9g, of which sugars 9.4g; Fat 13.5g, of which saturates 5.7g; Chol 25mg; Calcium 259mg; Fibre 4.1g; Sodium 454mg.

p149 | **Pumpkin soup with yogurt and melted butter** Energy 97kcal/406kJ; Protein 2.6g; Carb 9.3g, of which sugars 8g; Fat 5.8g, of which saturates 3.6g; Chol 14mg; Calcium 104mg; Fibre 2.5g; Sodium 51mg.

p150 | **Spicy red lentil soup with onion** Energy 203kcal/856kJ; Protein 11.1g; Carb 31.8g, of which sugars 7.3g; Fat 4.4g, of which saturates 0.6g; Chol 0mg; Calcium 45mg; Fibre 3.5g; Sodium 26mg.

p153 | **Lamb and yogurt soup** Energy 226kcal/943kJ; Protein 15g; Carb 14.4g, of which sugars 3.6g; Fat 12.4g, of which saturates 6.2g; Chol 88mg; Calcium 54mg; Fibre 1.4g; Sodium 87mg

p154 | **Classic tripe soup** Energy 101kcal/421kJ; Protein 4.8g; Carb 4g, of which sugars 0.2g; Fat 7.5g, of which saturates 4.2g; Chol 83mg; Calcium 41mg; Fibre 0.2g; Sodium 60mg.

p157 | **Tomatoes and peppers with eggs** Energy 190kcal/790kJ; Protein 8.6g; Carb 14.9g, of which sugars 12.4g; Fat 11.2g, of which saturates 3.5g; Chol 196mg; Calcium 65mg; Fibre 3.1g; Sodium 101mg.

p158 | **Simple eggs with garlic yogurt** Energy 345kcal/1438kJ; Protein 25.4g; Carb 19.1g, of which sugars 19.1g; Fat 19.8g, of which saturates 8.3g; Chol 400mg; Calcium 534mg; Fibre 0.1g; Sodium 393mg.

p161 | **Chickpea dumplings** Energy 416kcal/1760kJ; Protein 14.8g; Carb 73.7g, of which sugars 5.9g; Fat 9g, of which saturates 2.6g; Chol 71mg; Calcium 179mg; Fibre 5.9g; Sodium 360mg.

p162 | **Filo cigars filled with feta, parsley, mint and dill** Energy 311kcal/1291kJ; Protein 12.4g; Carb 11.2g, of which sugars 1.6g; Fat 24.4g, of which saturates 9.5g; Chol 92mg; Calcium 278mg; Fibre 1.6g; Sodium 838mg.

p165 | **Flat breads with spinach** Energy 246kcal/1033kJ; Protein 10.5g; Carb 27.9g, of which sugars 3.7g; Fat 11.1g, of which saturates 5.1g; Chol 21mg; Calcium 327mg; Fibre 2.5g; Sodium 493mg.

p166 | **Courgette fritters** Energy 207kcal/857kJ; Protein 8.3g; Carb 10.8g, of which sugars 4.7g; Fat 14.8g, of which saturates 2.4g; Chol 95mg; Calcium 104mg; Fibre 2.1g; Sodium 50mg.

p169 | **Deep-fried mussels in beer batter** Energy 439kcal/1827kJ; Protein 10.6g; Carb 24.6g, of which sugars 1.9g; Fat 33g, of which saturates 4g; Chol 89mg; Calcium 115mg; Fibre 1.5g; Sodium 502mg.

p170 | **Deep-fried squid with garlic bread sauce** Energy 636kcal/2668kJ; Protein 34g; Carb 56.2g, of which sugars 2.5g; Fat 31g, of which saturates 4.5g; Chol 394mg; Calcium 126mg; Fibre 2g; Sodium 296mg.

p173 | **Flat breads with spicy lamb and tomato** Energy 496kcal/2092kJ; Protein 20g; Carb 75.2g, of which sugars 8.1g; Fat 14.9g, of which saturates 6.1g; Chol 51mg; Calcium 167mg; Fibre 3.8g; Sodium 333mg.

p174 | **Minced meat and pine nut pie** Energy 463kcal/1920kJ; Protein 15.1g; Carb 16.5g, of which sugars 3.6g; Fat 37.9g, of which saturates 8.1g; Chol 97mg; Calcium 101mg; Fibre 0.9g; Sodium 94mg.

p179 | **Spinach with eggs and paprika** Energy 309kcal/1275kJ; Protein 18g; Carb 14g, of which sugars 11.3g; Fat 20.4g, of which saturates 6.6g; Chol 206mg; Calcium 693mg; Fibre 9.3g; Sodium 644mg.

p180 | **Smoked aubergines in cheese sauce** Energy 322kcal/1344kJ; Protein 14.1g; Carb 15.2g, of which sugars 9.3g; Fat 22.7g, of which saturates 14.5g; Chol 63mg; Calcium 415mg; Fibre 2.2g; Sodium 350mg.

p183 | **Stuffed poached aubergines** Energy 407kcal/1680kJ; Protein 3g; Carb 16.7g, of which sugars 14.1g; Fat 37g, of which saturates 5.1g; Chol 0mg; Calcium 67mg; Fibre 4.8g; Sodium 507mg.

p184 | **Stuffed leeks with a sauce** Energy 289kcal/1205kJ; Protein 17.3g; Carb 18.7g, of which sugars 4.6g; Fat 16.5g, of which saturates 6.9g; Chol 143mg; Calcium 122mg; Fibre 4g; Sodium 97mg.

p187 | **Peppers stuffed with aromatic rice** Energy 489kcal/2036kJ; Protein 9.1g; Carb 61.7g, of which sugars 23.6g; Fat 23.4g, of which saturates 2.8g; Chol 0mg; Calcium 108mg; Fibre 6g; Sodium 24mg.

p188 | **Baked stuffed apples** Energy 382kcal/1595kJ; Protein 5g; Carb 54.1g, of which sugars 18.8g; Fat 16.5g, of which saturates 1.9g; Chol 0mg; Calcium 26mg; Fibre 2.1g; Sodium 4mg.

p191 | **Aubergine stew** Energy 164kcal/685kJ; Protein 2.9g; Carb 20.7g, of which sugars 10.5g; Fat 8.3g, of which saturates 1.3g; Chol 0mg; Calcium 34mg; Fibre 3.7g; Sodium 23mg.

p192 | **Vegetable stew** Energy 166kcal/690kJ; Protein 4.4g; Carb 18.3g, of which sugars 17.3g; Fat 8.8g, of which saturates 1.4g; Chol 0mg; Calcium 68mg; Fibre 5.5g; Sodium 41mg.

p195 | **Carrot and apricot rolls with mint yogurt** Energy 401kcal/1673kJ; Protein 8.7g; Carb 46g, of which sugars 29.1g; Fat 21.5g, of which saturates 2.5g; Chol 48mg; Calcium 144mg; Fibre 8.5g; Sodium 145mg.

p196 | **Courgette, feta and mint patties** Energy 327kcal/1354kJ; Protein 12.3g; Carb 12.4g, of which sugars 5.4g; Fat 25.7g, of which saturates 7.9g; Chol 121mg; Calcium 214mg; Fibre 2.3g; Sodium 581mg.

p199 | **Potatoes baked with tomatoes and feta** Energy 243kcal/1016kJ; Protein 6.3g; Carb 27.5g, of which sugars 9.3g; Fat 12.8g, of which saturates 5g; Chol 19mg; Calcium 102mg; Fibre 2.9g; Sodium 447mg.

p200 | **Artichokes with beans and almonds** Energy 351kcal/1455kJ; Protein 8.2g; Carb 13.4g, of which sugars 8.3g; Fat 29.8g, of which saturates 3.6g; Chol 0mg; Calcium 110mg; Fibre 5.5g; Sodium 29mg.

p203 | **Green beans with tomatoes and dill** Energy 141kcal/588kJ; Protein 4.5g; Carb 16.5g, of which sugars 14g; Fat 6.8g, of which saturates 1.1g; Chol 0mg; Calcium 75mg; Fibre 5.7g; Sodium 20mg.

p204 | **Sweet-and-sour ladies' fingers** Energy 116kcal/482kJ; Protein 2.5g; Carb 6.6g, of which sugars 6.1g; Fat 9.1g, of which saturates 1.5g; Chol 0mg; Calcium 142mg; Fibre 3.5g; Sodium 7mg.

p207 | **Caramelised mushrooms with allspice and herbs** Energy 125kcal/517kJ; Protein 2.8g; Carb 1.2g, of which sugars 0.8g; Fat 12.2g, of which saturates 3.3g; Chol 8mg; Calcium 58mg; Fibre 2.5g; Sodium 37mg.

p208 | **Courgette and apple with a hazelnut and lemon sauce** Energy 365kcal/1513kJ; Protein 6.6g; Carb 13.3g, of which sugars 12.6g; Fat 32.1g, of which saturates 3.2g; Chol 0mg; Calcium 74mg; Fibre 4.2g; Sodium 5mg.

p211 | **Roasted courgettes and peaches** Energy 362kcal/1507kJ; Protein 11.7g; Carb 26.7g, of which sugars 26.3g; Fat 24.1g, of which saturates 3.7g; Chol 2mg; Calcium 284mg; Fibre 4.8g; Sodium 120mg.

p214 | **Lentils with carrots and sage** Energy 166kcal/696kJ; Protein 7.6g; Carb 21.1g, of which sugars 6.7g; Fat 6.2g, of which saturates 0.9g; Chol 0mg; Calcium 38mg; Fibre 4g; Sodium 22mg.

p217 | **Chickpea stew** Energy 178kcal/741kJ; Protein 5.3g; Carb 17.4g, of which sugars 10.6g; Fat 10.2g, of which saturates 1.5g; Chol 0mg; Calcium 136mg; Fibre 4.3g; Sodium 128mg.

p218 | **Chickpea patties with red onion and parsley** Energy 246kcal/1032kJ; Protein 10.2g; Carb 24.7g, of which sugars 2.3g; Fat 12.8g, of which saturates 1.7g; Chol 0mg; Calcium 118mg; Fibre 5.1g; Sodium 238mg.

p221 | **Beans with pastirma and lamb's lettuce** Energy 283kcal/1192kJ; Protein 21.4g; Carb 29.6g, of which sugars 9.6g; Fat 9.7g, of which saturates 2.3g; Chol 27mg; Calcium 112mg; Fibre 10.1g; Sodium 44mg.

p222 | **Borlotti beans with tomato and garlic** Energy 266kcal/1119kJ; Protein 12.4g; Carb 34.4g, of which sugars 14.4g; Fat 9.8g, of which saturates 1.5g; Chol 0mg; Calcium 103mg; Fibre 10.6g; Sodium 33mg.

p225 | **Black-eyed bean stew with spicy sausage** Energy 382kcal/1594kJ; Protein 18g; Carb 20g, of which sugars 6.7g; Fat 24.4g, of which saturates 10g; Chol 52mg; Calcium 55mg; Fibre 6g; Sodium 944mg.

p226 | **Broad bean purée** Energy 465kcal/1944kJ; Protein 17g; Carb 42.8g, of which sugars 6.2g; Fat 26.2g, of which saturates 3.8g; Chol 0mg; Calcium 89mg; Fibre 12.5g; Sodium 21mg.

p229 | **Bulgur wheat with yogurt** Energy 394kcal/1640kJ; Protein 11.1g; Carb 57.8g, of which sugars 6.6g; Fat 15.7g, of which saturates 8.2g; Chol 16mg; Calcium 154mg; Fibre 2.4g; Sodium 108mg.

p230 | **Anatolian bulgur with nuts and dates** Energy 412kcal/1719kJ; Protein 9g; Carb 54g, of which sugars 23.4g; Fat 19.1g, of which saturates 3.9g; Chol 11mg; Calcium 71mg; Fibre 3.4g; Sodium 74mg.

p233 | **Tomato bulgur with spicy lamb** Energy 541kcal/2259kJ; Protein 21.1g; Carb 86.1g, of which sugars 9g; Fat 15g, of which saturates 7.2g; Chol 64mg; Calcium 49mg; Fibre 3.3g; Sodium 110mg.

p234 | **Anchovy and rice dome** Energy 481kcal/2004kJ; Protein 19.5g; Carb 64g, of which sugars 3g; Fat 16g, of which saturates 3.1g; Chol 37mg; Calcium 178mg; Fibre 0.8g; Sodium 1982mg.

p237 | **Pumpkin stuffed with jewelled rice** Energy 345kcal/1443kJ; Protein 9.9g; Carb 50.1g, of which sugars 18.6g; Fat 12g, of which saturates 2.6g; Chol 5mg; Calcium 299mg; Fibre 9.6g; Sodium 93mg.

p238 | **Aubergine pilaff with cinnamon and mint** Energy 369kcal/1539kJ; Protein 6.1g; Carb 52.2g, of which sugars 11g; Fat 15.2g, of which saturates 1.8g; Chol 0mg; Calcium 38mg; Fibre 2.7g; Sodium 8mg.

p241 | **Rice with green peas, mint and dill** Energy 437kcal/1819kJ; Protein 10.5g; Carb 77g, of which sugars 2.3g; Fat 9.3g, of which saturates 3.8g; Chol 13mg; Calcium 57mg; Fibre 3.2g; Sodium 43mg.

p242 | **Sultan's chickpea pilaff** Energy 328kcal/1368kJ; Protein 7.1g; Carb 52.3g, of which sugars 1.2g; Fat 9.9g, of which saturates 4.4g; Chol 16mg; Calcium 36mg; Fibre 1.6g; Sodium 51mg.

p245 | **Sour cherry pilaff** Energy 295kcal/1231kJ; Protein 4.7g; Carb 54g, of which sugars 9.1g; Fat 6.5g, of which saturates 3.9g; Chol 16mg; Calcium 21mg; Fibre 0.5g; Sodium 46mg.

p246 | **Chicken liver pilaff with currants, pine nuts and almonds** Energy 430kcal/1790kJ; Protein 14.9g; Carb 54.8g, of which sugars 6.9g; Fat 16.6g, of which saturates 5.8g; Chol 179mg; Calcium 67mg; Fibre 1.9g; Sodium 38mg.

p249 | **Rice with spiced lamb** Energy 621kcal/2590kJ; Protein 30g; Carb 77.1g, of which sugars 4.2g; Fat 21.2g, of which saturates 9.5g; Chol 86mg; Calcium 51mg; Fibre 1.1g; Sodium 100mg.

pXXX | **Veiled pilaff** Energy 617kcal/2567kJ; Protein 27.4g; Carb 48g, of which sugars 2.1g; Fat 35.3g, of which saturates 4.6g; Chol 76mg; Calcium 100mg; Fibre 2.5g; Sodium 224mg.

p250 | **Anchovies poached in vine leaves** Energy 190kcal/788kJ; Protein 14.4g; Carb 2.5g, of which sugars 2.5g; Fat 13.6g, of which saturates 2.9g; Chol 0mg; Calcium 81mg; Fibre 1.1g; Sodium 84mg.

p256 | **Jewelled mackerel salad in a dome** Energy 575kcal/2383kJ; Protein 27.2g; Carb 9.5g, of which sugars 9.5g; Fat 47.8g, of which saturates 7.6g; Chol 66mg; Calcium 60mg; Fibre 2.2g; Sodium 121mg.

p259 | **Mackerel pilâki** Energy 270kcal/1127kJ; Protein 17.3g; Carb 22.9g, of which sugars 11.2g; Fat 12.7g, of which saturates 2.7g; Chol 40mg; Calcium 76mg; Fibre 4.1g; Sodium 115mg.

p260 | **Stuffed mackerel** Energy 520Kcal/2154kJ; Protein 20.2g; Carb 13.7g, of which sugars 10.1g; Fat 43.1g, of which saturates 5.5g; Chol 40mg; Calcium 86mg; Fibre 3.1g; Sodium 53mg.

p263 | **Baked sardines with tomatoes** Energy 219kcal/915kJ; Protein 11.7g; Carb 7.3g, of which sugars 7.3g; Fat 16.2g, of which saturates 3.1g; Chol 0mg; Calcium 57mg; Fibre 2g; Sodium 78mg.

p264 | **Stuffed sardines** Energy 265kcal/1098kJ; Protein 16.7g; Carb 4g, of which sugars 3.1g; Fat 20.3g, of which saturates 3.6g; Chol 0mg; Calcium 90mg; Fibre 0.4g; Sodium 88mg.

p267 | **Chargrilled sardines in vine leaves** Energy 300kcal/1245kJ; Protein 16.5g; Carb 5.3g, of which sugars 5.3g; Fat 23.7g, of which saturates 4.5g; Chol 0mg; Calcium 82mg; Fibre 1.5g; Sodium 101mg.

p268 | **Swordfish, lemon and red pepper kebabs** Energy 225kcal/940kJ; Protein 23.9g; Carb 7.8g, of which sugars 7.2g; Fat 11.1g, of which saturates 2g; Chol 51mg; Calcium 18mg; Fibre 1.9g; Sodium 177mg.

p277 | **Seared tuna with sage, parsley and dill** Energy 337kcal/1407kJ; Protein 38.6g; Carb 2.7g, of which sugars 2.3g; Fat 19.2g, of which saturates 3.4g; Chol 42mg; Calcium 224mg; Fibre 5g; Sodium 104mg.

p272 | **Sea perch baked on a tile with poppy seeds** Energy 684kcal/2840kJ; Protein 44.9g; Carb 5.4g, of which sugars 5.2g; Fat 53.8g, of which saturates 18.4g; Chol 213mg; Calcium 281mg; Fibre 4.1g; Sodium 309mg.

p275 | **Sea bass with rakı** Energy 236kcal/984kJ; Protein 24.5g; Carb 1g, of which sugars 1g; Fat 8.7g, of which saturates 1.3g; Chol 100mg; Calcium 172mg; Fibre 0.5g; Sodium 92mg.

p275 | **Deep-fried red mullet with rocket** Energy 275kcal/1146kJ; Protein 19.4g; Carb 9.7g, of which sugars 0.9g; Fat 17.9g, of which saturates 1.7g; Chol 0mg; Calcium 85mg; Fibre 0.5g; Sodium 97mg.

p276 | **Sea bass parcels with cinnamon and mastic** Energy 267kcal/1114kJ; Protein 21.7g; Carb 14.9g, of which sugars 12.5g; Fat 13.8g, of which saturates 4.6g; Chol 93mg; Calcium 167mg; Fibre 3.1g; Sodium 121mg.

p279 | **Cinnamon fishcakes with currants, pine nuts and herbs** Energy 317kcal/1324kJ; Protein 26.1g; Carb 17.8g, of which sugars 2.5g; Fat 16.2g, of which saturates 1.9g; Chol 99mg; Calcium 79mg; Fibre 1.6g; Sodium 169mg.

p280 | **Sea bass baked in salt** Energy 175kcal/737kJ; Protein 33.8g; Carb 0g, of which sugars 0g; Fat 4.4g, of which saturates 0.7g; Chol 140mg; Calcium 228mg; Fibre 0g; Sodium 1103mg.

p283 | **Baked bonito with bay leaves** Energy 281kcal/1168kJ; Protein 20.4g; Carb 11.4g, of which sugars 8.9g; Fat 17.4g, of which saturates 5g; Chol 59mg; Calcium 64mg; Fibre 2.8g; Sodium 108mg.

p284 | **Blue fish stew** Energy 290kcal/1214kJ; Protein 22.5g; Carb 21.7g, of which sugars 19.2g; Fat 13.3g, of which saturates 3g; Chol 8mg; Calcium 87mg; Fibre 4g; Sodium 96mg.

p287 | **Herb-stuffed squid with saffron** Energy 201kcal/842kJ; Protein 19.7g; Carb 10.6g, of which sugars 1.2g; Fat 7.8g, of which saturates 1.3g; Chol 263mg; Calcium 38mg; Fibre 1g; Sodium 144mg.

p288 | **Squid with olives and red wine** Energy 304kcal/1275kJ; Protein 30.3g; Carb 11.4g, of which sugars 6.8g; Fat 10.1g, of which saturates 1.7g; Chol 422mg; Calcium 62mg; Fibre 1.7g; Sodium 468mg.

p291 | **Baked prawns with tomatoes, pepper and garlic** Energy 388kcal/1413kJ; Protein 35.9g; Carb 11.2g, of which sugars 10.8g; Fat 16.9g, of which saturates 7.3g; Chol 274mg; Calcium 481mg; Fibre 2.9g; Sodium 585mg.

p292 | **Mussels stuffed with aromatic pilaff** Energy 319kcal/1328kJ; Protein 13.3g; Carb 32.7g, of which sugars 7.5g; Fat 15g, of which saturates 1.9g; Chol 33mg; Calcium 49mg; Fibre 0.5g; Sodium 237mg.

p296 | **Lamb kebabs in flat bread wraps** Energy 433kcal/1821kJ; Protein 34.3g; Carb 37.1g, of which sugars 4.4g; Fat 17.5g, of which saturates 7.9g; Chol 114mg; Calcium 83mg; Fibre 2.5g; Sodium 460mg.

p299 | **Lamb shish kebab** Energy 642kcal/2688kJ; Protein 35.2g; Carb 52.8g, of which sugars 24.1g; Fat 33.9g, of which saturates 15.1g; Chol 121mg; Calcium 253mg; Fibre 6.3g; Sodium 456mg.

p300 | **Lamb kebab in puff pastry** Energy 388kcal/1621kJ; Protein 15.6g; Carb 28.5g, of which sugars 5.1g; Fat 25g, of which saturates 4.8g; Chol 75mg; Calcium 58mg; Fibre 0.7g; Sodium 266mg.

p302 | **Lamb stew with roasted chestnuts** Energy 760kcal/3159kJ; Protein 28.3g; Carb 34.1g, of which sugars 10.6g; Fat 57.7g, of which saturates 26.5g; Chol 122mg; Calcium 62mg; Fibre 3.9g; Sodium 146mg.

p305 | **Aubergine musakka** Energy 479kcal/1993kJ; Protein 22.6g; Carb 24.4g, of which sugars 16.5g; Fat 33.1g, of which saturates 10.7g; Chol 145mg; Calcium 164mg; Fibre 4.2g; Sodium 130mg.

p306 | **Lamb cutlets with tomato sauce** Energy 683kcal/2822kJ; Protein 23.2g; Carb 7.4g, of which sugars 6.9g; Fat 62.4g, of which saturates 29.2g; Chol 122mg; Calcium 24mg; Fibre 1.7g; Sodium 114mg.

p309 | **Ladies' thighs** Energy 544kcal/2261kJ; Protein 30.5g; Carb 30.2g, of which sugars 3.2g; Fat 33.6g, of which saturates 10.3g; Chol 191mg; Calcium 84mg; Fibre 1.5g; Sodium 127mg.

p310 | **Meat-stuffed vine leaves** Energy 276kcal/1148kJ; Protein 14.6g; Carb 23.5g, of which sugars 6.6g; Fat 13.8g, of which saturates 4.4g; Chol 45mg; Calcium 88mg; Fibre 2.8g; Sodium 51mg.

p313 | **Meatballs with pine nuts and cinnamon** Energy 261kcal/1088kJ; Protein 11.4g; Carb 15.4g, of which sugars 5.2g; Fat 17.5g, of which saturates 4g; Chol 64mg; Calcium 40mg; Fibre 0.7g; Sodium 129mg.

p314 | **Mother-in-law's meatballs** Energy 484kcal/2011kJ; Protein 18.2g; Carb 40.8g, of which sugars 2.8g; Fat 28.8g, of which saturates 6g; Chol 40mg; Calcium 53mg; Fibre 2.2g; Sodium 89mg.

p317 | **Stir-fried liver with red onion** Energy 298kcal/1245kJ; Protein 27g; Carb 11.8g, of which sugars 4.3g; Fat 16.3g, of which saturates 3.3g; Chol 538mg; Calcium 37mg; Fibre 1.3g; Sodium 94mg.

p318 | **Spicy liver sausage** Energy 407kcal/1722kJ; Protein 15.4g; Carb 80.5g, of which sugars 61.7g; Fat 4.2g, of which saturates 1g; Chol 242mg; Calcium 68mg; Fibre 2.8g; Sodium 542mg.

p321 | **Chicken casserole with okra and lemon** Energy 386Kcal/1617kJ; Protein 47.3g; Carb 16g, of which sugars 13.1g; Fat 15.2g, of which saturates 5.7g; Chol 139mg; Calcium 224mg; Fibre 7g; Sodium 181mg.

p322 | **Chicken with green plums and grape syrup** Energy 316kcal/1325kJ; Protein 33.7g; Carb 10g, of which sugars 9.2g; Fat 16g, of which saturates 3.6g; Chol 163mg; Calcium 39mg; Fibre 1.8g; Sodium 153mg.

p324 | **Chicken stew with walnuts and pomegranate juice** Energy 867kcal/3591kJ; Protein 40.6g; Carb 17.4g, of which sugars 13.8g; Fat 71.1g, of which saturates 14.6g; Chol 176mg; Calcium 99mg; Fibre 4.6g; Sodium 180mg.

p327 | **Circassian chicken** Energy 222kcal/937kJ; Protein 34.1g; Carb 7.6g, of which sugars 1.6g; Fat 6.4g, of which saturates 3.3g; Chol 105mg; Calcium 53mg; Fibre 0.2g; Sodium 324mg.

p328 | **Lemon chicken thighs wrapped in aubergine** Energy 509kcal/2114kJ; Protein 34.7g; Carb 2.7g, of which sugars 2.3g; Fat 40g, of which saturates 8.4g; Chol 180mg; Calcium 67mg; Fibre 2.6g; Sodium 108mg.

p331 | **Roast wild duck with honey, thyme and almonds** Energy 776kcal/3241kJ; Protein 37g; Carb 45.9g, of which sugars 19.6g; Fat 50.8g, of which saturates 11.1g; Chol 166mg; Calcium 132mg; Fibre 2.5g; Sodium 492mg.

p332 | **Chargrilled marinated quails** Energy 288kcal/1207kJ; Protein 37.4g; Carb 5.8g, of which sugars 5.8g; Fat 13g, of which saturates 2.7g; Chol 0mg; Calcium 84mg; Fibre 0.5g; Sodium 111mg.

p335 | **Spicy rabbit stew with shallots and figs** Energy 456kcal/1906kJ; Protein 39.4g; Carb 28g, of which sugars 23.9g; Fat 21.5g, of which saturates 5g; Chol 139mg; Calcium 199mg; Fibre 4.2g; Sodium 109mg.

p338 | **Rose petal sorbet** Energy 222kcal/946kJ; Protein 0.3g; Carb 58.8g, of which sugars 58.8g; Fat 0g, of which saturates 0g; Chol 0mg; Calcium 30mg; Fibre 0g; Sodium 4mg.

p341 | **Mastic ice cream** Energy 742Kcal/3093kJ; Protein 8.9g; Carb 70.2g, of which sugars 70.2g; Fat 49.1g, of which saturates 30.7g; Chol 134mg; Calcium 332mg; Fibre 0g; Sodium 117mg.

p342 | **Poached apricots with buffalo cream** Energy 333kcal/1416kJ; Protein 4.6g; Carb 77.6g, of which sugars 77.6g; Fat 2.6g, of which saturates 1.4g; Chol 8mg; Calcium 139mg; Fibre 4g; Sodium 36mg.

p345 | **Pumpkin poached in clove syrup** Energy 317kcal/1353kJ; Protein 1.6g; Carb 82.1g, of which sugars 81.2g; Fat 0.3g, of which saturates 0.2g; Chol 0mg; Calcium 88mg; Fibre 1.7g; Sodium 5mg.

p346 | **Fresh figs baked with honey** Energy 198kcal/845kJ; Protein 2.3g; Carb 48.2g, of which sugars 48.2g; Fat 1g, of which saturates 0g; Chol 0mg; Calcium 155mg; Fibre 4.5g; Sodium 39mg.s and mix them with 30ml/2 tbsp caster (superfine) sugar.

p349 | **Sour cherry summer pudding** Energy 360kcal/1532kJ; Protein 6.6g; Carb 85.7g, of which sugars 50.2g; Fat 1.3g, of which saturates 0.2g; Chol 0mg; Calcium 108mg; Fibre 2g; Sodium 414mg.

p350 | **Classic almond milk pudding** Energy 404kcal/1693kJ; Protein 12.4g; Carb 44.4g, of which sugars 38.5g; Fat 20.7g, of which saturates 3.2g; Chol 9mg; Calcium 270mg; Fibre 2.5g; Sodium 91mg.

p353 | **Noah's pudding** Energy 289kcal/1229kJ; Protein 5.8g; Carb 65.4g, of which sugars 45.9g; Fat 2.2g, of which saturates 0.1g; Chol 0mg; Calcium 98mg; Fibre 4.2g; Sodium 24mg.

p354 | **Helva with pine nuts** Energy 568kcal/2388kJ; Protein 10.2g; Carb 78.3g, of which sugars 34.7g; Fat 26g, of which saturates 15.9g; Chol 67mg; Calcium 165mg; Fibre 1.2g; Sodium 227mg.

p354 | **Dried fruit compôte with rose water** Energy 238kcal/1001kJ; Protein 5.4g; Carb 34.6g, of which sugars 34.2g; Fat 9.6g, of which saturates 0.7g; Chol 0mg; Calcium 75mg; Fibre 4.4g; Sodium 12mg.

p357 | **Chilled baked rice pudding** Energy 364kcal/1520kJ; Protein 12.6g; Carb 49.7g, of which sugars 32.4g; Fat 13.1g, of which saturates 8.4g; Chol 47mg; Calcium 407mg; Fibre 0.1g; Sodium 145mg.

p358 | **Burnt chicken breast pudding** Energy 504kcal/2107kJ; Protein 12.9g; Carb 48.4g, of which sugars 38.4g; Fat 29.8g, of which saturates 18.4g; Chol 95mg; Calcium 224mg; Fibre 0.3g; Sodium 93mg.

p361 | **Cheese-filled pastry in lemon syrup** Energy 595kcal/2486kJ; Protein 13.7g; Carb 53.4g, of which sugars 39.9g; Fat 38.2g, of which saturates 18.2g; Chol 75mg; Calcium 259mg; Fibre 0.2g; Sodium 478mg.

p362 | **Yogurt cake in orange syrup** Energy 415kcal/1757kJ; Protein 10.5g; Carb 75.8g, of which sugars 61.5g; Fat 10.7g, of which saturates 4.5g; Chol 127mg; Calcium 217mg; Fibre 0.6g; Sodium 167mg.

p365 | **Ladies' navels** Energy 517kcal/2190kJ; Protein 6.3g; Carb 108.8g, of which sugars 78.9g; Fat 9.3g, of which saturates 4.9g; Chol 81mg; Calcium 93mg; Fibre 1.1g; Sodium 80mg.

p366 | **Baklava** Energy 973kcal/4059kJ; Protein 12.2g; Carb 89.9g, of which sugars 60.9g; Fat 65.2g, of which saturates 15.6g; Chol 47mg; Calcium 139mg; Fibre 3.1g; Sodium 141mg.

p369 | **Rose petal jam** Energy 1886kcal/8028kJ; Protein 14.9g; Carb 477.4g, of which sugars 477g; Fat 3.6g, of which saturates 0.5g; Chol 0mg; Calcium 1004mg; Fibre 9.4g; Sodium 657mg.

p371 | **Sour cherry jam** Energy 20kcal/18840kJ; Protein 14g; Carb 1160g, of which sugars 1160g; Fat 1g, of which saturates 0g; Chol 0mg; Calcium 660mg; Fibre 9g; Sodium 70mg.

p372 | **Dried fig and pine nut jam with aniseed** Energy 869Kcal/3693kJ; Protein 8.4g; Carb 197.5g, of which sugars 197.5g; Fat 10.5g, of which saturates 0.5g; Chol 0mg; Calcium 492mg; Fibre 13.4g; Sodium 115mg.

p375 | **Plum tomato and almond jam** Energy 948Kcal/4016kJ; Protein 11.3g; Carb 187.1g, of which sugars 186.1g; Fat 22.4g, of which saturates 2g; Chol 0mg; Calcium 204mg; Fibre 6.2g; Sodium 45mg.

# Index


alcoholic drinks 26, 93
allspice 85
almonds 55
Anatolian bulgur with nuts and dates 230
artichokes with beans and almonds 200
chicken with green plums and grape syrup 322
chicken liver pilaff with currants, pine nuts and almonds 246
classic almond milk pudding 350
dried fruit compôte with rose water 354
lemon chicken thighs wrapped in aubergine 328
plum tomato and almond jam 375
roast wild duck with honey, thyme and almonds 331
stuffed mackerel 260
veiled pilaff 250
anchovies 61
anchovies poached in vine leaves 255
anchovy and rice dome 234
haricot bean salad with eggs and anchovies 125
apples
baked stuffed apples 188
courgette and apple with a hazelnut and lemon sauce 208
apricots 48
carrot and apricot rolls with mint yogurt 195
dried fruit compôte with rose water 354
Noah's pudding 353
poached apricots with buffalo cream 342
pumpkin stuffed with jewelled rice 237
spicy liver sausage 318
stuffed mackerel 260
artichokes 38
artichokes with beans and almonds 200
vegetable stew 192
aşure 29, 353
aubergines 40
aubergine musakka 305
aubergine pilaff with cinnamon and mint 238
aubergine stew 191
fried vegetables with garlic yogurt 118
lemon chicken thighs wrapped in aubergine 328
smoked aubergine and yogurt purée 98
smoked aubergines in cheese sauce 180
stuffed poached aubergines 183
tangy charred pepper and smoked aubergine 109
vegetable stew 192
warm aubergine salad with pepper and tomatoes 121

baklava 8, 366
beans, dried
beans with pastırma and lamb's lettuce 221
see also individual varieties
beans, green see green beans
beef 63
ladies' thighs 309
meat-stuffed vine leaves 310
minced meat and pine nut pie 174
mother-in-law's meatballs 314
stuffed leeks with a sauce 184
see also pastırma
beetroot 41
grated beetroot and yogurt salad 137
bell peppers see peppers
births 31
black-eyed beans
beans with pastırma and lamb's lettuce 221
black-eyed bean stew with spicy sausage 225
blue fish stew 184
bonito 61
baked bonito with bay leaves 283
borlotti beans
beans with pastırma and lamb's lettuce 221
borlotti beans with tomato and garlic 222
bread 76–79
see also flat breads
broad beans 72
artichokes with beans and almonds 200
broad bean purée 226
Noah's pudding 353
bulgur wheat 72, 75
Anatolian bulgur with nuts and dates 230
bulgur wheat with yoghurt 229
fresh bulgur salad with mint and lemon 117
herb-stuffed squid with saffron 287
mother-in-law's meatballs 314
tomato bulgur with spicy lamb 233

cakes
yogurt cake in orange syrup 362
see also pastries, sweet
carrots 41
Anatolian bulgur with nuts and dates 230
carrot and apricot rolls with mint yogurt 195
carrot and caraway purée with yogurt 101
fish broth with celeriac 142
grated carrot and yogurt salad 137
lamb and yogurt soup 153
lentils with carrots and sage 214
mackerel pilâki 259
rice with spiced lamb 249
celeriac
fish broth with celeriac 142
mackerel pilâki 259
celery 41
celery and coconut salad with lime and yogurt dressing 134
cheese 68, 69
cheese-filled pastry in lemon syrup 361
flat breads with spinach 165
making cheese 69
smoked aubergines in cheese sauce 180
see also feta cheese
cherries 48
sour cherry jam 371
sour cherry pilaff 245
sour cherry summer pudding 349
chestnuts 55
lamb stew with roasted chestnuts 302
chicken 64
burnt chicken breast pudding 358
chicken casserole with okra and lemon 321
chicken with green plums and grape syrup 322
chicken liver pilaff with currants, pine nuts and almonds 246
chicken stew with walnuts and pomegranate juice 324
Circassian chicken 327
lemon chicken thighs wrapped in aubergine 328
veiled pilaff 250
chickpeas 75
chickpea dumplings 161
chickpea patties with red onion and parsley 218
chickpea stew 217
hot humus with pine nuts and melted butter 102
humus 97
Noah's pudding 353
sultan's chickpea pilaff 242
chillies 44, 87
cinnamon 85
circumcision 30
clotted cream 69
coconut and celery salad with lime and yogurt dressing 134
coffee 90
coriander seeds 86
courgettes 41, 43
courgette and apple with a hazelnut and lemon sauce 208
courgette, feta and mint patties 196
courgette fritters 166
fried vegetables with garlic yogurt 118
roasted courgettes and peaches 211
vegetable stew 192
couscous with yogurt 229
cream
burnt chicken breast pudding 358
mastic ice cream 341
poached apricots with buffalo cream 342
cucumbers 43
cucumber and mint salad 133
cumin 86

dairy produce 68–71
dates, Anatolian bulgur with nuts and 230
dill 86
dolma 47

dolmasi 113
drinks 90–93
duck 64
roast wild duck with honey, thyme and almonds 331

eggplants see aubergines
eggs 71
haricot bean salad with eggs and anchovies 125
simple eggs with garlic yogurt 158
spinach with eggs and paprika 179
tomatoes and peppers with eggs 157
etiquette, mealtime 20–21

fava beans see broad beans
feta cheese
courgette, feta and mint patties 196
fiery cheese and parsley dip 105
filo cigars filled with feta, parsley, mint and dill 162
leek soup with feta, dill and paprika 146
melon and feta salad with pastırma 130
potatoes baked with tomatoes and feta 199
salad with feta, chillies and parsley 129
figs 51
dried fig and pine nut jam with aniseed 372
fresh figs baked with honey 346
Noah's pudding 353
spicy rabbit stew with shallots and figs 335
filo see pastry
fish and shellfish 58–62
cinnamon fishcakes with currants, pine nuts and herbs 279
cooking methods 58
fish broth with celeriac 142
smoked cod's roe dip 106
see also individual types
flat breads 78–79
flat breads with spicy lamb and tomato 173
flat breads with spinach 165
lamb kebabs in flat bread wraps 296
pide 78–79
flavourings 84–89
fritters, courgette 166
fruit 48–53
fruit leathers 53
fruit molasses 53
see also jams; and individual fruits
funerals 31

garlic 87
grains and pulses 72–75
grapes 51
green beans 41
green beans with tomatoes and dill 203
vegetable stew 192
see also broad beans

haricot beans
beans with pastırma and lamb's lettuce 221
haricot bean salad with eggs and anchovies 125
Noah's pudding 353

hazelnuts 55
courgette and apple with a hazelnut and lemon sauce 208
helva 354
herbs 84–89
Hidrellez 30
history 12–17
honey 87
pickled pears, with saffron, honey and spices 82
roast wild duck with honey, thyme and almonds 331
hot snacks and street food
chickpea dumplings 161
courgette fritters 166
deep-fried mussels in beer batter 169
deep-fried squid with garlic bread sauce 170
filo cigars filled with feta, parsley, mint and dill 162
flat breads with spicy lamb and tomato 173
flat breads with spinach 165
minced meat and pine nut pie 174
simple eggs with garlic yogurt 158
tomatoes and peppers with eggs 157 humus 97
humus 97
humus, hot, with pine nuts and melted butter 102

ice cream, mastic 341
Islam 12–13, 25–26
Itfar 26

jams 53
dried fig and pine nut jam with aniseed 372
plum tomato and almond jam 375
rose petal jam 369
sour cherry jam 371

Kandil 29
kebabs 66
lamb kebab in puff pastry 300
lamb kebabs in flat bread wraps 296
lamb shish kebab 299
swordfish, lemon and red pepper kebabs 268
köfte 63, 66
Koran, The 25–26
Kurban Bayrami 29

ladies' fingers see okra
ladies' navels 365
lamb 64
aubergine musakka 305
classic tripe soup 154
flat breads with spicy lamb and tomato 173
ladies' thighs 309
lamb cutlets with tomato sauce 306
lamb kebab in puff pastry 300
lamb kebabs in flat bread wraps 296
lamb shish kebab 299
lamb stew with roasted chestnuts 302
lamb and yogurt soup 153
meat-stuffed vine leaves 310
meatballs with pine nuts and cinnamon 313

mother-in-law's meatballs 314
rice with spiced lamb 249
spicy liver sausage 318
stir-fried liver with red onion 317
tomato bulgur with spicy lamb 233
lamb's lettuce 43
beans with pastırma and lamb's lettuce 221
lamb's lettuce salad 133
leeks 43
leek soup with feta, dill and paprika 146
stuffed leeks with a sauce 184
lemons 51
cheese-filled pastry in lemon syrup 361
chicken casserole with okra and lemon 321
courgette and apple with a hazelnut and lemon sauce 208
lemon chicken thighs wrapped in aubergine 328
swordfish, lemon and red pepper kebabs 268
lentils 75
lentils with carrots and sage 214
spicy red lentil soup with onion 150
lima beans see butter beans
liver
chicken liver pilaff with currants, pine nuts and almonds 246
spicy liver sausage 318
stir-fried liver with red onion 317

mackerel 61
jewelled mackerel salad in a dome 256
mackerel pilâki 259
stuffed mackerel 260
mastic 87–88, 276, 341
meat and poultry 63–67
melons 51–52
melon and feta salad with pastırma 130
meze 21, 22
broad bean purée 226
caramelised mushrooms with allspice and herbs 207
carrot and apricot rolls with mint yogurt 195
carrot and caraway purée with yogurt 101
cinnamon fishcakes with currants, pine nuts and herbs 279
Circassian chicken 327
courgette and apple with a hazelnut and lemon sauce 208
courgette, feta and mint patties 196
fiery cheese and parsley dip 105
fried vegetables with garlic yogurt 118
green beans with tomatoes and dill 203
herb-stuffed squid with saffron 287
hot humus with pine nuts and melted butter 102
humus 97
ladies' thighs 309
meat-stuffed vine leaves 310
mussels stuffed with aromatic pilaff 292
peppers stuffed with aromatic rice 187
smoked aubergine and yogurt purée 98
smoked cod's roe dip 106
spicy walnut and red pepper dip 110

spinach with currants, pine nuts and yogurt 122
stuffed vine leaves 113
sweet-and-sour ladies' fingers 204
tahini and lemon dip 101
tangy charred pepper and smoked aubergine 109
tomato, pepper and chilli salsa 114
see also hot snacks and street food; salad
mint 88
muhammara 110
Muharrem 29, 353
musakka, aubergine 305
mushroom, caramelised, with allspice and herbs 207
mussels 62
deep-fried mussels in beer batter 169
mussels stuffed with aromatic pilaff 292

navy beans see haricot beans
nigella 88
nuts and seeds 55–57

offal 66
classic tripe soup 154
see also liver
oils, cooking 80
okra 43
chicken casserole with okra and lemon 321
sweet-and-sour ladies' fingers 204
olives 80
haricot bean salad with eggs and anchovies 125
orange and onion salad with olives 126
squid with olives and red wine 288
onions 44
oranges
orange and onion salad with olives 126
yogurt cake in orange syrup 362
oregano 88
Ottoman 15–17

parsley 86
pasta 79
pastırma (air-dried beef or veal) 67
beans with pastırma and lamb's lettuce 221
chickpea stew 217
melon and feta salad with pastırma 130
pastries, savoury 79
filo cigars filled with feta, parsley, mint and dill 162
lamb kebab in puff pastry 300
minced meat and pine nut pie 174
veiled pilaff 250
pastries, sweet 79
baklava 366
cheese-filled pastry in lemon syrup 361
ladies' navels 365
peaches and roasted courgettes 211
pears, pickled, with saffron, honey and spices 82
peas, green, with mint and dill 241
peppers, bell 44
aubergine stew 191
baked bonito with bay leaves 283
baked prawns with tomatoes, pepper and garlic 291
blue fish stew 284
fried vegetables with garlic yogurt 118
lamb cutlets with tomato sauce 306
peppers stuffed with aromatic rice 187
roasted courgettes and peaches 211
salad with feta, chillies and parsley 129
sea bass parcels with cinnamon and mastic 276
spicy walnut and red pepper dip 110
swordfish, lemon and red pepper kebabs 268
tangy charred pepper and smoked aubergine 109
tomato, pepper and chilli salsa 114
tomatoes and peppers with eggs 157
vegetable stew 192
warm aubergine salad with pepper and tomatoes 121
pickles 82
pilaffs
Anatolian bulgur with nuts and dates 230
anchovy and rice dome 234
aubergine pilaff with cinnamon and mint 238
bulgur wheat with yogurt 229
chicken liver pilaff with currants, pine nuts and almonds 246
mussels stuffed with aromatic pilaff 292
pumpkin stuffed with jewelled rice 237
rice with green peas, mint and dill 241
rice with spiced lamb 249
sour cherry pilaff 245
sultan's chickpea pilaff 242
tomato bulgur with spicy lamb 233
veiled pilaff 250
pine nuts 56
Anatolian bulgur with nuts and dates 230
anchovy and rice dome 234
aubergine pilaff with cinnamon and mint 238
baked stuffed apples 188
carrot and apricot rolls with mint yogurt 195
chicken liver pilaff with currants, pine nuts and almonds 246
cinnamon fishcakes with currants, pine nuts and herbs 279
dried fig and pine nut jam with aniseed 372
dried fruit compôte with rose water 354
helva with pine nuts 354
hot humus with pine nuts and melted butter 102
jewelled mackerel salad in a dome 256
meatballs with pine nuts and cinnamon 313
minced meat and pine nut pie 174
mussels stuffed with aromatic pilaff 292
Noah's pudding 353
peppers stuffed with aromatic rice 187
roasted courgettes and peaches 211
spinach with currants, pine nuts and yogurt 122
stuffed mackerel 260
stuffed sardines 264
stuffed vine leaves 113
pistachio nuts 56
Anatolian bulgur with nuts and dates 230
cheese-filled pastry in lemon syrup 361
classic almond milk pudding 350
mother-in-law's meatballs 314
pumpkin stuffed with jewelled rice 237
veiled pilaff 250
plums, green, with chicken and grape syrup 322
pomegranates 52
chicken stew with walnuts and pomegranate juice 324
sour pomegranate broth 141
potatoes
aubergine stew 191
fish broth with celeriac 142
lamb and yogurt soup 153
mackerel pilâki 259
potatoes baked with tomatoes and feta 199
prawns 62
baked prawns with tomatoes, pepper and garlic 291
fish broth with celeriac 142
prunes: dried fruit compôte with rose water 354
pul biber 87
pulses 72, 92–95
soaking and cooking 72
see also individual varieties
pumpkins 46
pumpkin poached in clove syrup 345
pumpkin soup with yogurt and melted butter 149
pumpkin stuffed with jewelled rice 237

quails 64
chargrilled marinated quails 332
quinces 52–53

rabbit stew with shallots and figs 335
rakı 93
sea bass with rakı 275
Ramazan 26
Ramazan Bayrami 26
red mullet 61
deep-fried red mullet with rocket 275
religious days and festivals 25–31
rice 72, 75
baked stuffed apples 188
chilled baked rice pudding 357
cooking rice 75
ladies' thighs 309
meadow soup with rice and mint 145
meat-stuffed vine leaves 310
Noah's pudding 353
peppers stuffed with aromatic rice 187
spicy liver sausage 318
stuffed leeks with a sauce 184
stuffed vine leaves 113
see also pilaffs
rose petals 53

rose water 89
dried fruit compôte with rose water 354
rose petal jam 369
rose petal sorbet 338

saffron 88
sage 89
Sahur 26
salads
celery and coconut salad with lime and yogurt dressing 134
cucumber and mint salad 133
fresh bulgur salad with mint and lemon 117
grated beetroot and yogurt salad 137
haricot bean salad with eggs and anchovies 125
jewelled mackerel salad in a dome 256
lamb's lettuce salad 133
melon and feta salad with pastırma 130
orange and onion salad with olives 126
salad with feta, chillies and parsley 129
warm aubergine salad with pepper and tomatoes 121
salep (beverage) 92
sardines 61
baked sardines with tomatoes 263
chargrilled sardines in vine leaves 267
stuffed sardines 264
sausage
black-eyed bean stew with spicy sausage 225
spicy liver sausage 318
see also sucuk
sea bass 62
sea bass baked in salt 280
sea bass parcels with cinnamon and mastic 276
sea bass with rakı 275
sea perch 62
blue fish stew 284
sea perch baked on a tile with poppy seeds 272
seeds and nuts 55–57
shakshuka 157
Seljuk 14–15
semolina
helva with pine nuts 354
ladies' navels 365
sesame seeds 56
93
shrimp see prawns
sorbet, rose petal 338
soups
classic tripe soup 154
fish broth with celeriac 142
lamb and yogurt soup 153
leek soup with feta, dill and paprika 146
meadow soup with rice and mint 145
pumpkin soup with yogurt and melted butter 149
sour pomegranate broth 141
spicy red lentil soup with onion 150
spices 84–89
spinach 46
chickpea stew 217
flat breads with spinach 165
spinach with currants, pine nuts and yogurt 122
spinach with eggs and paprika 179
squid 62
deep-fried squid with garlic bread sauce 170
herb-stuffed squid with saffron 287
squid with olives and red wine 288
sucuk (sausage) 67
black-eyed bean stew with spicy sausage 225
chickpea stew 217
sumac 89
sunflower seeds 56
sweet dishes 20
burnt chicken breast pudding 358
chilled baked rice pudding 357
classic almond milk pudding 350
dried fruit compôte with rose water 354
fresh figs baked with honey 346
helva with pine nuts 354
mastic ice cream 341
Noah's pudding 353
poached apricots with buffalo cream 342
pumpkin poached in clove syrup 345
rose petal sorbet 338
sour cherry summer pudding 349
see also cakes; pastries, sweet
swordfish 62
swordfish, lemon and red pepper kebabs 268

tahini and lemon dip 101
tarama 106
tea 92
herbal and fruit teas 92
thyme 89
tomatoes 46
aubergine pilaff with cinnamon and mint 238
aubergine stew 191
baked bonito with bay leaves 283
baked prawns with tomatoes, pepper and garlic 291
baked sardines with tomatoes 263
beans with pastırma and lamb's lettuce 221
black-eyed bean stew with spicy sausage 225
blue fish stew 284
borlotti beans with tomato and garlic 222
chargrilled sardines in vine leaves 267
chicken casserole with okra and lemon 321
chickpea dumplings 161
chickpea stew 217
flat breads with spicy lamb and tomato 173
green beans with tomatoes and dill 203
jewelled mackerel salad in a dome 256
lamb cutlets with tomato sauce 306
lamb shish kebab 299
mackerel pilâki 259
plum tomato and almond jam 375
potatoes baked with tomatoes and feta 199
roasted courgettes and peaches 211
sea bass parcels with cinnamon and mastic 276
stuffed poached aubergines 183
tomato bulgur with spicy lamb 233
tomato, pepper and chilli salsa 114
tomatoes and peppers with eggs 157
vegetable stew 192
warm aubergine salad with pepper and tomatoes 121
tripe, soup 154
tuna 62
seared tuna with sage, parsley and dill 271
Turkish culinary history 12–17
Turkish delight 8–9, 30–31
Turkish food traditions 18–20
Turkish kitchens 32–35

vanilla 89
vanilla sugar 346
vegetables 38–47
cooking methods 47
see also individual vegetables
vine leaves 46–47, 267
anchovies poached in vine leaves 255
chargrilled sardines in vine leaves 267
meat-stuffed vine leaves 310
stuffed vine leaves 113

walnuts 56
baklava 366
chicken stew with walnuts and pomegranate juice 324
Circassian chicken 327
deep-fried mussels in beer batter 169
mother-in-law's meatballs 314
spicy walnut and red pepper dip 110
stuffed mackerel 260
watermelons 51–52
waters, scented 89
see also rose water
weddings 31

yogurt 70–71
bulgur wheat with yogurt 229
carrot and apricot rolls with mint yogurt 195
carrot and caraway purée with yogurt 101
celery and coconut salad with lime and yogurt dressing 134
cucumber and mint salad 133
fried vegetables with garlic yogurt 118
grated beetroot and yogurt salad 137
grated carrot and yogurt salad 137
lamb and yogurt soup 153
lamb's lettuce salad 133
making yogurt 70–71
meadow soup with rice and mint 145
pumpkin soup with yogurt and melted butter 149
roasted courgettes and peaches 211
simple eggs with garlic yogurt 158
smoked aubergine and yogurt purée 98
spinach with currants, pine nuts and yogurt 122
yogurt cake in orange syrup 362
yufka 14, 32

zeytinyağlı 47
zucchini see courgettes

**About the author** | Writer, broadcaster, and food anthropologist, Ghillie Başan has worked in different parts of the world as an English teacher, ski instructor, cookery writer, restaurant critic and journalist. With a degree in Social Anthropology and a Cordon Bleu Diploma, her interest in and research into different culinary cultures has culminated in many books, some of which have been nominated for the Glenfiddich, Guild of Food Writers, and the Cordon Bleu World Food Media Awards. They have also appeared regularly in the 'Best of the Best' and 'Top 50' lists; and she has been described as one of the 'finest writers on Middle Eastern food'. Her food and travel articles have appeared in the Sunday Times, Sunday Herald, Daily Telegraph, Sunday Tribune, Press & Journal, BBC Good Food Magazine, Diet & Nutrition USA, and various Middle Eastern and internet magazines, and she is one of the presenters on BBC Radio Scotland's Kitchen Café.

This edition is published by Lorenz Books
an imprint of Anness Publishing Ltd
www.lorenzbooks.com
www.annesspublishing.com
info@anness.com



A CIP catalogue record for this book is available from the British Library.

Publisher: Joanna Lorenz
Design: Simon Daley, Giraffe Design
Photography: Martin Brigdale
Food styling: Fergal Connolly and Sunil Vijayakar
Nutritional consultant: Clare Emery
Index: Marie Lorimer

With thanks to Alamy (13t, 13b, 14t, 14b, 15, 16b, 18b, 20t, 27t, 28t, 33t, 39t, 48b, 54t, 73b, 92t and 92b) and Shutterstock.

Previously published as *The Food and Cooking of Turkey*, updated and revised.



## Cook's notes

Bracketed terms are intended for American readers.

For all recipes, quantities are given in both metric and imperial measures and, where appropriate, in standard cups and spoons. Follow one set of measures, but not a mixture, because they are not interchangeable.

Standard spoon and cup measures are level. 1 tsp = 5ml, 1 tbsp = 15ml, 1 cup = 250ml/8fl oz.

Australian standard tablespoons are 20ml. Australian readers should use 3 tsp in place of 1 tbsp for measuring small quantities.

American pints are 16fl oz/2 cups. American readers should use 20fl oz/2½ cups in place of 1 pint when measuring liquids.

Since ovens vary, you should check with your manufacturer's instruction book for guidance.